THE PREHISTORY OF
AFRICA

J. Desmond Clark

48 PHOTOGRAPHS
62 LINE DRAWINGS
10 MAPS

THAMES AND HUDSON

THIS IS VOLUME SEVENTY-TWO IN THE SERIES

Ancient Peoples and Places

GENERAL EDITOR: DR GLYN DANIEL

First published 1970
© *J. Desmond Clark 1970*
*Filmset by Keyspools Ltd, Golborne, Lancs and
printed in Great Britain by The Camelot Press Ltd, Southampton.
Not to be imported for sale into the U.S.A.*

ISBN 0 500 02069 8

Ancient Peoples and Places

THE PREHISTORY
OF AFRICA

General Editor

DR GLYN DANIEL

ABOUT THE AUTHOR

John Desmond Clark, having graduated with First Class Honours at Christ's College, Cambridge in 1937, was appointed Curator of the National Museum of Zambia (then Northern Rhodesia) and later, as Director, initiated and ran a country-wide Antiquities Service there. In 1961 he became professor at the University of California, Berkeley, where he teaches African prehistory. He has carried out excavations in a number of African countries, and returns almost every year to continue archaeological work in the continent. Professor Clark is a Fellow of several distinguished institutions including the British Academy and the American Academy of Arts and Sciences, and holds the diploma of the Museums Association. He has published a dozen or more books and some 125 papers in scientific journals.

CONTENTS

CONTENTS

5

Preface

THE INCREASING INTEREST being shown today in the peoples and continent of Africa turns naturally also towards a closer acquaintance with and understanding of the processes of cultural and economic change evidenced in the continent's history and the two and a half million years or more of prehistoric time over which the record has now been extended.

This book is an attempt to provide an up to date account of this prehistoric evidence and its interpretation in the light of prevailing thought. So rapidly, however, is new material being recovered as a result of the volume of research being carried out in many related fields, that any such book must be out of date almost as soon as it is published. Although, on the one hand, this is a disadvantage that only regular revision can overcome, it is also a reflection of the intensity and energy with which the basic research is being undertaken.

The present text is based upon those prepared for the Anna Howard Shaw Lectures given at Bryn Mawr College, Pennsylvania, in the earlier part of 1969 and I wish to thank the Principal and College authorities for this much appreciated invitation as also Professor Frederica de Laguna and other faculty and student members of the Department of Anthropology there for the stimulating discussions which were of material help in preparing the final text of the book.

It is neither possible nor desirable in a general work such as this to give the detailed evidence on which many of the statements made here are based but those who wish to will be able to follow this up through the Annotations and other information given at the back of the book.

I wish to record my best thanks to the many colleagues and friends who have assisted either directly or indirectly in the writing of this book. In particular to those who have provided help with the illustrations—Dr and Mrs L. S. B. Leakey for permission to reproduce the Olduvai material, Mrs Janette Deacon for the drawings of the Howieson's Poort artifacts and all those whose names are recorded in the List of Acknowledgements. I wish to record my grateful appreciation and thanks to Drs Sherwood L. Washburn, Glynn Ll. Isaac and C. Garth Sampson who read various sections of the text and made suggestions for its improvement. Their help is most gratefully acknowledged here as also the benefits deriving from discussions with them and with Professors Brian Fagan, Jacques Nenquin, Merrick Posnansky and Thurstan Shaw and Drs Francis van Noten, Sheryl Miller and others.

I wish to thank also Mrs Mary Sampson for the many excellent illustrations and Mr Brian O'Connor for many of the photographic prints used in the book. The typing of manuscripts and much of the preparation work connected with getting the text and illustrations together was undertaken by my wife and my greatest debt and thanks are, as always, to her.

J.D.C.

To
Miles Burkitt
whose teaching and enthusiasm led so many, like myself,
to take up the rewarding study of Africa's past.

taking place today are fast bringing about the obliteration or drastic modification of the old ways of life, of the patterns of behaviour and technologies that have their origins buried in the centuries and millennia through which the archaeologist now traces the record of African cultural development back to the very emergence of man himself. Much of this corpus of ethno' graphic data, made more meaningful by the systematic investiga' tions of anthropologists and others since the beginning of this century, is highly relevant for understanding the invariably incomplete archaeological evidence and for attempting to recon' struct the behaviour of the people whose activities this represents.

Ethnography is, however, but one of the many disciplines to which archaeology is turning today for assistance and to which, in return, it is able to contribute temporal depth and perspective. Such interdisciplinary studies are, or should be, the basis of prehistoric research the world over and the record of the last few years shows that Africa is not behindhand in applying new methods and new conceptions to the unearthing of the unique record of human activities preserved beneath the African bush.

There are few corners of this ancient land mass that have not now been geographically explored and mapped, but the investi' gation of Africa's *past* is opening up a whole new dimension and has already brought about a fundamental readjustment in the conceptions of man's origins and biological and cultural evolu' tion. Besides, it is also providing a large part of the source material for writing the history of Black Africa.

The prehistorian's chief concern lies in seeking to understand the changing cultural patterns relating to those periods of time before the appearance of written records. His main source for doing this lies in the artifacts and other products of man's handi' work that have survived the whittling process of time by reason of their imperishable nature—stone or potsherds, for example— or because of the favourable circumstances that contributed to the preservation of other materials (wood and skin, for example),

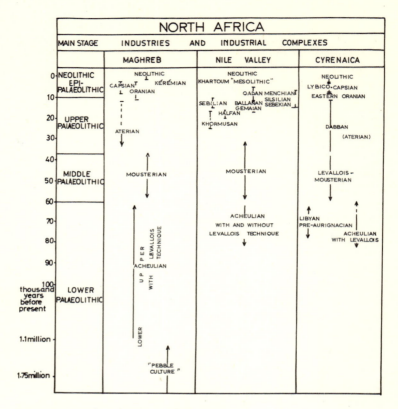

Fig. 1   *Chronological table of African prehistory*

such as the arid deserts of northeast Africa or the occasional buried and perpetually waterlogged sites by some tropical lakes and rivers.

If, therefore, the prehistorian is working essentially with *artifacts*, he is now learning to make increasingly better use of the associations that these have with one another and with other features, both artificial and natural. With expert assistance from other disciplines, such study can go a long way towards recreating the economy of the people who once occupied a site and the nature of the activities they practised there.

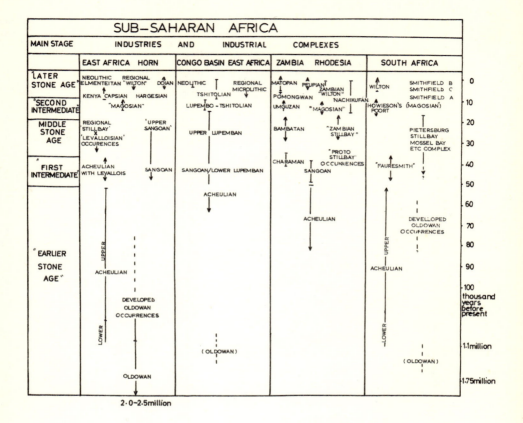

Although the archaeologist works with *things*—(what we know as material culture)—his concern is with *people* and he extracts from his excavation and makes skilled and rigorous use of every scrap of data he can find about the things he digs up so that he may understand the mind and ability of their makers. As Sir Mortimer Wheeler has so eloquently said, 'However much he may analyze and tabulate and desiccate his discoveries in the laboratory, the ultimate appeal across the ages, whether the time interval be five hundred or five hundred thousand years, is from mind to intelligent mind, from man to sentient man. Our graphs and schedules mean nothing if they do not ultimately mean that, of our scraps and pieces we may say, with Mark Anthony in the market place,—"You are not wood, you are not stones, but men".'[1]

The archaeologist's business, then, is to recreate the past. However, before we look at some of the methods and techniques he adopts and some of the sources he draws upon to do this, a word of caution is necessary. It must not be too readily assumed that the archaeologist of today exhibits the same uncritical and simplistic approach that motivated his antiquarian grandfather, or the ingenuity and experimental acumen that marked the activities of his archaeologist father. Today it is easy for us to criticize and to forget that the precision which, since the second World War, is fast turning archaeology into a discipline, could not before then have the same meaning that it does now. The over-simplistic analogies that were once drawn between prehistoric culture and ethnographic example, though they sometimes show more unrestrained ingenuity than the present-day prehistorian is entitled to exercise, have, nevertheless, had a very salutary effect on the way such data are being used today.

Africa provides a ready crop of fanciful interpretations. If these are not always as prolix and erudite as those of Mr Pickwick and his fellow antiquarians in their interpretations of the stone that bore the words 'Bill Stumps, his mark', yet they cannot fail to appeal to the more imaginative and, perhaps, the more romantic side of our natures. For example, the grindstones found on coastal sites were interpreted by one South African investigator as 'gravy dishes for the epicures among the natives'.[2] Another saw in the tree trunks of a former *Podocarpus* forest, now buried beneath the sands of the Cape Flats, the timbers of the galleys used by Pharaoh Necho's Phoenicians when rounding the Cape.[3] Incidentally, how they completed their journey, we are not told!

Plate 48

The Zimbabwe ruins in Rhodesia have probably produced more misinformed interpretations than any other monument in the continent. Rather like the Three Jolly Huntsmen, one saw the elliptical building as a *foetus in utero*; another he said 'nay' and found that this 'had been set on a series of curves whereof the radius was a mystical number, embodied in the relation between the large and small cones'; and the third discerned it as an 'enormous gnomon' which permitted the computation that Zimbabwe had been built in 1100 BC.[4]

Fortunately, few believed in these interpretations except their creators, and the popular imagination was caught, back in 1872 as it is today, by the interpretation expressed by the geologist Carl Mauch, the first to describe the ruins: 'I do not think that I am far wrong if I suppose that the ruin on the hill is a copy of Solomon's temple on Mount Moriah and the building in the plain a copy of the palace where the Queen of Sheba lived during her visit to Solomon.'[5] To the chagrin of the adherents of this myth, that fragment of Hebrew or Himyaritic script, or the seven-branched candlestick needed to clinch the matter, have so far eluded the search. The best that could be produced was a *ushabti* figure from Dynastic Egypt that subsequently turned out to have been brought into the country by a miner at the end of the last century.

Enough has been said to show that there is no room for this sort of reasoning in prehistoric studies today. As Edgar Allan Poe said, 'The ingenious man is often remarkably incapable of analysis,' and, indeed, *sound* analysis is the outcome of objective observation and arrangement of all the data available at a prehistoric site. In this way the facts are allowed to speak for themselves, can be compared with models and are not made to fit any preconceived notion of the investigator. As Poe also tells us, 'It would have been wiser, it would have been safer, to classify (if classify we must) upon the basis of what man usually or occasionally did, and was *always* occasionally doing, rather than upon the basis of what we took it for granted the Deity intended him to do.'

ARCHAEOLOGICAL METHODS

Whether he is concerned with the Pleistocene or with the last two thousand years, the archaeologist working in Africa must deal with four main problems. The methods that he has evolved for doing this, or that have been developed for him by others are a direct result of the need to tackle these problems realistically, using, where available, the aid of collaborators in the physical and natural sciences.

The four issues are:
1. the temporal relationship and age of the material;
2. the nature of the palaeo-environment and its effect upon culture;
3. the associations and analysis of the total archaeological content within the Archaeological Horizon in which it is found; and
4. the interpretation of these data and their empirical use for reconstructing the culture pattern.

Let us now look briefly at each of these major issues.

DATING ARCHAEOLOGICAL MATERIAL

We will begin with the problem of *temporal relationships*—in other words, the age, both relative and absolute, of the objects the archaeologist finds. Almost from the start in Africa the difficulty has been how to place in *relative sequence* the many diverse assemblages of stone artifacts that were found there in great quantity from the end of the nineteenth century onwards. It was early realized that the threefold division of culture into Stone, Bronze and Iron ages adopted in the nineteenth century for Europe had no validity in Africa outside the Nile valley. Of course, the various methods of relative dating of the finds adopted for Africa have a validity that is world-wide and not merely confined to that continent.

(a) Relative Dating

Firstly, relative dating may be arrived at by determining *the relative stratigraphic position in which the cultural assemblage occurs.* This depends upon the identification and description of stratigraphic rock units which are lithologically distinct and have a top and a bottom that can be clearly seen. These may be found preserved in vertical stratigraphic sequence as at the Olduvai Gorge in northern Tanzania (the site made famous by Louis and Mary Leakey's discoveries) or at the Kalambo Falls in northern Zambia; or in *échelon* where the morphological relationship of the different units can be precisely defined. Examples of this are the famous Moroccan coastal sequence at Casablanca, or that in the Vaal river in South Africa. These sedimentary rock units—sands, silts, gravels, screes, breccias or tuffs—can be classified into beds, members, formations and groups and for their identification and definition the archaeologist nowadays relies upon his geological colleagues.

Plate 5

Fig. 2

The result of the study of the sedimentary rock units will be a succession of strata the ages of which are known relatively, the one to the other. As a corollary, of course, this establishes the relative age of any associated fossil material, whether faunal, floral or cultural.

Dating by the associated fauna is the next most important method although this is not always possible, either because, as is the case with almost nine-tenths of the sites in the continent, there is no fauna preserved; or because there is an insufficient amount; or because what exists there is undiagnostic.

The African Pleistocene faunas can be divided into five main stages. Because there is no clear-cut division between one so-called 'stage' and the next, this term is not a very good one and has recently been abandoned in favour of 'faunal span' to which a locality name is given.[6] This conveys better the gradual nature of the change. A representative assemblage of fossils from a given bed will determine to which of the five faunal spans the

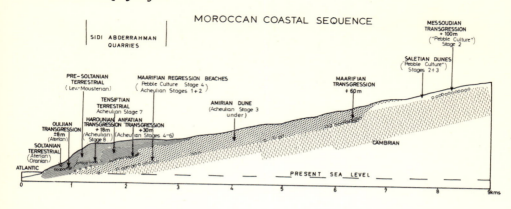

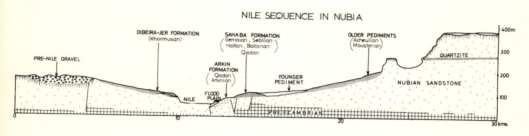

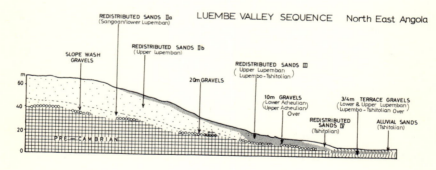

Fig. 2   The stratigraphic and cultural sequences in coastal Morocco (after P. Biberson, 1963); in the Nile Valley (after J. de Heinzelin, 1968) and in northeastern Angola (after J. D. Clark, 1963)

assemblage belongs and, provided it is a truly representative one with a range of genera and species, this provides one of the best means of relative dating for associated cultural material.

However, there are problems, especially where it comes to correlation of faunal units between regions—for example between east and South African early Pleistocene faunas, where there are few common forms. There are open, dry savanna faunas in east Africa and cave faunas in South Africa but there are few common species found in such contrasting habitats.

Certain genera showed remarkable evolutionary diversification in the Pleistocene and so are much better chronological indicators than others—for instance, elephants, pigs and some bovids which are especially good. Some genera are less useful in this way as they show little or no change—such as crocodiles, rhinos and, to some extent, hippos.

Again, it is necessary to have diagnostic parts of the beast to be sure of correct identification and also to have enough of it. Teeth, jaws, horn cores, carpel or tarsal bones are good, but wrong identifications can be made where only isolated fragments are used as was found to be the case at the Olduvai Gorge.

Of course, the associated fauna on a living site of early man has much more to contribute than just to provide a relative age for the occurrence, as we shall see later.

At one time, almost the commonest method of dating used in sub-Saharan Africa was by means of associated cultural material the age of which had been previously determined. It was the practice, in fact it still is, to pick upon what was believed to be a *fossile directeur* and to say that, 'because this is present, therefore the assemblage is of such and such an age'.

This method is still very commonly practised in Europe and it may have more validity there than it does in Africa. Certainly in Africa today recent work has shown that there are very, very few, if any 'zone fossils' that can be used in this way. It used to be considered that 'Earlier', 'Middle' and 'Later Stone Age' tool-kits were mutually exclusive but the excavation of sealed living sites has shown how completely erroneous this idea is. The best example is, perhaps, the living floors in Bed II at the Olduvai Gorge where *outils écaillés* and other small tools, previously thought to be characteristic of 'Later Stone Age' assemblages, occur in deposits that are of Middle Pleistocene age.[7]

On the other hand, the *sequence dating method*, using pot forms, developed by Petrie for establishing a relative chronology for the Egyptian Neolithic and Predynastic cultures, is still generally accepted. So far as I am aware, sequence dating of this kind has not been used in any other part of Africa except very recently in Rhodesia where seriation of Iron Age wares has shown relationships not previously recognized. Today Egyptologists are themselves beginning to have doubts about the validity of this method in the Nile valley and it seems inconceivable, but nevertheless true, that there is no reliable sequence of radiocarbon dates there against which to check it.

For Iron Age times in sub-Saharan Africa, the exotic imports found on coastal or inland sites have been used to establish an approximate age for the associated, locally manufactured artifacts. Thus, glazed Arab and Persian earthenware, Sung and Ming porcelain, glass trade beads and other imports have been used. The time when such materials were being made is sometimes known and these thus provide a maximum or minimum age for the horizon in which they are found. Thus, the Dutch gin bottle in the foundation deposit at the DhloDhlo ruins in Rhodesia satisfactorily dated that site to not earlier than the middle of the eighteenth century. In other cases, however, especially those of beads, there is no firm dating, since the manufacturing centres are not identified, nor does the composition of the glass always show the place of origin. Steps are being taken to remedy this by refined methods of glass and pottery analysis by the X-ray spectrometry and neutron activation methods which it is to be expected will yield data on origins and age.

Finally, relative dating of organic materials can be established by *chemical analysis* methods which have been used in particular in connection with dating human fossils. The determination of the fluorine and nitrogen content and the percentage of uranium present in a bone and the comparison of the results with assays on associated animal bones will show whether a specimen is contemporary with, or younger or older than the main assemblage. Thus, some human skulls, such as those from Saldanha or Broken Hill, have been shown to be contemporary with the fauna with which they were found; while others, for example the Kanam mandible fragment, have been shown to be younger than the apparently associated fauna.[8]

(b) Chronometric Dating

All these techniques and methods permit one to fix the relative position of the human and cultural material when *two or more* of them are used in conjunction. Of very far-reaching consequence, however, has been the development of various *chronometric methods of dating in terms of years before the present*, within the margin of error of the method adopted. Not only do these make the relationship between cultures more meaningful and more precise than is possible by any relative dating method, but they also give for the first time the approximate time span during which tool kits were used and the rate of cultural and physiological evolution.

So far as Africa is concerned, two of these methods stand out in importance beyond all others—the potassium/argon and the radiocarbon methods.

Let us first take a brief look at *potassium/argon* dating results in Africa. The usefulness of this method is really confined to the regions of volcanicity, which means the Rift Valley. From the point of view of the archaeologist, this method is most important for the later Tertiary and earlier Pleistocene although single, isolated dates are not of much use and runs of dates are required to show the span of probability. We now have runs *and* single dates from localities ranging from the Miocene to the beginning of the Middle Pleistocene and these show that the Plio-Pleistocene boundary was between three and four million years ago.

Dates from the Lower Omo Basin in southwest Ethiopia[9] and from the Olduvai Gorge show that the Lower Pleistocene lasted for about two-and-a-half million years (from *c*.3.75 to less than 1.1 million years ago). The second of these dates was obtained from a tuff sample believed to come from the base of Bed II at Olduvai.[10] The Miocene is now known to have begun more than twenty-six million years ago and the Pliocene to have started about seven million years ago.[11]

These dates have opened up a long chronology for hominid evolution and permit a vastly better appreciation of the time taken and of the importance and influence of tool-making in hominid biological evolution.

Now to consider *radiocarbon*. If such old samples are enriched, the lower limits of this method begin about sixty thousand years ago. As yet, potassium/argon has not produced any very satis-factory results for later times and there is, thus, a gap in the chronometric record that has not yet been adequately filled. From sixty thousand years before the present (BP) onwards, however, we have an increasingly more precise time scale and a series of dates from cave and open sites which shows the relative duration of the industrial stages that have been set up. We now have good data from east and South Africa, an increasingly large number of results from west Africa and the Sahara and an excellent series from Nubia.

There are, of course, some serious gaps. We have nothing very much from the Egyptian Neolithic, for the early Holocene industries of northwest Africa or for the Aterian, the 'Middle Stone Age' culture of that region.

At the same time some important anomalies in cultural evolution have been shown up, such as the late survival in some regions of the Final Acheulian, or the irregular and much earlier appearance of punched-blade technology in sub-Saharan Africa than had previously been believed.

As a result, the picture of cultural succession in the Stone Age is becoming increasingly clearer as is the degree of variability between occurrences that can now be shown to be approximately contemporary. Similarly, the Iron Age in southern Africa is now known to have a respectable antiquity reaching back to the beginning of our era instead of to the fifteenth century, as was thought at one time.

Other relative and chronometric dating methods have been used—such as *palaeo-magnetism, uranium fission track* or *thermo-luminescence*. Although their use has been less frequent and less satisfactory, they sometimes provide support for potassium/argon and radiocarbon dates.

DETERMINING THE PALAEO-ENVIRONMENT

Let us now take a look at the second of the archaeologist's problems—that of determining the palaeo-ecology and the effects this might have had on human culture. At one time it seemed that climatic fluctuation in the African Pleistocene could be adequately explained by the theory of periods of increased rainfall —called Pluvials—separated by periods of lesser rainfall or Interpluvials. It has now been shown, however, that agencies other than climate—tectonic movements, for example—were also able to produce the results and kinds of evidence on which the Pluvial hypothesis was based. For this and other reasons, therefore, it has been abandoned as unproven and other lines of investigation have had to be developed to determine the nature of climatic changes during the Pleistocene. These methods are now producing results of increasing interest. Most of the data relate to the last sixty to one hundred thousand years and, although micro-climates at individual sites dating to earlier Quaternary times can occasionally be reconstructed, we have as yet no means of

Fig. 3

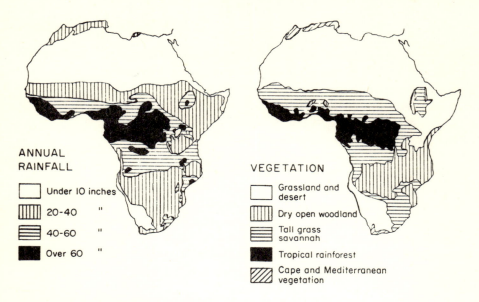

ANNUAL
RAINFALL

☐ Under 10 inches
▥ 20-40 "
▤ 40-60 "
◼ Over 60 "

VEGETATION

☐ Grassland and desert
▥ Dry open woodland
▤ Tall grass savannah
◼ Tropical rainforest
▨ Cape and Mediterranean vegetation

Fig. 3   African rainfall and vegetation (after J. D. Clark, 1964)

knowing the sequence and extent of the continent-wide climatic fluctuations before the Upper Pleistocene.

Firstly, let us take *palaeo-botanical evidence*. Since the 1940's it has been found that the right kinds of deposit do exist in Africa for the preservation of pollens, mostly, though not all, from the Upper Pleistocene onwards. Pollens are preserved in the dry Sahara but not usually in tropical Africa because of the seasonal rainfall and the acid soils, though they can be preserved in perpetually wet sites. They have been found on the high mountains of east Africa and on the interior plateau and in the deposits of lakes, springs and rivers. By determination of the species of plants from which the pollens come it is possible to get an over-all picture of the type of vegetation represented and, thus, an idea of the kind of climate that must have prevailed in order for it to have flourished. At some plateau sites, such as the Kalambo Falls in northern Zambia, there is a direct association of pollens, human culture and macro-plant remains. Sometimes significant changes in climate, as shown by cores from mountain lakes, can be dated by radiocarbon and tied into the archaeological sequence by this means.[12]

Plates 12, 14

Fig. 4

In this way it has been possible to learn a considerable amount about the type of climate that prevailed at various times during the Pleistocene, though there are, of course, still anomalies which we are not always successful in explaining.

Pollen spectra are of vital importance in showing the palaeo-environment of the main industrial stages and also whether changes in vegetation pattern were contemporary with cultural changes. The difficulties consist in the shortage of trained workers, in the fact that not enough is yet known of the present-day pollen

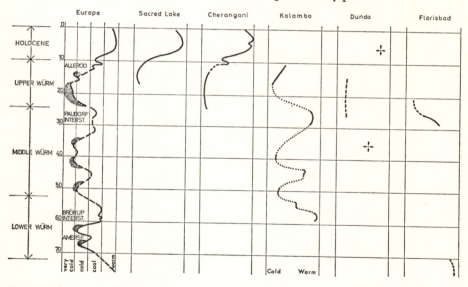

Fig. 4 Comparison of the temperature curve published by Woldstedt (1962) for the European Upper Pleistocene and Holocene with pollen-analytical results from sub-Saharan Africa (age in thousands of years). (Courtesy of E. M. Van Zinderen Bakker, 1967, and the Wenner-Gren Foundation)

in the rain-forest regions and much of the savanna and in the incompleteness of the pollen diagrams due to breaks in the sequence when no pollens are preserved. In any case we have nothing much before the beginning of the Upper Pleistocene.

Secondly, let us take the evidence from *faunal analysis* when, if a good assemblage is available, it should be possible to get an idea of its habitat by determining the range of habitats for the same species today. Usually microfauna gives a more accurate picture than do large animals since the former is more often dependent on a specific habitat. So the fauna from Bed I at the Olduvai Gorge gives the impression of savanna/steppe vegetation very like that of today but with swamp and rain-forest on the volcano slopes.[13]

The fauna from the Broken Hill cave in which Rhodesian Man was found (at $\pm$ 40,000 years BP) has certain forms— giraffe, wildebeeste and gazelle—that do not occur in the area today and thus show that the country was then a much more open one than is the woodland savanna existing there now.[14]

There are several problems in interpretation. Some of the genera or species may have changed their behaviour—for example, the okapi and the bongo have markings that suggest that initially they may have been savanna-dwelling animals. Certain animals also are known to have a great tolerance in the matter of habitat and so are not good indicators of environment. Such animals are, for instance, the hippo, leopard and elephant. Some forms may be over-represented at archaeological sites due to the hunting preferences of the hominids. Occasionally some species, especially large animals, are not represented at all at the living sites as the butchery was done where the kill was made and the bones were not carried back to the home base.

Zoo-geography or *plant geography* can also provide information about the vegetation and climate of regions in the past. Where there is today discontinuous distribution and where species are now isolated by many miles from the next nearest occurrence, they must at one time have been joined by a continuous corridor. Sometimes these are the same species or forms with only sub-specific differences and may be plants, birds, mammals and even insects—for instance, certain butterflies. Such discontinuous distribution shows that there has been movement of vegetation belts partly in response to climatic change. The problem is to know when or how often this took place.

A study of *minerals* and *sediments* can also provide data on climatic conditions in the past since they may have become chemically or lithologically altered and so show indications of drier or wetter conditions compared with those of the present day. For instance, zeolites, which are hydrous, aluminium silicate minerals and are indicative of saline, alkaline water can be seen today forming in the delta of the Peninj river in the Lake Natron Rift on the Kenya/Tanzania border. In the Olduvai Group of Beds, certain zeolite-cemented red beds were reddened and cemented after deposition, so indicating the presence at that time of saline water in the area over the beds.[15] Again, laterite, an iron-rich, residual weathering product derived from many different rocks under strongly oxidising and leaching conditions, is forming today in regions of high rainfall and thick vegetation cover. Thus, when we find laterite in an archaeological horizon, we know something about the climate during the time of its formation.

Sedimentation studies have been carried out in the Transvaal caves where a comparison of the sandy fractions in the Ape-Man deposits with modern hillwash soils permits the counting of the percentage of wind-blown to residual grains and so the gauging of how much wetter or drier the climate was than that of today.[16] *Fig. 5* The angularity of sand grains can also be used to estimate the amount of rainfall—the grains are super-angular with more than forty inches of rain; with from forty to twenty inches of rainfall there is a decrease in angularity; and below fifteen inches of rainfall the grains are again angular but with a carbonate coating.

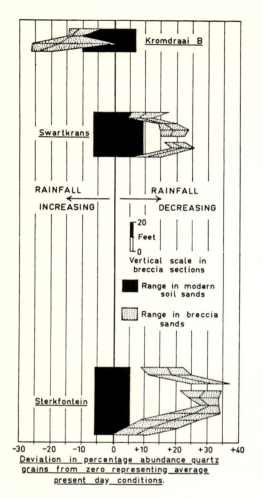

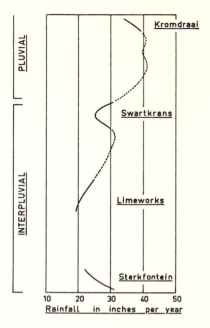

RAINFALL INCREASING ← | → RAINFALL DECREASING

20
Feet
0
Vertical scale in breccia sections

■ Range in modern soil sands

▨ Range in breccia sands

Kromdraai B

Swartkrans

Sterkfontein

-30 -20 -10 0 +10 +20 +30 +40
Deviation in percentage abundance quartz grains from zero representing average present day conditions.

PLUVIAL

INTERPLUVIAL

Kromdraai

Swartkrans

Limeworks

Sterkfontein

10 20 30 40 50
Rainfall in inches per year

Fig. 5 Diagrams showing, left, the suggested correlation of the Transvaal Australopithecine sites based on the relative abundance of chert and quartz grains in sand samples isolated from the breccias; and, above, the suggested rainfall changes inferred from analyses of the various cave deposits. The Sterkfontein Extension site (not shown here) falls between Limeworks (Makapan) and Swartkrans. (Courtesy of C. K. Brain, 1958, and the Transvaal Museum, Pretoria)

For example, in the Cave of Hearths, again in the Transvaal, the angularity of the sand grains is greater than it is for the modern hillside soil (except in two places) and this indicates an increased rainfall for the greater part of the time represented by the deposits.[17]

Fig. 6

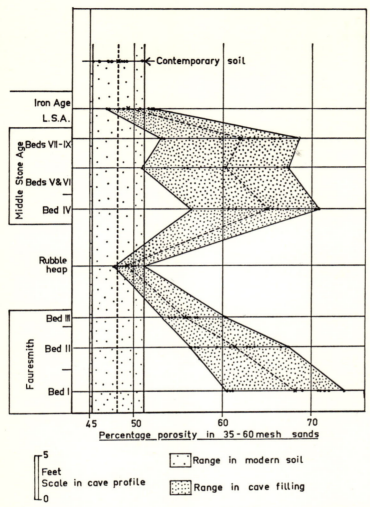

Fig. 6 Comparison of the percentage porosity of the sand component of the modern hillside soil with that from the Cave of Hearths at Makapansgat shows that the angularity of the cave samples is higher than that of the contemporary soil, except on two occasions in the past, demonstrating that the rainfall during most of the time was greater than it is today. (Courtesy of C. K. Brain, 1967, and the Wenner-Gren Foundation)

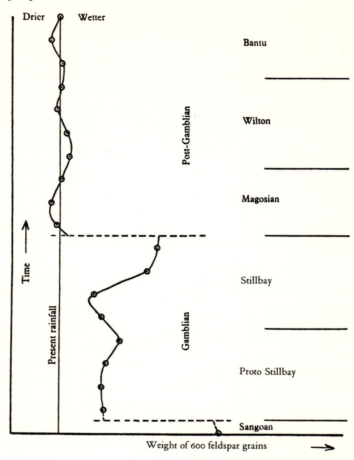

Fig. 7 Analysis of feldspar grain weights from granite hillwash at Khami, Rhodesia, has been used to estimate climatic fluctuations during later Pleistocene and Recent time. The break in the centre part of the curve indicates that rainfall and so run-off exceeded deposition at this time. Feldspar grain weights from immediately below this break compared with those of modern samples are in the ratio of 3 : 1 and so provided the basis for rainfall calculations. (Courtesy of G. Bond, 1957)

At Khami, in Rhodesia, work has been done on the variation, through a vertical section, in the weathering and breaking-down of feldspar crystals in the colluvial soil of a site in granite country with several cultural horizons and this permits the reconstruction of the Upper Pleistocene and Holocene rainfall curve. The sediment is entirely formed from disintegration of bedrock and heavier weights for feldspar samples indicate wetter conditions.[18]

Fig. 7

With regard to the effect of climatic change on the distribution of human culture, it was not until the publication in 1967 of the *Atlas of African Prehistory* that cultural distributions had been correlated on a continent-wide basis. However, the cultural and palaeo-ecological maps of the *Atlas* now permit us to compare and see to what extent changes in lithic technology and typology coincide with natural changes in geography, vegetation, climate, etc. The problems are centred in the unknown areas; in the fact that we still need a more accurate assessment of palaeo-climatic extremes; and that we must develop more rigorous definitions for industrial designations.

ANALYZING THE ARCHAEOLOGICAL
AND ASSOCIATED MATERIAL

Thirdly, we must consider the archaeological corpus which will be done from two viewpoints: namely, analysis and terminology and the techniques now employed for the recovery of the material.

To take first analysis and terminology—archaeology in Africa is striving to develop into a more exact science. It has become apparent that this will not advance very far until some general agreement has been reached on the employment of more precise techniques of analysis and more meaningful definitions to identify and describe all the components of an assemblage. This is applicable as much to archaeologists working with Pleistocene material, where not much other than stone and bone has usually survived, as to those working on the later periods.

Up to the end of the second World War the cultural material from a dig—tools, utilized artifacts and the waste products of flaking—was usually selected and not everything was saved. Descriptions were based on these selected elements which were considered sufficient to show the main typological and technical characteristics of the whole assemblage. Moreover, descriptions were mostly in general terms, even though tool lists might be included. There thus existed a degree of imprecision that rendered it impossible to make comparisons with assemblages from other areas except at a general and not very meaningful level. Thus the inferred similarity of an industry from, say, Kenya or the Horn of Africa, to one from South Africa, on the the basis of the presence in both of certain 'type fossils'—in this case bifacially worked foliate points—led to the wide geographical expansion of the South African terminology, established in 1927, throughout the whole of the continent south of the Sahara. For example, we find 'Middle Stone Age' assemblages in all these regions described as 'Stillbay' after the type site on the South African south coast where the characteristic tools were first found. Outside the type area in the southwestern Cape these similar industries are distinguished by the addition of a regional prefix such as 'Kenya Stillbay'. The same process has occurred in the case of other cultural units, for example, 'Abyssinian Fauresmith' or 'Transvaal Lupemban' and so on. In many cases these terms are still used since redefinition will only be possible after further work in the field and laboratory.

After the war and following the lead in analysis techniques coming from Europe, African archaeologists began to make systematic analyses of the *total* component of their assemblages and to make meaningful deductions on the data obtained from measurement and recording of the attributes of the artifacts, and their associations in the field.

There is today, also, a growing use of graphic presentation in one form or another, again based upon analysis of the whole component. This gives for the first time a much more precise basis for comparison between individual aggregates and assem-blages. In general, however, there is little about African archaeo-logical material that is formal and stereotyped, so that it is more of a problem here than in Europe to fit it into any rigid classifi-catory system, such as the 'Système Bordes'. Since tool classes often merge, definition is perhaps best made on the basis of attributes, a method that is already yielding valuable results.

Such methods enable comparisons to be made between one aggregate and another but they do not help with the ordering of the data from many sites and localities which would previously have been taken care of by standard prehistoric nomenclature. Unfortunately, confusion has often resulted from the many different terms that have been used in Africa in the past so that, in 1965,[19] an attempt was made to obtain more general uniformity of usage. A graded series of four terms was proposed designed to show the precise nature of the cultural unit being described and these are used, where appropriate, in this book. The smallest cultural unit *in its context* that can be defined is an *Archaeological Horizon* or *Archaeological Occurrence*, the artifacts themselves forming an 'aggregate' or 'assemblage'. Where several aggregates from archaeological occurrences can be shown to be closely related and to be distinct from other entities these are grouped into a *Phase*. Phases may succeed each other through time or may be contemporary; the term 'facies' has sometimes been used to describe the recurrent differences recognizable within larger cultural units. Groups of related aggregates, whether or not they have been grouped into phases, which share a number of tech-nical and typological features in recurrent associations and are more diversified than the members of a Phase, are classified as an *Industry*. Industries having specific traditions in common form an *Industrial Complex*.

More precise definition of artifact assemblages is now resulting in more meaningful comparative studies and a revision of the

Fig. 1

Plate 17

Plate 18

regional cultural sequences. This greater precision has pointed up differences between assemblages not previously apparent, so making advisable, at least for the time being, a much greater use of local terms. Figure 1 shows the various African cultural units to which reference will be made, their chronological setting and the current terminology for Africa north and south of the Sahara.

Turning now to *excavation techniques*, it is not necessary to say much about the recovery of the vertical stratigraphy, where a succession of cultural levels is found. Well-established methods apply here and more and more attention is now being paid to the non-cultural data that can give information on the palaeo-ecology of the site—soil profiles, erosional features, sediment studies and so on. In these cases excavation is by natural stratigraphic units or, where these are thick and uniform, by arbitrary spits within them. A fine example of this is the Haua Fteah excavation in Cyrenaica, where 45 feet of deposit contained material dating back to about one hundred thousand years BP.[20]

A regional yardstick in the form of a long stratified sequence such as is found at the Cave of Hearths in the Transvaal, Montagu Cave at the Cape or the Kalambo Falls on the Zambia/ Tanzania border, will permit comparison of the individual occurrences with isolated horizons from other sites and may enable the archaeologist to fit these into the regional sequence.

What should be stressed here is the development that has taken place in Palaeolithic archaeology for recovering the pattern of the scatter of cultural material on a single horizon. So far as I am aware, the first work of this kind was carried out in Africa on Acheulian sites. Although, of course, it is the invariable way of digging any settlement site from the Mesolithic upwards, it does not appear to have been attempted before for the Palaeolithic. The excavation of ancient occupation areas in the open in east and southern Africa provided the opportunity of knowing, for the first time, something of the distribution patterns of artifacts on sites of hunters and gatherers, back to the beginning of the Pleistocene.

There is an enormous richness of cultural remains on such sites and the material is often fresh and undisturbed. The excavation of a part or the whole of such an occupation horizon, as, for example, part of an Acheulian living floor at the Kalambo Falls, shows many interesting features and variations. Of importance is the situation of the site—whether near water, such as a lake shore, or among sand dunes; its over-all dimensions (whether it is large or small); the relationship of the groups of artifacts—shaped tools to waste and utilized pieces—and the association of these with food debris such as smashed bone. Equally important are the features that may be exposed—hearths, empty areas, etc.—and the association of natural stones and 'manuports' (which are stones that could not naturally have got onto the site and which, therefore, must have been carried in by man) as well as signs of dispersal by natural agents and so on. Evidence of this kind has been obtained mostly from sites dating from the earliest Upper Pleistocene backwards in time. At the Olduvai Gorge, where the occupation debris was rapidly buried and superbly preserved, there are a number of such floors and similar floors are also preserved at Olorgesailie in the Kenya Rift and at a number of other east and South African sites.

Plate 7

The amount of variability is considerable and presumably reflects activity differences. Some sites can be shown to be butchery sites. Others are clearly living or manufacturing places and still others appear to combine the products of several activities. Sometimes detailed differences in the individual classes of tool, as with contemporary Acheulian handaxes and cleavers, may well reflect individual idiosyncracies and preferences.

INTERPRETING THE EVIDENCE

Now let us look at the archaeologist's fourth problem namely that of interpretation and reconstruction. Naturally, this cannot be attempted until he has done everything possible to provide answers to his first three problems.

The further a site is removed from the present the more difficult becomes the reconstruction of behaviour on the basis of the preserved cultural and non-cultural materials. Such reconstruction is mostly built up on the scatter patterns and relationships of artifacts, the association of the artifacts with food waste and features of the site, the physical remains of the population and on a study of the wear patterns on tools. The whole content of the site is then critically compared with ethnographic parallels, based upon a study of the relationships of individuals and of the group to their material culture, and of the decay and dispersal rates of materials on abandoned settlements. The use of ethnographic data can sometimes be supplemented by that available from the rock art some of which may be seven thousand years old.

Unfortunately, much of what has been written on African prehistory does not adequately keep separate and distinguish between what is fact, on the basis of what has been found on an excavation, and what is the author's interpretation of these finds. In consequence, there has recently been a move away from oversimplified synthesis and conjectural interpretation towards no interpretation at all. This is largely due to the realization that many of the earlier site records are imprecise and unreliable and that much of the work will have to be done again in the light of current thought and methods to determine the exact nature of the aggregate in its stratigraphic setting, before meaningful comparisons can be made.

Africa, however, provides an unique opportunity for the reconstruction of the way of life of past populations in the continent since there are still peoples there who preserve behaviour, techniques or activities which sometimes stretch far back into the past. There are still today hunting and gathering communities, such Plate 39 as Bushmen in the Kalahari or Hadza in east Africa living in steppe and savanna; Nemadi in the Mauretanian desert, Pygmy

groups in humid rain-forest in the Congo; and acculturated Batwa
groups in swamps in central Africa. There are people in various
stages from pure pastoralism, such as the nomads in Mauretania,
to incipient cultivation and the full village farming way of life
practised by the Bantu-speakers from northern Malawi. There
are pure agriculturists and there are political systems that range
from groups with no chiefs to the powerful, centralized, political
unit.

Plate 36
Plate 47
Plate 42

It should be possible, indeed it has been found to be so, to
identify some of these patterns of behaviour in the archaeological
record. Especially is this the case for Iron Age sites since, in many
instances, the present-day peoples are the direct descendants of
earlier Iron Age populations.

With Bushmen and other hunting peoples the correlation is
not so sound, as those who survive now occupy only the unfavourable areas that no one else wants. Thus, comparison between
them and 'Later Stone Age' peoples in a favourable environment
is not as meaningful in some respects as it might be. The over-all
pattern is still preserved, however, and we can see the same
exploitation in depth of the resources of the habitat and a technology that is the outcome of selective choice within the frame-
work of a long, regional adaptation. Studies of present-day
social and economic patterning, based on existing and abandoned
camps, provide a major advance in permitting the archaeologist
to make valid use of the ethnographic data.

In the same way specific traits of behaviour found today may
have special relevance for helping us to understand behaviour
in earlier times, even back into the Pleistocene. Kinds of structures, hunting equipment such as animal-head masks which
can also be seen in the rock art, burial customs, or manufacturing
techniques for which evidence occurs in the prehistoric record
may be interpreted in the light of still existing examples—pit
dwellings, for instance, wind breaks, skin- or mat-covered, light
framed huts, thatched beehive or pole and daub, conical huts

Plate 38

Plate 25

and the techniques of a modern gun-flint worker observed at Dundo in Angola.

The observation of modern, human scavenging practices helps to show how early man could have obtained the meat of large animals; and various ways of driving game still in use—bogging the animals in mud, driving by the use of fire and smoke, trapping and snaring—also help in understanding the ways of prehistoric peoples and the time at which these practices appear in the record. A study of the uses of wild vegetable foods or the preparation of initially unpalatable foods; of building or metallurgical practices and other skills—all these contribute to our understanding of the preserved remains of the past.

Studies of the bone debris from human and carnivore occupation sites can be used to throw light on the so-called Osteodontokeratic ('Bone, tooth and horn') culture of the South African Australopithecines or Man-Apes.[21]

Studies, by controlled experiment and observation, of the ways in which natural agencies fracture stone or cause dispersal of occupation waste on a site, are all pertinent for understanding prehistoric distributions.

Another line of approach that is just coming into use is the study of wear patterns on the edges of stone tools. Of course, the specimens for study must show no signs of natural weathering or abrasion and must come from a primary context. Work of this kind has been done on specimens from the Kalambo Falls site and several of the Acheulian and Sangoan core-scrapers show wear facets and there is one grindstone with the Acheulian. Later Pleistocene core-axes from the Congo often show damage of the working end and, in some cases, intentional resharpening for re-use. In Angola, experiment has shown that the polished ends of some of these core-axes resemble the polish that results from use for digging in the ground. This is an intriguing line of evidence that could have even greater significance if biochemists can identify whether the organic traces—amino acids, for example—absorbed by the working edges of the stone, come from animal or vegetable sources.

The archaeologist is, therefore, part of an interdisciplinary team of scientists all of whom are equally concerned to know the effects of past climatic changes on the African flora and fauna, on the vectors of diseases, on water sources, and to find the answers to many other questions that can only be solved by the pooling of knowledge and by collaborative effort.

Research and discussion, the application of a rigorous, though flexible, methodology, reconstruction and publication of the 'bits and pieces' are the steps by which the prehistorian populates the past. These are the ways in which he finds out what his people were doing and why they were doing it; and in which, also, he seeks to determine the time and manner of the differentiation of the human line and then the increasing biological and cultural specialization of man, firstly as a tool-user and then as a tool-maker of ever greater efficiency through the millennia. Finally, the prehistorian can join forces with the historian to clarify and document those developmental but prehistoric stages that lie behind the culture and personality of every nation in the African world today.

About whether tropical Africa was the only place in which the transmutation from proto-hominid to man took place it would, at this stage, be rash to make any categoric statement. Up to now, however, it has certainly produced the most significant, indeed unique, evidence of what the Restoration playwright Congreve calls 'a branch of one of your antediluvian families, fellas that the flood could not wash away'. What we already have, exciting as it is, is but an earnest of that much greater and more complete body of evidence that still awaits discovery beneath the African savannas for, indeed, Africa looks more and more like the place where it all began.

CHAPTER II

The Emergence of Man the Tool-maker

THE GEOGRAPHICAL ZONES OF AFRICA

Figs. 1, 8 THE ABUNDANCE OF fossil remains of early man and his immediate ancestors that have been brought to light during the last thirty years—often in spectacular circumstances—amply confirms Charles Darwin's belief that it would be in the tropics —perhaps in Africa—that man would prove to have evolved from a simian ancestor. It is in Africa that man's closest relatives among the great apes are found—the chimpanzee and the gorilla—and recent studies are showing that we are appreciably closer biologically to these African apes than had at one time been thought. For this reason primate studies, especially those concerning the anatomy and behaviour of the gorilla and chimpanzee, are directly relevant to an understanding of the biological nature and behaviour of the early hominids.

Before discussing the evidence and its implications, however, we need to consider the factor of environment since this varyingly affected the way of life of the human populations occupying the five main biogeographical zones. For climatic reasons these zones are complementary north and south of an equatorial, tropical region but undergo modification on account of topography, winds and ocean currents.

In equatoria is the humid, evergreen rain-forest—'that towering multitude of trees . . . all perfectly still' of which Joseph Conrad writes so graphically in *Heart of Darkness*. These forests are undergoing steady destruction at the hands of slash-and-burn cultivators and have done so for the past three thousand years. To the north and south and throughout much of the eastern area

Plates 4, 19 are the savanna lands—open forest, woodland and grass savanna

46

—which support an ungulate fauna fantastically rich, both in species and in the extreme size of the populations. Here also, on the higher plateaux, ridges and mountains, are found the high altitude evergreen forest and the montane grasslands that replace it when man interferes. The African savanna is one of the richest

Fig. 8   African topography, main rivers and lakes

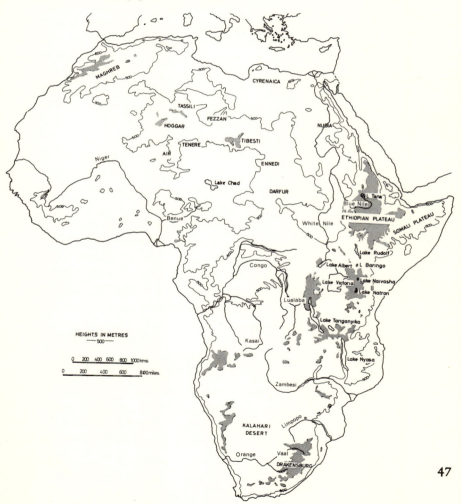

47

habitats in the world and stretches from the Atlantic to the Indian Ocean and from the southern border of the Sahara to South Africa's south coast.

The third of these biogeographical zones is the dry steppe country—the Sahel areas north and south of the Sahara, and the Karroo and Kalahari regions in the south of the continent. The vegetation of the steppe country consists of short, dry grass, succulents, low bushes and thorn trees. It is often rich in food reserves and supports a mammalian fauna of medium to small-sized animals.

Plate 1

Fourthly, there is the desert of which, again, there are several kinds—salt steppes, semi-desert and the dune fields and stony pavements of the desert proper. These are among the most unfavourable parts of the continent for human settlement but are, nevertheless, capable of supporting populations of economically self-sufficient hunters and herdsmen.

Fifthly, in the extreme north on the Mediterranean coast and in the southwestern parts of the Cape at the other end of the continent, there is country enjoying a winter rainfall and supporting a Mediterranean vegetation of evergreen forest and macchia. In north Africa generally this Mediterranean zone has had a profound effect upon the course of cultural development.

As was mentioned before, each of these zones has, in the past, undergone modification on several occasions, its boundaries expanding and contracting in response to fluctuations of climate which are best seen through fossil pollen evidence. In pre-Pleistocene times the vegetation pattern was markedly different from that of the present.

THE EARLIEST FOSSILS: HOMINOIDS AND HOMINIDS

Fig. 9

Evolutionary theory shows how the hominid line derives from an arboreal ancestor; and the chimpanzee and the gorilla are both forest-dwellers so that it is to be expected that it might be in the forested or formerly forested regions of Africa that the fossil

forms intermediate between ape and man will mostly be found.
This is, in fact, what has now transpired in those parts of east
Africa that are, or were once, covered by forest or a mosaic of
forest and savanna vegetation. Very important fossil material is

*Fig. 9   The main faunal and fossil man localities in Africa (Miocene and earlier Pleistocene).
(After J. D. Clark, 1967)*

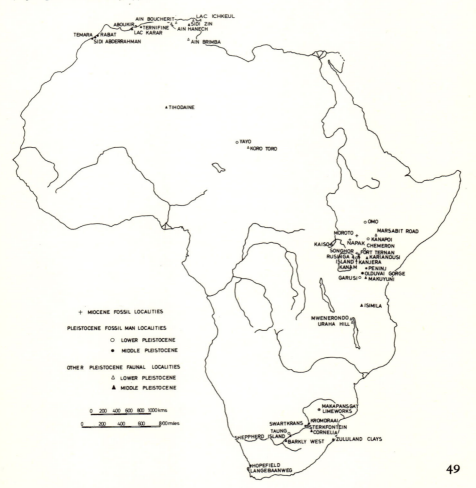

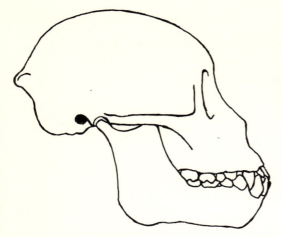

Fig. 10   Reconstruction of the skull of Dryopithecus (Proconsul) afri- canus. *(Courtesy of W. E. LeGros Clark and Chicago University Press, 1967)*

also known from the Fayum Depression in Egypt thus showing the former extent of the forests during the mid-Tertiary in a region that is now desert.[1]

Unfortunately, it is only in a comparatively few parts of the continent that fossils of the past twenty-five million years are preserved and there is, for example, hardly a bone from the whole of the west African forest zone or the Congo basin. Similarly, vast areas of savanna on the central plateau and in the east and south are also devoid of any fossil material because of the acid nature of the soil and the ground-water.

The main fossil-bearing regions are the Maghreb (northwest Africa), the east African region of the Western and Gregory Rifts, certain localities in South Africa, and a few isolated localities in Egypt, the Sahara and Rhodesia. Far the richest of these is the east African region. Here the formation of deep troughs, basins and volcanoes, the rapid accumulation of sedi- ments and burial of the fossils have combined to preserve a unique record extending back to the earlier Miocene, some twenty- two million years ago.

Man is distinguished from other primates by his upright posture, bipedal locomotion, peculiarly prehensile fore-limbs, his large brain and the ability to make and use many kinds of tools. Each of the parts of the body here distinguished appears to have evolved separately and at different times: thorax and arms first, then pelvis, legs and feet and, lastly, the head and brain. Man's humanity shows itself in the many complicated social and cultural patterns that are unique to his kind. Some of the stages whereby this transformation from a quadrupedal ancestor was effected can be adduced from a study of the fossil record that is now coming to light in east Africa and Egypt.

During the early to mid Tertiary, some fifteen to twenty-five million years ago, there existed in Asia, Europe and Africa a number of *Dryopithecus* ape forms. These fossils show modification of the limb bones and face, indicating that they were adapted to living *primarily* in the trees, although *also* on the ground.[2] Judging from their wide distribution, these pre-brachiators, as they have been called,[3] must have been living in a very favourable environment which was one of forest that, in Africa, constituted a mosaic with the savanna. This is well established by the finds of uniquely preserved fruits, seeds and insects of this time-period from the Miocene deposits on Rusinga Island in Lake Victoria and those on the slopes of the volcanoes.[4]

Fig. 10

By some fourteen million years ago, however, a more evolved form was present in India and east Africa, known as *Ramapithecus*.[5] Whereas the dryopithecines were unspecialized apes, morphological features point to *Ramapithecus'* having been a hominid. Unfortunately, the remains consist mostly of fragments of the face and teeth and nothing is known of the rest of the skeleton. However, the face has undergone considerable modification and has been reduced in length, the teeth having an arrangement and pattern that are essentially human. Therefore, it has been inferred from this that *Ramapithecus* must have walked upright and must have had fore-limbs adapted to using simple tools.

The remains of the later Miocene/Pliocene hominids are known only from rather small fragments of the face and from individual teeth and it has been pointed out that the face may have become modified at a different time from the limbs. When, therefore, remains of these are found they may not be as evolved as has been suggested.[6] Such observations are also very relevant for the interpretation of fossils of this kind *(Kenyapithecus africanus)* recovered by Leakey in a Lower Miocene context at Rusinga Island and Songhor, which suggest the possibility that hominids were present some eight to ten million years earlier still.[7] Recently good reason has been shown to think that man and apes may have shared a ground-dwelling, knuckle-walking existence up to the time that the human line developed bipedalism.[8] Whether, therefore, the hominid line had become separated from the common ancestor with the Pongids as early as the mid-Tertiary must remain in doubt until more complete fossil material becomes available. Rather does the recent work on chromosomes, serum proteins and hemoglobin[9] and on the calibration of the immuno-logical distance between man and other primates indicate that the separation of the Hominid and Pongid lines more probably took place as recently as four to five, certainly no earlier than ten

Fig. 11

million years ago—that is to say in the Pliocene.[10]

The suggestion has been made that the late Miocene/Pliocene ancestor *(Ramapithecus)* may have been a ground-dwelling, knuckle-walker, like the modern African great apes and that, like them, he escaped the extinction that overtook the smaller Miocene apes through competition with the forest-dwelling monkeys, by reason of his greater weight and his adaptation to ground-dwelling in addition to tool manipulation.[11] Since the gorilla and chimpanzee are forest-dwellers, it is most likely that this was also the habitat of *Ramapithecus*—a habitat that then stretched from east Africa across to northern India. *Ramapithecus* is associated in India with plant and animal fossils indicating a habitat of broad water-courses bordered by forest, giving place to savanna away from the rivers. As also at Fort Ternan evidence indicates that there was considerable migration of land

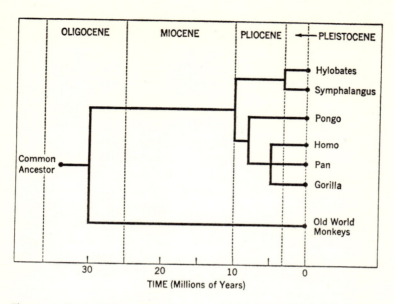

Fig. 11   Times of divergence between the various hominids as estimated from immunological data. The time of divergence of hominids and Old World monkeys is assumed to be 30 million years. (Courtesy of V. M. Sarich and A. C. Wilson and Science, 1967). Copyright by the American Association for the Advancement of Science

mammals between Africa and Eurasia in later Tertiary times, it is likely that the environment was similar in both continents. If this was, indeed, so it demonstrates to some extent the fundamental changes in climate and biome (ecological unit) that have taken place, particularly in the Arabian peninsula and southwest Asia generally since the later Tertiary.

The east African form of *Ramapithecus (Ramapithecus [Kenyapithecus] wickeri)* from the Fort Ternan site east of Lake Victoria[12] may have made and used simple tools. This site also provides evidence of what are believed to have been bone-bashing activities: a lump of lava with a battered and bruised edge was found associated with a long-bone with a depressed fracture.[13]

Further evidence is necessary to confirm this type of activity, but existing finds certainly suggest that *Ramapithecus* [*Kenyapithecus*] *wickeri* was a meat-eater.

It is interesting also that, in the parts that are preserved, there is no very significant difference between *Ramapithecus* and the Australopithecines that characterize the next hominid stage, and continued selection for increased use of the rear-limbs for bipedal locomotion and of the fore-limbs for tool manipulation could have been responsible for the developments to be seen in the anatomy of the Australopithecines in the earlier Pleistocene some two million or more years ago.

If *Ramapithecus wickeri* is a hominid, these morphological developments took place over a period of about ten to twelve million years. On the other hand, using the chronology based on the immunological scale,[14] there are between three million and one-and-a-half million years during which the Hominidae, now separated from the Pongid (or ape) line, were evolving the lower limbs toward efficient bipedalism and the upper limbs toward more complex tool use and manufacture. If the latter estimate is correct then *Ramapithecus wickeri* would have been an aberrant ape with fortuitous dental resemblances to the hominids. Unfortunately, very few deposits of Pliocene age are known from Africa so that we possess as yet no fossils of this time other than the Mio-Pliocene ones from the Fort Ternan site. During 1968, however, a new Middle Pliocene formation together with a hominid tooth were discovered to the north of Lake Baringo in Kenya, so that other finds may now be expected which will throw light on the biological character of the Pliocene hominids.[15] It is not going to be easy to recover evidence for tool-use at this time since, as will appear later, intentional and consistent fracture of stone to make a more efficient tool is likely to have been minimal or non-existent and, in any case, only stone and bone, of any of the materials that *may* have been used, can be expected to have survived. More convincing evidence is likely to be forthcoming from the association of natural fragments, sometimes modified by use, with hominid and other bone showing artificial modification, on land surfaces to which these materials could not have been transported by geological or animal (other than hominid) agencies.

There is every reason to suppose that this mode of tool-using behaviour and omnivorous feeding habits would have made available many more resources and so provided a greatly enriched environment which encouraged experimentation and so, in turn, brought about more rapid evolutionary change than would have been possible without the use of tools.

LOWER PLEISTOCENE FOSSILS

During the later Miocene and Pliocene crustal movement began to disrupt the earlier Tertiary pattern of internal drainage basins, replacing it with the present hydrographic system. At the same time there was faulting, deep rifting, orographic and volcanic activity along the line of the Great Rift Valley and certain other unstable parts of the continent. The later stages of these processes and, possibly, the fragmentation of the evergreen forest vegetation coincided with a significant lowering of temperature in Europe and the onset of the Pleistocene Period. The later Tertiary also saw the accumulation of the Kalahari Sands over much of the western half of the subcontinent during a time of more arid climate, and drier conditions were generally widespread during the Pliocene. It may have been at this time also that the xerophytic Karroo vegetation spread over a large part of southern Africa at the expense of the lowland humid tropical forest.

Plate 1

It appears likely that these events played a not unimportant part in accelerating hominid evolution some nine to six million years ago. The fossil record from the Lower Pleistocene is very much better known than is that of the Pliocene in Africa. The now famous Australopithecines, or Man-Apes, dating from the early Lower Pleistocene are known chiefly from limestone caves in the Transvaal in South Africa and from certain sites in east Africa, in particular the Olduvai Gorge in Tanzania. An advanced Australopithecine has recently come to light in Chad and there is an enigmatic fossil—*Meganthropus*—from Java that may belong in this group also though in some respects it is further advanced.[16] The discovery of the Australopithecines we owe primarily to three men—Dr Raymond Dart, the late Dr Robert Broom and Dr Louis Leakey—whose tireless and persistent researches have resulted in so much material being available today; in fact, no other fossil hominid genus is so well known as *Australopithecus*.

Without doubt, these are early tool-making hominids combining a small brain (435–562 cc.) with a large and massive jaw which was the feature that made scientists first consider them to be fossil apes, related more closely to the modern apes than they were to man. The discovery of a nearly complete foot at Olduvai and of a number of the bones of a hand, together with a reasonably complete vertebral column and pelvis from Sterkfontein in South Africa, and of complete and fragmentary limb bones from both regions, show that the Australopithecines walked erect and used their hands for manipulating tools and so foreshadowed the later hominids of the Middle Pleistocene.

Two races of Australopithecines are represented in the South African caves—a slenderly built and smaller form, *Australopithecus africanus*, and a robust, larger form, *Australopithecus robustus*, originally named *Paranthropus*.[17] The gracile form occurs at three sites—Taung, Makapan and Sterkfontein—and the robust form at two sites—Swartkrans and Kromdraai. They are found cemented in breccia filling old caves in the limestone and are associated with many animal bones.[18] Palaeontological evidence,[19, 20] suggests that Taung, Sterkfontein and Makapan are the oldest, followed by Swartkrans and then Kromdraai and the rhythm of climatic fluctuations obtained from sedimentation studies done on the breccias[21] shows the consistency to be

Plate 26
Plate 22

Plate 10

expected when based upon this sequence. *Australopithecus africanus*, the gracile form, therefore, precedes *Australopithecus robustus*.

These discoveries were mostly made in the 1930's to 1950's but in 1959 Leakey made the first discovery of a hominid fossil from Bed 1, the lower part of the long lacustrine and terrestrial sequence of beds at the Olduvai Gorge. This discovery was the famous 'Nutcracker Man'—*Zinjanthropus boisei*, now called

Fig. 12

Plate 27

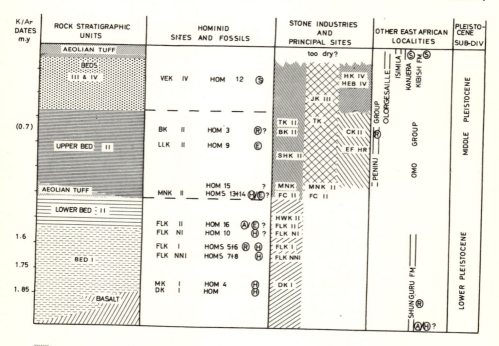

Fig. 12 Stratigraphy, hominids and stone industries at Olduvai Gorge

Australopithecus boisei.[22] The fossil was found in close association with a buried occupation site with broken animal bones and stone tools of which 'Nutcracker Man' was at first hailed as the maker.

In 1964 an almost perfect jaw, with teeth, of the robust Australopithecine was found eroding from beds of Middle Pleistocene age at Peninj, west of Lake Natron on the Kenya/ Tanzania border.[23]

Plate 28

In 1960, remains of another hominid had been found at Olduvai from a level slightly below that from which *Zinjan-thropus* came and near the same locality. These remains comprised parts of the side and back bones of the skull of a juvenile, that had been broken prior to fossilization. With them were a collar bone and fifteen hand bones from two individuals, an adult and a juvenile, and most of the bones of the foot of an adult individual. With these remains were ten worked stone tools and evidence of carnivore activity. The cranial fragments have been shown to belong to a somewhat larger-brained hominid (680 cc.) with a dental pattern different from that of *Australopithecus boisei* (or *Zinjanthropus*), but not very different from that of *A. africanus.*[24]

The associated hand and foot bones show close comparability to those of man, though with certain primitive features suggesting, so far as the foot is concerned, that its owner was adapted to running but not, perhaps to striding. Unfortunately, the ends of the toes had been chewed off, but a toe bone from higher up and near the top of Bed II shows that by this time striding was possible.[25] The hand falls into a position immediately between that of *Homo sapiens* and the apes and the great flexure and muscularity of the finger bones confirms the near ancestry with knuckle-walkers. The Olduvai hand was small and has been described as having an opposable thumb[26] that was not only capable of the power grip, but also probably of the 'precision grip' that made possible finer manipulation of objects in addition to the manufacture of simple tools.

Plate 32

Plate 23
Plate 24

Leakey and his associates who have studied these remains have described them as belonging to a new species of the genus *Homo* which they have named *Homo habilis*—meaning 'Man having the ability to manipulate tools'—and stone artifacts are found associated with these remains from the bottom of Bed I into the lower part of Bed II.[27]

Plate 29

In addition to the finds from the type locality (FLK NNI) there are a number of others—individual teeth from Bed I and more complete cranial and jaw material from the lower part of Bed II (from sites MNK II and FLK II)—that have been ascribed to this form. The only nearly complete limb bones are a tibia and fibula from the same site that produced *Australopithecus boisei*.[28] They are well adapted to bipedal walking though differences suggest that the manner in which these early men did so may not have been very like our own striding gait. Because teeth similar to those of *Homo habilis* were also present on this horizon, these leg bones are attributed to that form rather than to the robust Australopithecine. As yet no complete thigh bone has come to light but fragments are known from the caves in the Transvaal and they generally confirm the bipedal though clumsy gait of these early hominids.[29]

The other finds attributed to *Homo habilis* at Olduvai Gorge include a large part of the vault of a skull and the greater part of a lower jaw and parts of the upper jaw from one site (MNK II); and at another locality (FLK II: Maiko Gully) a skull, rendered fragmentary by an inconsiderate herd of Masai cattle that had passed over it as it lay exposed by erosion. Both these finds came from the lower part of Bed II and belong probably in the earlier part of the Middle Pleistocene.[30] They are considered to be morphologically more advanced than those from Bed I but no detailed descriptions have yet been published. Thus, the *Homo habilis* fossils as currently defined span a long range of time, perhaps a million years, and clearly, when comparisons are made with *Australopithecus africanus*, we must use the earlier fossils.

Plate 31

Fossils from two other regions confirm that there was at this time a more advanced hominid present, contemporary with the robust Australopithecine. These are the front part of a skull and face from the Chad basin[31] and a crushed jaw, palate and other fragmentary remains from the Cave of Swartkrans in the Transvaal, where they occur together with stone implements and *Australopithecus robustus*.[32] The Swartkrans remains have been attributed to a small species of *Homo erectus* though LeGros Clark and others consider they could well fall within the possible range of *Australopithecus africanus*. The remains from Chad are said to be transitional between *Australopithecus* and *Homo erectus*.

Controversy ranges mostly round whether the *Homo habilis* remains and those just referred to from Swartkrans can be included within, or whether they lie outside the range of *Australopithecus africanus*. Some, like Sir Wilfrid LeGros Clark, as has been said, maintain that they can be included within the possible range of the Man-Apes. Others, including Leakey, consider that they are too advanced and so lie outside this range and represent the oldest true *Homo*.

A look at the relative ages of these and other recent finds will help to explain better what was probably happening during this time—in the earlier part of the Pleistocene. Recent work by American and French teams shows that the gracile and the robust Australopithecines were *both* living in the Omo basin, north of Lake Rudolph, in the late Pliocene to early Pleistocene, between 3.5 million and 1.8 million years ago, on the evidence of the potassium/argon dates.[33]. The Olduvai sequence overlaps slightly the upper end of the Omo Beds but, while the robust Australopithecine is present unchanged at Olduvai, the other contemporary form is now *Homo habilis*.

Although no detailed description has yet appeared, it has been suggested that the *Homo habilis* fossils from Bed II at Olduvai are more advanced than those from Bed I and nearer to *Homo erectus*—a large-brained form of which occurs at a site (LLK II) in the upper part of Bed II. On the other hand, the robust Plate 34 Australopithecine, *Paranthropus*, continues apparently unchanged into the upper part of Bed II and thereafter disappears from the record.

The interpretation of this evidence is complicated by the uncertainty surrounding the age of the Australopithecine cave breccias in South Africa where there are few fossil animal forms in common with those of the east African open savanna sites and for which there are no chronometric dates. Re-examination of the associated fauna suggests that the sites with *Australopithecus africanus*[34] may be older than Bed I at Olduvai and could, therefore, be contemporary in part with the Omo Beds. The sites with *Paranthropus* (Swartkrans and Kromdraai) and the enig-matic *Homo erectus* fossil, on the other hand, are later and the possible equivalent of the lower part of Bed II at Olduvai; they have also yielded stone tools. Any suggestion, moreover, that the robust form might have evolved from the gracile in the Lower Pleistocene can now be shown to be unfounded on the basis of the new finds from Omo, where the two are contemporaneous.

If the South African fossils are not later than has been indicated, all this evidence can best be explained by the view that the gracile form evolved into *Homo habilis* and so into *Homo erectus*, by reason of the fact that it early developed the ability to make more efficient and complicated tools; whilst the robust form remained a tool-user only and so stayed biologically unchanged, eventually succumbing to competition with the tool-maker. If, on the other hand, the older sites in South Africa (Taung, Sterkfontein and Makapan) are contemporary and later than those in Bed I at the Olduvai Gorge, then the gracile Australopithecine fossils they contain cannot lie in the direct line of descent of man and would represent late survivals of the likely ancestor of *Homo habilis*. The first hypothesis would seem the most likely but whether it will stand the test of time, only time itself will show;

however, every year new discoveries make the evidence more complete and interpretation easier. If the intermediate position of the *Homo habilis* fossils between *Australopithecus africanus* and *Homo erectus* is confirmed it is not of too great significance whether they are classified as an advanced Australopithecine or a lowly form of *Homo*, though the cultural evidence seems to favour inclusion with *Homo*.

Fig. 13

Potassium/argon dating indicates that it would have taken about one million years or more to complete the transition (represented by the *Homo habilis* stage) from the gracile Australopithecine to *Homo erectus*. Such evolutionary developments could have been possible only through the medium of culture and the feed-back mechanism brought into play between physiological and cultural development. If this time-range is substantiated, the changes that have come about in the bony structure show how truly significant was the acquisition of culture.

With two doubtful exceptions, deposits older than Bed I at Olduvai have as yet produced no flaked stone tools, though, on the Omo evidence, the gracile Australopithecine was present at least a million-and-a-half years earlier. If further work confirms the absence of flaked stone tools from deposits older than two to two-and-a-half million years, we would be justified in associating the tools with *Homo habilis* more specifically and can, therefore, expect the rate of evolutionary change to have been appreciably slower, while the transformation occurred that changed a knuckle-walking to a fully erect posture and effected the coincidental increase in brain size and changes in the hand which made conceptual and skilled stone working and utilization possible, in the later part of the Lower Pleistocene. The immunological time-scale suggests that it could have taken as little as from one to three million years to evolve from the ancestral form common to Man and the African apes to a fully bipedal hominid form.[35]

Of course, it should not be imagined that this was a simple process of unilinear development, since the behavioural adaptations that would have been called for in the transition from a Pliocene forest-dweller to a savanna-dweller in the Lower Pleistocene, must surely have resulted in some diversification, though only the most successful survived. Similarly, in the initial stages of tool manufacture more than one form may have made simple tools, though only one, in which developing brain size permitted increasing complexity of artifact manufacture, made the transition to *Homo erectus*.

Fig. 13   Two possible interpretations of hominid evolution

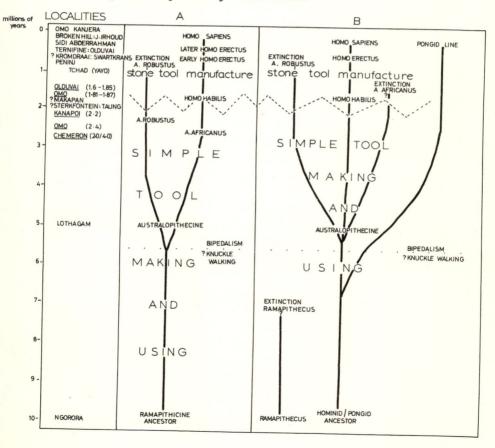

AUSTRALOPITHECINE BEHAVIOUR

The chief sources of evidence on which to attempt to understand and reconstruct the behaviour of the earliest tool-makers are the fossils themselves, the associated artifacts, animal remains and features of the sites on which these occur and, last but not least, chimpanzee and gorilla behaviour. To these should also be added any palaeo-climatic evidence that can be deduced from a study of the lithology of the beds in which the remains are found.

On the palaeo-climatic evidence from the Transvaal cave breccias there can be little doubt that the Australopithecines were living in a habitat somewhat drier than that of the region today but becoming wetter at the upper end of the sequence.[36] At Olduvai the habitat has been shown to be not unlike the Serengeti Plains today—open and adjacent to a brackish or saline shallow water lake—while that of Chad was savanna associated with forest galleries and occasional patches of evergreen forest.[37] This is a far cry from the forest or forest fringe environment occupied by the Later Tertiary ancestral forms, so that considerable adaptability can be postulated for successful existence in dry savanna by this time. It is probable, since the social patterns of the great apes—in particular of the African ones—do not show a great range of variation, that these did not differ very much from those of the common ancestor they shared with man. Moreover, if the separation took place as recently as the immunological approach suggests, then chimpanzee and gorilla behaviour is especially relevant to understanding that of the earliest hominids.

We know from the work of Baroness Jane van Lawick-Goodall and others[38] among the free-ranging chimpanzees in the Gombe Stream Reserve in Tanzania, that chimps are highly social animals and also make and use a number of simple tools. They select twigs for getting at termites; sticks to break open tree-ant nests and get out honey; sponges to mop up water from holes in hollow trees; and they are capable of using stones to break nuts.

Plate 21

They have been observed throwing sticks and stones, both over- and under-arm, in several different kinds of display against predators or at times of excitement.[39] Moreover, they are reasonably adept at carrying objects and they construct sleeping platforms. Interpretation of Man-Ape behaviour must, therefore, take into account this and other aspects of chimpanzee behaviour as well as the closer anatomical relationship to ourselves shown by the Australopithecine fossils. In other words, the greater brain size and character of the post-cranial skeleton show that what the chimpanzee does the Australopithecine must have done a good deal better and much more besides that the chimpanzee cannot do.

The chimpanzees at the Gombe Stream Reserve live in open groups that vary between thirty-three individuals and nine or less; the groups are constantly changing in size and composition. Sometimes they comprise males, females and juveniles; sometimes males only or only females with young; sometimes adult males and females. The males in particular are long-ranging for purposes of foraging and when food is plentiful the groups are largest. When food is obtained the group is called together by vocalization and drumming and there is some evidence that the food is shared. The most permanent association is between mother, infant and juveniles. Adult males are attracted, however, not so much for sexual reasons as by the mother-infant relationship. The greeting ceremonies when individuals or small groups come together (both among chimpanzees and gorillas) indicate the open nature of these societies, which is greater in the case of the chimpanzees than of the gorillas. In other words a returning member of the group is welcomed and a new arrival must be 'vetted', as it were, before the group accepts him.

A change from life in a forest to one in a savanna would necessitate an alteration in the dietary habits from a primarily vegetarian to an omnivorous diet in which meat eating acquired increasing importance. The Gombe Stream chimpanzees are, as yet, the only ones that have been observed to hunt and kill fairly large animals for food. This practice is, however, now known to be commoner than was previously thought, though whether it is a general characteristic of chimpanzee behaviour, not only in savanna/forest mosaic, as at Gombe, but also in forest[40] is not yet known, due to lack of adequate observation. It is, however, to be expected that the greatly increased source of animal protein available in the savanna and the less continuous supply of fruits would have served to encourage any hunting propensities possessed by the early hominids.

Another possible cause of the greater emphasis on animal foods now discernible, may have been the need to supplement the dwindling vegetable resources in an environment that was becoming increasingly drier. Whether or not continent-wide climatic deterioration was a factor in bringing this about cannot, however, be shown as yet since the evidence for these changes is too poorly documented. But there is no doubt that the micro-environment at the Olduvai Gorge in which the early hominids were living was essentially an arid one, though forest on the volcano slopes cannot have been far away. Whatever the process, therefore, it is certain that the possession of culture by the hominids ensured their success as predators and had by this time permitted groups of them to occupy a range of habitats outside the forest.

As our knowledge of the free-ranging behaviour of the African apes grows, it becomes increasingly apparent that the Australopithecines were not the aggressive 'armed killers' that one school of thought has so vividly represented them to be. The desire to interpret has overstretched the facts. The Transvaal caves cannot yet be shown to have been the places where the Man-Apes lived, neither can the assemblages of broken animal bone with which they are associated be proved to have resulted from the predatory and aggressive habits of the Man-Apes themselves.[41] It still remains to be shown that the differential preservation of the various skeletal parts in these caves was not due to the natural selective agencies that have recently been so effectively distinguished,[42] or that the so-called wear on certain bones was not, similarly, a naturally controlled phenomenon. Some very persuasive voices have been raised in support of the idea that 'man is a predator whose natural instinct is to kill with a weapon'. The associations of bones and hominids in the tropical caves and lake-side camps is used by these prophets of primeval violence as mute evidence of the 'courage and cunning' that was said to be already part and parcel of our heritage two million years ago.[43]

Defence of territory lies behind the aggressiveness of many animals and of modern man, but the African apes do not appear to engage in vigorous defence of their territory and, as we have seen, their groupings are essentially open ones, the composition of which is frequently changing. Territoriality in human societies is very likely, therefore, to have come about appreciably later in the Pleistocene. The stone implements at the occupation sites can, therefore, better be seen as evidence of man's reliance on artifacts of his own selection and manufacture, primarily for obtaining and preparing food and for defence. Thus, leaving aside for the moment the controversial, so called 'implements' of bone from the South African caves, we find indisputable manufactured tools of stone that relate to life at the home base and represent, not weapons, but domestic equipment. The industry to which they belong has been termed *Oldowan* from the type site at the Olduvai Gorge. If there is thus little evidence to substantiate Hobbes' thesis that the natural state of man was one of '. . . warre, as if everyman against every man', there is just as little reason for crediting the earliest tool-makers with the compassion and humanity of Rousseau's 'gentle savage'.

The occupation sites of this time are found in Bed I and at the base of Bed II at the Olduvai Gorge and are unique in providing information on the nature of the early hominid living-places.[44] These sites are small concentrations of occupation débris. One such oval area (FLK I with which *Zinjanthropus* was associated)

Plate 9

measured twenty-one by fifteen feet and contained a quantity of broken bone fragments, stone implements and chipping waste. At these sites are collected natural stones (manuports) and others that have been used for hammering and bashing. There are a number of flaked stone tools: choppers worked from one or both faces giving the tool an irregular chopping edge; polyhedrals, discoids, scrapers, burins and spheroids as well as a number of utilized flakes. Many unmodified flakes also occur. Three basic forms of worked stone predominate—polyhedral bashing stones, choppers and flake knives. There is nothing esoteric about their manufacture and they are all small implements with no 'formality' about them. They show, however, clear evidence of a rudimentary knowledge of working stone for the production of flakes and chopping edges. Assemblages such as these must lie very close
Fig. 14   to the beginnings of stone-working.

It is a common misconception that the Oldowan tools were made from pebbles and the term 'Pebble Culture' has been used as synonymous with Oldowan. Where pebbles and cobbles abounded, these were frequently used but the Olduvai evidence shows that angular lumps and flakes of lava and quartz were equally selected for making into tools. There are very few other sites in addition to the Olduvai Gorge where well-dated Oldowan artifacts have been found. They occur in the oldest sediments of the coastal sequence of Atlantic Morocco and in stream sediments at Ain Hanech in Tunisia where a number of polyhedral spheroids and a few choppers are associated with a late Lower Pleistocene (Upper Villafranchian) fauna. A very few artifacts have been found also in lake beds in east Africa—at Kanam in the Lake Victoria basin and at Kanyati in the Lake Albert Rift. The associated fauna dates these to the earlier part of the Lower Pleistocene—earlier, therefore, than the beginning of the Olduvai sequence. 'Pebble tools' have been reported from a number of other sites, usually from river gravels, but the evidence is insufficient or too incomplete to confirm their Lower Pleistocene

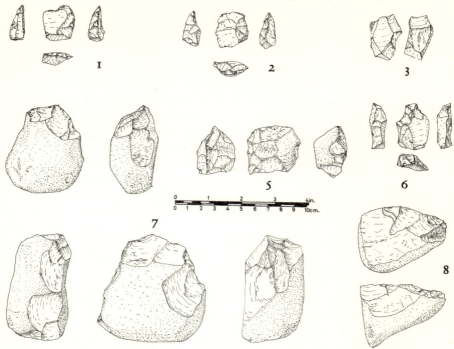

Fig. 14   Tools of the Oldowan Industry from Bed I, Olduvai Gorge: 1, 2   minimally re-touched flakes; 3   modified chunk with utilised notch; 4, 5   bifacially worked choppers; 6   flake scraper; 7   proto-handaxe; 8   unifacial chopper. Quartz and lava

age. Of course pebbles continued to be used for making tools in some regions until modern times.

Vegetable foods form about 60–80% of the food of hunters and gatherers today in warm and temperate climates.[45] Such foods, however, leave very little evidence in the archaeological record. It is, nevertheless, possible to regard the numerous polyhedral and other heavier stones, not only as tools for breaking animal bones and dealing with tough parts of the skin (also eaten

69

by present-day hunters) but also for breaking open nuts and preparing the otherwise unpalatable parts of plants by the break-ing-down of the fibrous portions. Experiment shows the so-called choppers to be effective for pointing a stick to use for digging out buried plant foods or small burrowing animals as well as for cutting, by means of a sawing action. Unmodified flakes form very efficient knives for skinning and cutting. Occasionally wear on a bone also suggests use, though not intentional shaping, by hominids. Two broken bones with Oldowan aggregates from Bed I (FLK NNI and FLK north) show striations and polishing similar to the kind of wear resulting from rubbing a hide or digging in the ground. A few of the 'Osteodontokeratic' bones show this kind of wear and there are others that cannot be readily explained as due to natural causes.

The Oldowan artifacts thus comprise the basic equipment necessary for obtaining a varied and unselected supply of plant and animal foods which were carried back to the home base. Ample evidence of this collecting behaviour is provided by the animal remains on the sites but as yet the full details have not been published. At one site (FLK I) the remains have been described as coming mostly from small to medium-sized animals, though bones from larger animals are also present.[46] Usually individuals are represented by only very incomplete remains and this is particularly so in the case of the few large animals that occur. This may, perhaps, indicate the importance of scavenging as a means of supplementing the meat supply though it could also reflect the habits of the hunters in that the animals may have been butchered and partly eaten or distributed away from the home base. There are also sites (DK I and FLK NI) where the full range of large to small animals is present. Thus, while it may be postulated that the Australopithecines and early tool-makers were hunting mostly small game and scavenging larger animals, the evidence is as yet insufficient to provide the necessary con-firmation.

Two butchery sites of large animals are known at the Olduvai Gorge from the top of Bed I (FLK NI, Level 6) and the base of Bed II at the same site. At the first, the nearly complete skeleton of an extinct elephant (*Elephas reckii*) was associated with one hundred and twenty-three artifacts and at the second the barely disarticulated remains of a Deinotherium had thirty-nine artifacts associated. However these creatures met their death, and they may equally have died from natural causes as have been killed, there is no doubt that by this time the makers of the Oldowan Industry had learned how to deal with the meat from large animals.

The degree to which hunting formed an essential part of Australopithecine behaviour is open to debate, but it need not have amounted to much more than the individual capturing of small mammals—young antelopes, pigs for example, or lizards —by running them down and killing them with the bare hands or the aid of a stick or stone, as is still done today by some African peoples. However, some animals can hardly have been taken except by organized group hunting skills and the recent evidence on chimpanzee hunting methods shows that group hunting must by now have formed an integral part of the behaviour pattern. Successful hunting organisation need not necessarily imply any complex communication system or the existence of language. The group hunting practised by wild dog packs, though it makes little use of vocalization, is, nonetheless, highly successful. Chimpanzees are known to make use of some twenty-three distinct calls or vocalizations, besides a number of gestures, facial expressions and bodily postures and it is a legitimate assumption that tool-making hominids would have had an even larger range of sounds and gestures at their command.

The *home base* is one of the most significant features of the early hominid sites since it represents a place of continuous, though temporary, occupation. The existence of a home base can prob-ably be explained by the prolongation of pre-adult life and the

greater dependence of the young upon the adults which emphasizes the mother/infant relationship. On the evidence of the erup-
tion cycle of the teeth in Australopithecines, this dependence continued for much the same length of time as in modern man.[47]
Primate studies show that this stretching-out of the period before
full maturity is reached is closely related to the learning of skills
and behaviour necessary for adult life. The young chimpanzee
becomes independent at between seven and eight years of age
and the transmission of the more complex learned skills of the
Man-Apes must have required an even longer time. The home
base can, therefore, be seen as the answer to the constraint
imposed upon the mobility of the group by this longer period
of learning. One particularly interesting base of this kind
(DKI) from the very bottom of the Olduvai sequence contains
a sharply defined area of stones with the usual stone and bone
waste and Oldowan tools. This suggests an intentional piling,
perhaps as some form of shelter or hide.[48]

Plate 6

There is no good means of estimating the size of a hominid
grouping at this time, but the area covered by the home base
suggests that the bands were not large, though it may be expected
that the actual numbers and individuals underwent fairly
continuous change. It has been calculated that the Australopithecine fossils from Swartkrans represent between fifty and
seventy individuals but, of course, this has to be spaced over the
time taken for the breccia to accumulate.[49] Bands probably
consisted of members of two or three compatible families of
mothers and juveniles and perhaps three or four adult males.
All these individuals were mutually dependent and shared the
results of their hunting and foraging activities; indeed, food-
sharing is the basis of human society and one of the most fundamental differences between human and mammalian behaviour.
That it is practised by chimpanzees (and, to a lesser extent, by
wild dogs) is of great interest but this is only a minor part of a
very varied pattern of behaviour; their society does not depend

upon it as does human society. This is in marked contrast to the picture of the club-wielding aggressor that is usually painted.

If most of the females were concerned with looking after infants and juveniles and with foraging for plant foods in the vicinity of the base, the males and the females without young would have been directly engaged on hunting and the carrying-back of the proceeds of the chase. The variety and number of individual animals represented on the living-sites shows that these were not places of purely ephemeral occupation but must always have served as a base for at least several days. There is not much of a problem in carrying small or medium-sized animals and larger ones can be cut up and the pieces divided among the hunters. But the gathering of vegetable products—fruits, nuts, roots and seeds, for example—requires the use of some kind of receptacle if any quantity is to be gathered. It seems that one of the things that most infuriates a chimpanzee is his inability to carry away more bananas than he can hold in his arms, so that it is likely that, even at this early time, the Man-Apes will have evolved some simple form of carrying device—a piece of bark or skin, a hollow tree burl or a tortoise shell—more specifically for the collection of vegetable foods.

These early sites are all close to water and this could reflect man's inability to live far away from a permanent water supply. Certainly such localities were the most favoured by man as well as animals. Probably no adequate way existed of storing and carrying water and waterside sites provided not only the best opportunities for hunting but (since the meat was, of course, not cooked) a regular supply of water to slake the thirst that invariably follows the eating of raw meat.

Such sites may have been sought-after for these reasons but probably also their popularity may have been connected with the thicker vegetation and tree growth usual at waterside localities in the tropics. Not only would this have provided vegetable foods in greater abundance but would also have admitted of tree-climbing as one means of protection from the larger predators. Quite clearly, also, the use of sticks and stones must have been one of the ways in which the Man-Apes sought to protect themselves and the reduction in the size of the canine teeth that is a feature of Australopithecine dentition was coincident with, and a direct outcome of the increasing and more efficient use of tools. As we have seen, chimpanzees have been observed to throw sticks and to use them as clubs against leopards as well as to throw stones. Many natural stones—'manuports', as the Leakeys call them—occur on the living-sites and the circular concentration of natural stones at the DKI site at the base of Bed I at the Olduvai Gorge could, besides any other purpose they may have served, have provided a reserve supply of ammunition with which to keep away scavengers from food stocks, especially during the hours of darkness.

Plate 6

One of the dangers for interpreting the stones and bones that constitute the cultural remains associated with the earliest hominids on the living sites, lies in the difficulty we experience in escaping from the preconceived notions that derive from membership in the evolved but rigid social system in which we live today. The opportunity of understanding the psychology and motive agencies that lie behind the behaviour of present-day hunting-gathering peoples like the Bushmen and the Hadza, is undoubtedly of the greatest relevance for understanding the behaviour of prehistoric groups at a similar economic level, though few such studies have yet been made. But even the most lowly of present-day hunter-gatherers are far in advance of *Homo habilis* physiologically, intellectually and culturally.

On the other hand, if we approach prehistory from the other direction, as it were, through studies of primates, in particular of man's closest living relative, the chimpanzee, we have a means of gauging the minimal intellectual and cultural achievements possessed by the early Pleistocene hominids. The truth lies between these two, though probably closer to the chimpanzee.

The close association between the development of the brain and the evolution of technical skills has been stressed[50] and as these skills advanced, more efficient adaptive behaviour resulted. In turn, this was made possible by the development of those parts of the brain connected with motor skills and the ability to communicate, so that culture and brain growth stand in a feed-back relationship to one another. The comparative speed with which (it is inferred) *Australopithecus africanus* changed into *Homo habilis* while *A. robustus* remained biologically unchanged until overcome by competition, can only be due to skilful tool-making and use originated by the gracile form.

The picture that now emerges, therefore, is one of small-brained, bipedal tool-makers, spread widely across the continent and living in small but variable, highly social, open groups existing by collecting vegetable foods and by organized hunting, the proceeds of which were shared with the other members of the group. The success of this behavioural adaptation lay in the way the learned skills of tool-making were transmitted from parent to offspring and the increasing experimental use to which the tools were put that led to new parameters, new adaptive behaviour and parallel biological evolution.

CHAPTER III

Unspecialized Hunting Societies

MORE ADVANCED HOMINIDS

To SPEAK OF HUNTING societies immediately suggests that hunting was not only the main activity of the group but also the chief way in which these populations obtained their food. It should be emphasized from the beginning, therefore, that no such implication is intended here. Ethnography shows that the total bulk of vegetable foods consumed by tropical peoples at a hunting and gathering stage of culture greatly exceeds that of meat and evidence from the Central Kalahari Bushmen and the Hadza, for example, shows, as was mentioned on page 69, that 60–80% of the food supply of these hunting peoples is vegetable.

Over many millennia, however, hunting and meat-eating have had a very great attraction for man and, still in our modern, advanced societies the hunter is held in high repute. There is much evidence of the age-long significance attached to the hunting way of life, to the consumption of meat and the utilization of the other by-products of the chase. Among early hominid populations it would seem quite likely that a minimal consumption of raw meat was essential to ensure a balanced diet. If, therefore, hunting is stressed at this stage in the evolution of culture, it is because it appears as a comparatively new and now very significant element in the pattern of behaviour of early man as seen in the more numerous remains of food bones scattered around on his camp sites.

In the previous chapter we saw something of the evidence, with its interpretation, for understanding the origins and behaviour of the earliest hominids—small-brained Australopithecines or Man-Apes whose upright stance and agility in handling tools made it possible for them to ensure the survival of the group in the African savanna. This they were able to do by exploiting both vegetable and animal food sources as well as by developing reasonably effective mechanisms for protection from the large predators. It was suggested that the deliberate flaking of stone to make tools was directly related to meat-eating, and that the greatly increased possibilities that the intentional manufacture of cutting and chopping equipment provided were both the outcome of and the agency for accelerated biological evolution.

The same evolutionary processes that gave rise to *Homo habilis* from, it is believed, the gracile Australopithecine form, in the later part of the Lower Pleistocene, some time prior to two million years ago, were also responsible for the genetic changes that gave rise to *Homo erectus* in the succeeding one million years, and for the technological advances shown by his stone tools.

The result of these evolutionary processes can again best be seen in east Africa. Here the accumulation of sediments in the troughs of the Rift Valley lake basins and their rapid burial and preservation under volcanic dejecta, document an unique record of this biological and cultural change.[1] This is best seen at the Olduvai Gorge where, in the long time period represented by Bed II, the simple Oldowan tool-kit is supplemented by the Acheulian type of assemblage. The Acheulian is so called by reason of the presence of tools similar to the handaxes and other large cutting tools which were first recognized last century in the assemblages recovered from St Acheul and other sites in the north of France. At the Olduvai Gorge the first Acheulian assemblages occur abruptly above a layer of aeolian tuff that separates Bed II into an upper and a lower half and which may also coincide with the extinction of certain archaic species of animals.[2] Below this break the physical type is that of *Homo habilis* (from site FLK II) and the industry is Oldowan but above the break, one site (MNK II), low down in the stratigraphic sequence, has yielded a hominid form provisionally assigned to *Homo habilis* but having, it has been suggested, some features that link it with the small-brained *Homo erectus* from the Djetis beds in Java.[3] A third site (LLK II), higher in the sequence and *above* the aeolian tuff, has produced the skull cap of a large-brained *Homo erectus* form (cranial capacity about 1000 cc.) and here the industry is Acheulian.[4]

Homo erectus can also be directly connected with the Acheulian cultural tradition at three sites in northwest Africa—at Casablanca and Rabat on the Moroccan coast and at Ternifine on the Algerian plateau. The oldest are three fossil jaws and one of the parietal bones of a skull from Ternifine and, somewhat later in age, are jaw and skull fragments from Casablanca and Rabat. The variability to be seen in the different tool-kits being used at this time during the Middle Pleistocene shows that *Homo erectus* was intellectually and technologically capable of a number of new cultural adaptations.

Plate 30

The Acheulian Industrial Complex is the most widespread and, apart from the Oldowan, the longest-lived cultural tradition that we know but, as yet, we have no completely satisfactory means of dating very exactly the period of time during which it was practised. No really acceptable chronometric dates are yet available from Olduvai that are younger than 1.6 million years and these are associated with the Oldowan industry and *Homo habilis* near the top of Bed I. However, in the adjacent Lake Natron basin a series of sediments (known as the Humbu Formation) was dated to 0.7 million years approximately by palaeo-magnetic reversal chronology. These sediments contain a robust Australopithecine mandible and, at a slightly higher level, a Lower Acheulian assemblage that is comparable to those from immediately above the aeolian tuff in Bed II at the Olduvai Gorge.[5] A single potassium/argon date for the Humbu Formation is 1.4–1.6 million years. This is compatible with estimates for the age of the Lower Acheulian at Olduvai.[6]

Plate 28

At the other end of the time-scale we have dates from the site of Kalambo Falls at the southern end of Lake Tanganyika that come just within the lower limit of the radiocarbon method and show that the final Upper Acheulian assemblages there are about sixty thousand years old.[7] Elsewhere this tradition is thought to have continued in an evolved form until about forty thousand years ago, though it had by then acquired a more specialized and regional character. The Acheulian Industrial Complex probably lasted, therefore, for as long as one million years.

There are no other satisfactory early chronometric dates for this time from African sites but the geomorphological relationship of archaeological occurrences in the Moroccan coastal sequence provides a means of correlation (through marine fluctuations) with the European sequence.[8]

Homo erectus was a man with an expanded brain (between 775 and 1225 cc.) and the skull to contain it. His face was much more like our own than it was like that of the Man-Apes though it was still massive. He had a post-cranial skeleton that shows few significant differences from our own and he possessed a much more extended range of abilities and indulged in a greater variety of activities than the evidence suggests to have been the case with *Homo habilis*.[9]

The Man-Ape and *Homo habilis* fossils found so far are confined to the tropical parts of the continent—east and South Africa and the Lake Chad basin. Whether these hominids were also located farther afield, occupying several different ecological niches, we have as yet no means of knowing. Most probably they were widely distributed in Africa, if we can use the evidence of the Oldowan tools and it is not improbable that they will also be found in the tropical regions of Asia and perhaps in southern Europe too. What is apparent, however, is that, by the beginning of the Middle Pleistocene—that is, around one million years ago—stone tool-making hominids had spread widely, not only in the African continent but also into southern Europe and Asia.

THE CULTURE OF HOMO ERECTUS

Homo erectus fossils are now known from southern Africa (Swartkrans) to central and western Europe, Indonesia and China. The very diversity of these habitats suggests that this form of man was capable of a considerable degree of ecological adaptation ranging from the cold temperate conditions of Choukoutien in northern China, and VertesZöllös in the central Hungarian plain to the tropical forest/savannas of Java and the grassland savannas of Africa. This degree of adapta-bility not only resulted in biological variability but also can be seen reflected in the composition of the tool-kits. It is in large part from a study of the stone tools and their relationship to associated remains on the camp sites, as well as from studies of the nature of the camps themselves, that we can attempt to reconstruct the behaviour patterns of Lower Palaeolithic times.

The questions to be answered are, for instance, how intensely and over how long a period were the camp sites used? How many people were involved? What were the patterns of settlement? or of movement? of territorial range? economic activity? com-munication and inter-group relationships? These and others can only be resolved after much more detailed excavation of complete camping places, recording of the relationships of the associated finds and analysis of the respective tool-kits. However, a start, at least, can be made now and will serve to throw into relief those lines of research which can best help towards a more com-plete understanding of behaviour.

It might be expected that in so long a time as that covered by the Acheulian tool tradition, some modification of the com-position and complexity of the tool-kits would have taken place. This has, indeed, happened but the degree of change is not of the magnitude that might be thought likely over more than half a million years and all the evidence points to an extremely slow and gradual rate of cultural evolution. Attempts have been made to establish a series of cultural stages with regional significance, such as that in use in Morocco or those formerly employed at Olduvai or in the Vaal river basin, based on stratigraphic or geomorphological data. Today, however, it is more generally recognized that the Lower Palaeolithic is divided into only three main culture stages: an Oldowan, followed by a Lower and an Upper Acheulian. More sites of the Upper Acheulian are known than belong with the Lower stage, the components of which are chiefly characterized by the bold nature and small number of the flake scars as well as by the lack of refinement which comes from using a hard hammer or anvil of stone for working the tools. Otherwise Lower Acheulian aggregates fairly closely resemble those of the Upper and later stage.

In the upper part of Bed II in the Olduvai Gorge, above the aeolian tuff, three kinds of assemblage have been shown to occur.[10] Firstly, there is a continuation of the Oldowan tradition of a flake and chopper type of industry that was the only sort of tool-kit present in the lower part of the sequence. In the upper part of Bed I and in Bed II, there is some, though very little, development as compared with the assemblages from the lower part of the sequence at Olduvai. To the range of tools already noted (page 68), there is here added a kind of simple pointed chopper, known as a proto-handaxe, rough bifacial forms and rare handaxes together with some more evolved scraper forms and other small tools which, when made of fine-grained stone, take on a surprisingly sophisticated appearance. Spheroids are also present and if, as has been suggested (page 69), the battering they have suffered comes from pounding foodstuffs to make them edible, these tools now imply a prolongation or regular resumption of such activities at the sites where they are found as well as a longer period of occupation.

As well as these Developed Oldowan assemblages there are now also found others in a contemporary tradition which is that known as the Acheulian. As yet there are analysis details from only one Lower Acheulian site at Olduvai (Site EF-HR), from

Fig. 15

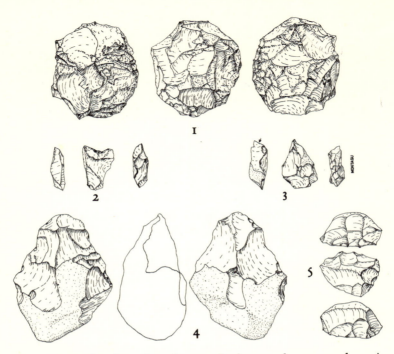

1

2   3

5

4

the middle of Bed II, though several others are known and await
excavation. The large cutting tools (handaxes and cleavers)
which characterize the Acheulian Industrial Complex, comprise nearly thirty-nine per cent of the retouched tool classes and
this is increased to over forty-seven per cent if the large scrapers
are included. The other classes comprise choppers (10.5%),
spheroids (11.5%), utilized heavy duty equipment (21%) and
the remainder are hammerstones and some miscellaneous specimens. This tool-kit was associated with a large percentage (78%)
of unmodified flakes in a total of 434 artifacts. The most significant feature about this Acheulian tool-kit is that its appearance
in the record is quite sudden and that it is made from large flakes
struck from cobbles or boulders, in this case of lava.[11] This is in
marked distinction to the Oldowan and Developed Oldowan,
all of which are made from appreciably smaller fragments or
cobbles.

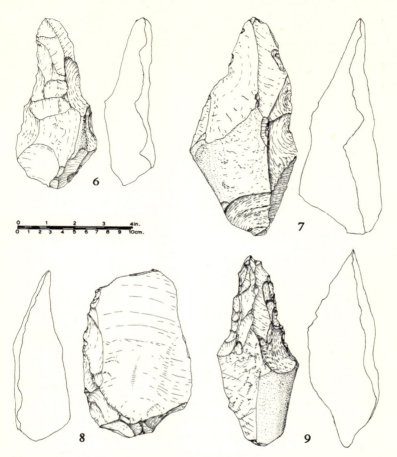

Fig. 15 Developed Oldowan and Lower Acheulian implements. Developed Oldowan: 1 multi-facetted polyhedral, limestone (Pré-Acheuléen) Ain Hanech, Algeria; 2 double notched scraper, chert; 3 flake with utilised notch and burin scar, chert, Locality HWK II, Olduvai Gorge; 4 denticulate core scraper, quartz, Locality BK II, Olduvai Gorge; 5 proto-handaxe, quartzite, Sterkfontein Extension breccia, Transvaal. Lower Acheulian: 6 handaxe (ficron type with chisel end) Ternifine, Algeria; 7 trihedral (pick-like hand-axe) STIC Quarry, Casablanca, Morocco; 8 cleaver on a Kombewa flake, Ternifine, Algeria; 9 trihedral, STIC Quarry, Casablanca, Morocco. 6–9 all quartzite

The third type of assemblage that is present in Bed II combines both Acheulian and Developed Oldowan forms, though the handaxes are generally present only in small numbers and are, on the whole, less well made. Characteristic are the numbers and variety of the small scraping tools made on flakes and fragments.

Acheulian tool-kits did not evolve from the Oldowan in east Africa. The only other region with a comparable, long, cultural and stratigraphic sequence is the Moroccan coast and here also the earliest Acheulian assemblages make an equally sudden appearance in the succession in the beach gravels of the receding sea level brought about by the onset of the Mindel glaciation. Judging from the wide distribution of the handaxe tradition, the most likely explanation would seem to be that this large tool element represents the addition of a new and important activity to the previously established way of life. The very nature of such an invention necessitates a sudden manifestation of its presence— large flakes result from breaking large blocks of stone, though whether this technique originated in east Africa is unknown. At the same time the ability successfully to strike off large flakes also represents an important technological development, a major step forward in man's mastery of his raw material. It can be expected, therefore, that, once invented, knowledge of this technique would spread rapidly throughout the Acheulian world.

At first the cores were randomly struck but it was not long before special techniques were developed for the removal of large flakes for making into handaxes and other tools from boulders too large to be broken up in the normal manner. We find, therefore, what are called the proto-Levallois and Levallois methods of core preparation and another—the Kombewa method—giving the curious flake with double bulb of percussion. These occur with the Acheulian, both inside and outside Africa, wherever the size and nature of the raw material make it necessary; but which of these, or other basic methods, would,

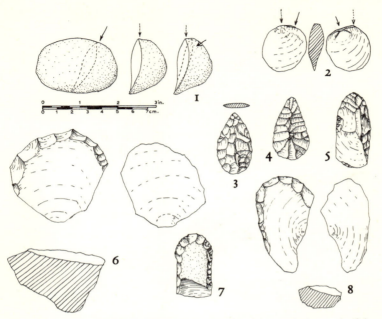

Fig. 16 Acheulian flaking techniques : 1 the Kombewa method ; 2 the flake with two bulbar surfaces ; 8 Proto-Levallois I, and 6 Proto-Levallois 2 cores and derived flakes. 3–5, 7 handaxes and cleavers made from these flakes. (After L. Balout, 1967 and C. van Riet Lowe, 1937)

in fact, be used appears to have depended on traditional choice and the flaking properties of the material itself.

Fig. 16

The three cultural phases or facies that we have just noted from Olduvai are found widely in the continent and persist from the beginning to the end of the Acheulian Industrial Complex; that is to say, into the beginning of the Upper Pleistocene. It has been suggested that the Bed II evidence from Olduvai can be interpreted as showing the existence of two or more contemporary hominid forms representing separate phylogenetic streams.[12] While the evidence is too incomplete to rule this out, it would be necessary to postulate that these two forms were each occupying

85

separate ecological niches where they did not come into com-petition, since had they done so, the less efficient must have been eliminated. The persistence of the robust form of Australo-pithecine during the earlier half of the Middle Pleistocene is likely to have been possible only because there was no com-petition and, as soon as *Homo erectus* started to experiment and so begin to exploit the habitat of *Australopithecus robustus*, the latter's extinction was inevitable. Progress, therefore, as Herbert Spencer has said, 'is not an accident. . . . It is a part of nature.'

A more likely explanation, therefore, for these three cultural facies is that they are related to different activities—the large cutting tools being used for a purpose other than were the small flake tools or the choppers and spheroids. This explanation is strengthened by the clear evidence of selection in the use of raw materials. The large cutting tools of the Acheulian are more often than not made from tough hard rocks such as quartzite or various kinds of lavas. The small flake tools, on the other hand, are generally made from fine-grained rocks—quartz or chert, for example—that produce a sharp but brittle cutting edge and are more easily retouched to form a scraping edge. This is a pattern that is reflected throughout the Oldowan sequence also and can be seen at a large number of Upper Acheulian sites north and south of the Sahara. There can, therefore, be little doubt that we have here an intentional selection of raw materials best suited to the work for which the tools made from them would be used. Both the tool-kits in which the large cutting tools pre-dominate and those in which they are mixed with Developed Oldowan forms are here designated as Acheulian: most assem-
Figs. 17, 18 blages are of the second type.

There are, as the map shows, many more Upper than Lower Acheulian sites known. However, their general geographical situation is the same, though the degree of technical skill evidenced in the tool assemblages is greater with the later ones. Archaeo-logical Occurrences of the earlier part of the Middle Pleistocene

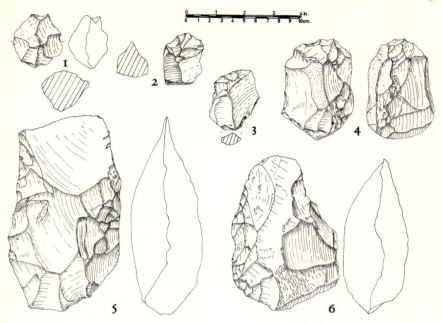

Fig. 17   Mixed Acheulian/Developed Oldowan tools from Cornelia, Orange Free State, stated to be associated with the Vaal/Cornelia fauna : 1   disc core ; 2, 3   end scrapers ; 4   chopper ; 5   cleaver ; 6   handaxe

which include those with both Lower Acheulian and the Developed Oldowan tool-kits, are more widely distributed in Africa than are Occurrences with adequately attested Oldowan assemblages. They are present in northwest Africa, in east and South Africa but there are few living-places like those at Olduvai that remain undisturbed and in most cases the assemblages are contained in lakeside, river or marine sediments. The handaxes are usually either lanceolate or taper to a chisel-like end. Pointed, pick-like forms with a trihedral cross-section and cleavers with parallel sides and square butts are characteristic of the north

87

African Acheulian sites of this time. One of the undisturbed sites is probably that which is referred to as the STIC quarry at Casablanca, where a fine series of tools and food waste was found along the edge of a watercourse stratified above the sea-shore deposits of the Maarifian regression (= Cromerian interglacial period of Europe), and sealed by the great consolidated dune rock deposits coeval with the Mindel glaciation in Europe.[13]

Another important site is Ternifine on the grass-covered Algerian plateau. Here the artifacts, both large and small, came from horizons now below water level and lay on the bank and down the slope of a small lake fed by artesian water. Over fifty per cent of the tools were worked pebbles and there were 107 cleavers and 110 handaxes out of a total of 652 artifacts; small tools were also present.[14] This assemblage was associated with much bone food waste and three mandibles and a parietal bone

Plate 30

of a north African race of *Homo erectus*.

At Peninj, in the Lake Natron basin, two further early Acheulian sites are situated on what was open and grassy flood plain on sandy ground, adjacent to a seasonal stream course. Here fresh water would have been available and perhaps some tree growth would have provided shade along the stream as there is along the Peninj river today; the two aggregates are similar to that described above from the Olduvai Gorge.[15]

At the Olduvai Gorge the Acheulian sites (those, as we have seen, where there is a preponderance of handaxes and cleavers) are situated near to stream courses and gravel beds but away from the margin of the shifting *playas* or pans which had replaced the formerly stable salt lake.[16] By contrast, the sites where the Oldowan assemblages were found lie on the lake-shore flats, close to streams of fresh water draining into the lake from the slopes of the adjacent volcanoes. This may show some major change in the choice of habitation sites but it could be related to Acheulian man's need for suitable boulders from which large flakes could be struck.[17]

In South Africa, a mixed assemblage of nearly three hundred Developed Oldowan (Acheulian) tools was found in breccia at the Extension Site at Sterkfontein, immediately adjacent to the older Type Site breccia which yielded the gracile Australo-pithecine fossils.[18] There were 287 artifacts and manuports; the

Plate 10

Fig. 18   Distribution of Oldowan and Acheulian sites. (After J. D. Clark, 1967)

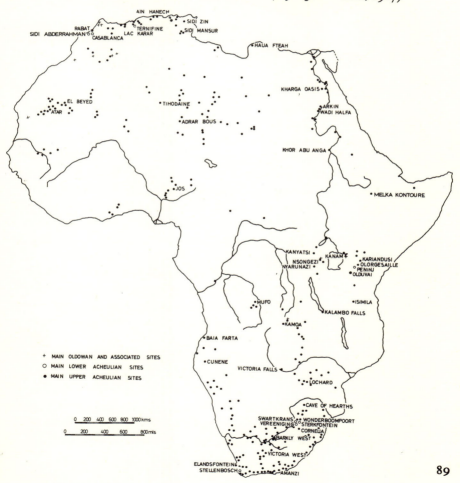

+ MAIN OLDOWAN AND ASSOCIATED SITES
O MAIN LOWER ACHEULIAN SITES
• MAIN UPPER ACHEULIAN SITES

89

artifacts being mostly bifacially worked choppers and polyhedral forms together with two possible handaxes. These artifacts cannot be regarded as coming from a living-site, since, apart from seven flakes, there is no flaking waste present. Nevertheless, they were brought into the limestone cave for use, the quartzite cobbles being derived from the near-by Blaaubank stream. The few hominid teeth associated have been variously considered as representative of the gracile Australopithecine and of *Homo habilis*.[19] Similar tools come from the near-by cave breccia at Swartkrans associated with the robust *Australopithecus* and some fragmentary fossil material which has been ascribed to *Homo erectus*.[20]

Other, though disturbed, Lower Acheulian assemblages (Three Rivers and Klipplaatdrif) are found at the junction of the Klip river with the Vaal in South Africa, a little to the south of those just described.[21] Here the artifacts are found within or resting on river gravels and are, many of them, fairly heavily abraded but the same tool forms are manifest as are present at the other sites that have been mentioned. There are handaxes and, more rarely, cleavers, crude, pointed, pick-like tools and often trihedral forms, spheroids, choppers and a varying number of small, scraper-like artifacts on flakes. The retouch is by means of a stone hammer or anvil, the flakes are thick and broad while the negative scars on the large cutting tools are similarly bold and deep. As with other Lower Acheulian aggregates, these handaxes mostly show a minimal number of flake scars—often not more than eight or ten—while the edges are irregular, not straight.

Some bone and ivory fragments, split and minimally trimmed by percussion, are also found with Developed Oldowan (Site MNK II)[22] and Acheulian (Site SHK II)[23] aggregates at the Olduvai Gorge and an especially convincing small, parietal bone fragment from Sterkfontein Extension Site shows fine striations and polishing that can only result from use.[24]

The Acheulian sites that belong in the later part of the Middle Pleistocene show a greater diversity of retouched tools and an appreciable refinement in the technique employed for fashioning them. Handaxes and cleavers are now made by what is called a 'soft' hammer technique (that is, by using a hammer of hard wood, bone or antler instead of stone). This results in the removal of thinner and longer flakes and a considerably more refined end-product with straight, regular sides on which much more labour and skill have been lavished than was strictly necessary to make a usable tool. These finely finished large cutting tools (handaxes and cleavers) may be some of the first evidence of an aesthetic sense in man and, although the general shape of the tool varies, they are the first 'formal' implements made to a regular pattern to appear in the cultural record. Additional evidence of the greater 'awareness' of *Homo erectus* may also, perhaps, be seen in the piece of red colouring matter—haematite—carried onto one of the Developed Oldowan sites (BK II) at the top of Bed II at Olduvai.[25]

Fig. 19

Now also, considerably more refinement in the retouch of the working edge can be seen in the various scraper forms with the later Acheulian. The trimming is probably the result of more continuous use of the edge, which thus needs to be resharpened by flaking when it becomes blunt, together with a more skilful use of the tool on the material being worked. Although there are still many of the rough polyhedral spheroids on the camping sites, there are also now others that are more perfectly shaped. Whether these formed part of some missile weapon, as has been suggested, is not known, but if their primary use was not for battering and bashing, this was, nevertheless, the method by which they were shaped. This carries with it implications for the pounding of vegetable foods and also for bone-breaking and splitting, since these spheroids and broken bones occur together. What is again significant here is that continued treatment by the 'bouncing' action of stone on stone, which is the technique by

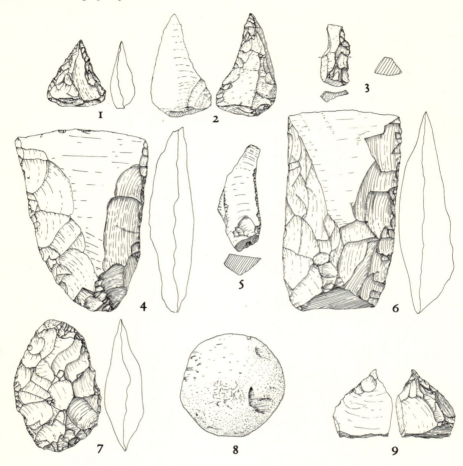

which these spheroids were rounded (whether by intention or not) needs quite some time to bring about the reduction and rounding shown by some of them. Either, therefore, the camping places were now being occupied more intensively and for longer stretches or they were being reoccupied seasonally over a longer period of time.

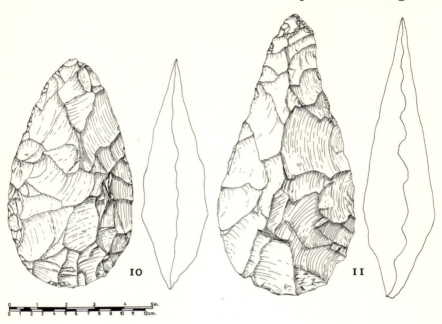

*Fig. 19   Upper Acheulian tools from Kalambo Falls, large tools quartzite, small tools chert:
1 convergent scraper; 2 concave side scraper; 3 denticulated side scraper; 4 divergent edged
cleaver; 5 flake knife with marginal retouch; 6 parallel edged cleaver; 7 ovate handaxe;
8 spheroid; 9 awl or bec; 10 elongate ovate handaxe; 11 lanceolate handaxe. Dated to
60,000 years BP and earlier*

THE WAY OF LIFE OF HOMO ERECTUS

Let us now look at the camping places themselves, where they
are found and what they can tell us concerning the behaviour
and composition of the group that occupied them. Firstly, there
are now many more sites of this time (Upper Acheulian) than
of any previous period and they occur mostly along stream and
river courses, round lakes and on the sea-shore. They are found

in country that is today grassland, woodland savanna, semi- or complete desert; but they are generally absent from the forest zones. Most of the sites belong to what is now drier savanna and grassland where water and grazing are plentiful—in other words, where the greatest concentrations of the large herbivorous and gregarious game herds are found. Those camp sites situated in the Sahara and other desert regions are invariably associated with sediments that show their contemporaneity with wadi courses or springs or with shallow pans, lakes or marshes between the dunes. Caves were also sometimes occupied—over long periods of time as the thirty feet of deposit at the Cave of Hearths in the northern Transvaal shows. The later Acheulian appears to have been associated with a long, fairly stable, period of somewhat wetter and more humid climatic conditions than those of the present time and it is probable, though as yet unproven, that the earlier stages were contemporaneous with a series of wet and dry fluctuations.

Not too much is known about the over-all size of occupation sites since problems of removing large thicknesses of overburden have, up to now, generally precluded the excavation of a complete concentration of occupation waste. We have, however, for comparison at least one Oldowan 'floor' at the Olduvai Gorge (that which yielded *Zinjanthropus*) where the occupation débris —worked stone and broken bones—was concentrated within an area of roughly three thousand square feet. If we use as a criterion a recent estimate of the requirement of the central Kalahari !Kung Bushmen of about one hundred and forty square feet per person, we arrive at round about twenty, or perhaps fewer, as the number of individuals using this FLK I (*Zinjanthropus*) site. If, however, we take the evidence for the median requirement of the Californian Indians, which is twenty-five square feet per person per house, and use *this* to calculate how many people may have been using the area of higher bone and stone density in the centre part of the FLK I concentration (an area about twenty-

Plate 9

one by fifteen square feet) we can estimate a group of some ten to twelve individuals at this site.[26] If we use the same two criteria for the complete later Acheulian concentration at Olorgesailie in the Kenya Rift Valley (DE/89 Horizon B), we get, using the Bushman figure, a total of not quite nine individuals and, using the much smaller requirements of the Californian Indians, we arrive at a total of about fifty people for an area of roughly twelve hundred and fifty square feet. Obviously, estimates of this kind must remain highly speculative in our present state of knowledge, but they may, at least, suggest some possible increase in over-all group size.

Plate 7

There is also now some indication that structures of some kind may at times have been built. Some of the sites, as at Olorgesailie, show such a sharp delineation of the outer margin of the occupation waste as to suggest its having been contained within some fence or wind-break, though, admittedly, the mechanisms for natural concentrations are as yet only imperfectly understood.[27] A semicircle of stones on one of the occupation floors at the Kalambo Falls may have formed the base of a wind-break[28] and, looking outside the continent for the moment, the limestone blocks on the Latamne site in Syria may be indicative of some more substantial structure.[29] At the recently excavated site at Nice (Terra Amata), Lower Acheulian implements of stone and bone are associated with habitation places within an oval floor area of about 15×36 feet marked by post holes and stone blocks; there are also hearths associated.[30]

An interesting and puzzling feature at some of the African sites is the accumulation of stony rubble that is associated with the artifacts. Mostly this rubble is concentrated in the same way as are the artifacts. In these instances there can be no doubt that the rubble was carried to the site by man and did not accumulate by natural means and it occurs on only some of the occupation floors. It has been suggested that this rubble may have provided the foundation for a home base situated in swampy ground as protection from predators; that it may have been used to hold down the base of a wind-break or that it was ammunition for keeping away scavengers and predators (see page 74).

The *Zinjanthropus* 'floor' (FLK I) at Olduvai and the Olorgesailie concentration DE/89 Horizon B are what have been termed 'living-sites'. There are, however, other kinds of site known from this time which show that *Homo erectus* engaged in several different kinds of activities that left as record several different sorts of tool-kit. Firstly, there are the sites we have just mentioned where several different kinds of activities were being carried on and the tool-kits are of the mixed Oldowan and Acheulian type, together with unmodified waste from the making of the tools.

Next, there are sites where the purpose of the tool-kits was for butchering one or more large animals. Such, for example, are those found at Isimila in Tanzania (Sands 4 Horizon)[31] and one of the lower surfaces at Olorgesailie (Basal Bed A, Locality 1: 3)[32] where disarticulated and incomplete hippopotamus carcases are associated with rare heavy-duty or occasional large cutting tools and small collections of flakes, only some of which show minimal modification and retouch. Similar assemblages with butchered large animals are better known from Europe, as at Torralba and Ambrona in central Spain, at the latter site associated with the remains of over twenty straight-tusked elephants, and there is little doubt that in all these cases the equip-ment represents the tools made for use in butchering the animals.

Again, other sites have concentrations of large cutting tools with varying proportions of light-duty equipment but little or no bone. Such is the case on a partly excavated surface at Melka Kontoure in Ethiopia,[34] or again, at the waterside site of Latamne in northern Syria where large cutting and light-duty tools were associated with large limestone blocks which, as we have said, suggested some kind of shelter construction: at each of these sites there was very little bone.

Other Archaeological Occurrences closely resemble the Developed Oldowan from Bed II at the Olduvai Gorge. A site in Bed III at Olduvai (JK III).[35] others from Olorgesailie (Basal Bed B[LSI], L.H.S. or 'Hog' [LSXI]) and another from Broken Hill in Zambia[36] have numbers of light-duty, small tools but few and poorly-made large cutting tools.

Yet another facies can probably be distinguished by the number of rather crudely-made heavy-duty tools—pick-like forms, some parallel-sided bifaces and large flakes—but the general lack of well-made handaxes and cleavers. Such assemblages are found in the peripheral parts of the Congo basin in northeast Angola and the Lower Congo and may be characteristic of localities of thicker vegetation and higher rainfall.[37]

Other sites, again, were specifically workshops, and examples of this kind are known from the Vaal river (Canteen Kopje),[38] from the Transvaal (Wonderboompoort),[39] the Kalahari (Nakop)[40] or the Sahara (Tazazmout)[41] where small concentrations or huge spreads of débris lie adjacent to the sources of the raw material—river boulders, an outcrop or a scree at the base of some scarp.

Each of these three or four main kinds of tool-kit, when it is broken down into its component parts, shows a considerable amount of variation in the number of the individual tool forms. Sites such as Isimila and Olorgesailie or Kalambo Falls show this in the several successive Acheulian horizons they each preserve. They show also that there is considerable variety in the attributes of the large cutting tools which may be pointed and long in one horizon while, in the succeeding level, they will be ovate in plan form. It has been suggested that such variability may reflect the idiosyncratic variation that was possible between individual groups or bands of tool-makers both contemporaneously and through time.

Estimation of the length of time a site was occupied is even more difficult than trying to determine the number of individuals

Fig. 20

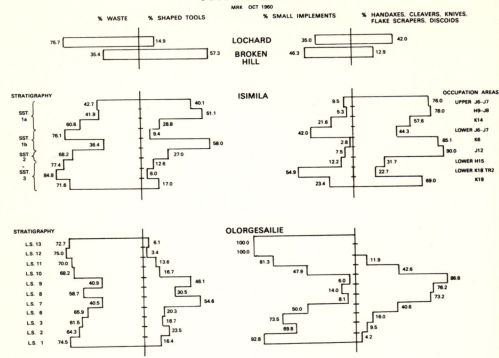

Fig. 20 Comparison of the percentage frequencies of various artifact classes in Archaeological Occurrences at four Upper Acheulian occupation sites. (Courtesy of M. R. Kleindienst, 1961)

who may have used it. Sometimes, as at the Kalambo Falls, the thin spread of sandy sediments that separates one concentration from another is likely to have been deposited in one season but, where such microstratigraphic evidence is lacking, the problem is more difficult. On the Olorgesailie floor (DE/89), referred to earlier, were found the remains of sixty-five giant baboons, the bones of which had been broken up, presumably for the marrow. It seems unlikely that these were all killed during one season's

Plate 11

98

occupation of the site and it is probable that such sites, favourably situated close to suitable sources of food, water or other resources, were regularly visited over an extended period of time.[42] The Hadza, incidentally, hunt baboons at night by surrounding their sleeping-places and then letting fly with all available weapons.[43]

Regular visits over a period of years may account for the large number of elephant remains at the Lower Acheulian sites in central Spain or for the large concentrations of handaxes and cleavers on the gently sloping rocky surface leading down to the river at Power's site on the Vaal near Kimberley in South Africa.[44] At the Kalambo Falls some seven or more occupation concentrations are found overlying each other separated by sandy and gravelly sediments; this is the case also at a number of other sites of this time, both in the open and in caves, showing that some favourable localities remained in use for quite long periods.[45]

The quantities in which the large cutting tools are often found (for instance they can be counted in hundreds at the famous 'catwalk' site at Olorgesailie where there are more than five hundred handaxes and cleavers) suggest, either a large population occupying the site on one occasion, which we have seen to be unlikely, or occupation and manufacture over a more extended period of time. Once the basic techniques of 'hard' and 'soft' hammer have been mastered, stone-flaking is not laborious or difficult and it is likely that, when the band moved and since hunters must of necessity travel light, most, if not all of the stone tool equipment was left at the camp where, at the favourable sites that were revisited, it accumulated over the years and was available for re-use.

Unfortunately, we have, as yet, no direct means of knowing what many of these tools were used for. We are now in a position to show a connection between light-duty tools (flake knives, small scrapers and chopping tools) and butchery practices, but the large cutting tools appear to be only incidentally associated with meat-eating.[46] It seems more probable that they were general-purpose tools connected with the collection of vegetable foods and animal food preparation rather than primarily meat mattocks and flensers for cutting the flesh from the carcases of large animals as has been previously suggested; they may, therefore, have been carried away for use on another occasion. Plant materials are rarely preserved in the early sites but gathering must always have been an important, indeed, the major source of food and, at the Kalambo Falls various edible fruits, seeds and nuts are found associated with the Acheulian living sites.

Plate 14

Similarly, there is no precise way of estimating the area of country over which an Acheulian hunting band would range. A very approximate estimate can be obtained by establishing the location of the nearest source of a particular raw material found on an Acheulian occupation site. The distances established vary usually between three to five miles with a maximum of forty miles. By this means we arrive at an estimated range over an area of something less than twenty square miles at Olduvai for the periods represented by Beds I and II, and a range of between fifty and over twelve hundred square miles for Upper Acheulian sites in Africa and Europe. The maximum figure obtained derives from a Rhodesian watershed site at Lochard.[47]

Meat has now become a regular and important item of diet judging by the number of large and medium-sized animals represented by the bones on the camping places. Some of this meat was undoubtedly still obtained by scavenging but most of it can more probably be seen as the direct outcome of the adoption of more efficient methods of hunting. Wooden spears with a simple point are known from two Middle Pleistocene sites in Europe, Clacton-on-Sea (England) and Lehringen (North Germany), and it is a fair supposition that the spear was also used in Africa at this time. Stone-throwing is likely to have been the most effective means of attack and defence and large quantities of collected natural stones are present, as we have seen, at the camping places.

Evidence of fire has not yet been found on Acheulian sites in Africa except at the very latest. Its use is well attested from several sites in Europe and Asia during the earlier Middle Pleistocene and in the colder, high-latitude regions—from Choukoutien, Torralba, Ambrona, Hoxne and other places.[48] It certainly seems probable that such a fundamentally important source of heat and power was similarly employed in the tropics but the resulting charcoals have probably been broken down and dispersed by soil fauna and so are not preserved.

Plate 13

The attraction that contained fire has for many animals and birds and the obvious potentiality for *Homo erectus* (if not for *Australopithecus*) must early have led to experimentation in the use of fire—for protection, for tool-making and, perhaps, for hunting by setting fire to the grass and driving game as, for example, at Torralba. In this method of hunting it is not only the fear of the fire but also the blinding effect of the smoke that accounts for the kills.[49] It is easier to accept the hypothesis put forward recently that man may have been responsible for the extinction of a number of the earlier Pleistocene faunal species, if this was accomplished through the destruction of their habitat and food supply by the continued and uncontrolled use of fire, than if it had been achieved by his killing them off by the more conventional use of hand weapons.

There may be a much wider range of animals represented at the Acheulian than at the Oldowan sites and a greater concentration of large and medium-sized animals. The large animals were butchered where they died, a method still often adopted by Bushmen. Analysis of the bone waste on these Acheulian sites suggests that the smaller animals were usually dismembered, in part eaten where they were killed and, in part, carried back to camp in the same way as the Bushmen and Hadza do today, thus accounting for the partial remains of individual beasts among the food waste. Hunting activities on the scale suggested by the number of butchered *Pelorovis* and *Libytherium* remains at the

BK II site at the top of Bed II at the Olduvai Gorge,[50] by the giant baboons at Olorgesailie and the elephants at the Spanish sites, indicate that some kind of better organized group hunting was probably practised. Communal hunting on such a scale as well as the flaking skills and formal retouch exhibited by the stone implements imply some improved form of communication over that of the Man-Apes and it has been suggested that these skills could only have been possible through the ability to speak, that is, the possession of language.

Speech implies certain musculatory modifications of the mouth which came about with the shortening of the jaw and the co-ordinated use of larynx, tongue and lips to articulate sounds. But, as Bernard Campbell has said, 'Speech . . . is more than complex sound. It is the act of codifying thought into sets of controlled and connected sounds, and such codification occurs in the cerebral cortex.'[51] Since it is in the Middle Pleistocene that man's cranial capacity begins to increase more rapidly, it seems likely that it was during this time that those parts of the cerebral cortex that control speech ability—notably the inferior, posterior, parietal area—were undergoing genetic selection for communication by speech.

The cultural evidence suggests, however, that if Middle Pleistocene man were, indeed, possessed of the ability to speak, this was doubtless at a lower level of expression than language as we know it today. While hunting and the excitement that this engenders in the participants may have been one of the cultural stimulants to verbalization, efficient hunting, at least in its initial stages, can certainly be carried on with only minimal vocalization between the hunters. Wild dogs, hyaenas and lions use very little vocalization, certainly to begin with and, though hunting chimpanzees are undoubtedly more vocal, it is not necessary for quite efficient hunting that the communicative ability of Middle Pleistocene man should have been very much more complex than that of Australopithecines or of chimps. That it *was* in advance can surely be postulated from the increasing brain size as well as the learning and mastery of the stone-flaking techniques and steadily expanding range of activities manifest in the different tool-kits at this time.

One of the most striking things, however, about the broad cultural pattern of the Middle Pleistocene is its general 'sameness' within the limits imposed by the stone industries. The over-all similarity in pattern between the Acheulian and Developed Oldowan cultural assemblages wherever they are situated calls for a common level of behaviour. Idiosyncratic differences and variation in the frequency with which the particular classes of artifact occur are very evident, as we have seen, but there is nowhere the fundamental, regional specialization in the tool-kits that is present in the Upper Pleistocene. Handaxes from Europe, South Africa, or peninsular India are all basically similar tools and this is also true for the rest of the heavy-duty and the light-duty elements. At the same time this 'sameness' about the stone artifacts suggests that, although the period of learning necessary to become proficient in making them may have been drawn out, there is no reason to suppose that some, at least, of this skill could not have been learned by observation, experimentation and imitation rather than by direct instruction. On the other hand, the degree of 'standardization' shown by the handaxes and cleavers, for example, argues for at least limited instruction and so perhaps for some rudimentary form of speech.

While, therefore, the wide distribution of occupation sites in the Old World shows the ability of man in the Middle Pleistocene to adapt to a large range of ecological conditions, the absence of regional specialization and the over-all standardization of the tool-kits suggest a general pattern of behaviour that was every-where, throughout the occupied world, at much the same level of efficiency. The very slow rate of cultural change over more than half a million years and the limited range of activities implied by the different tool-kits and the contexts in which they are found suggest that *Homo erectus*, though he exploited a wide range of resources, did so only at a very low level of efficiency and with minimal ability to specialize.

However, although the rate of cultural evolution was extremely slow during the Middle Pleistocene, it was, nonetheless, one of continuing and quickening tempo and, by the time the Acheulian Industrial Complex came to an end, there is evidence that man had achieved social stability and intellectual abilities that led to more rapid diversification in many different directions and placed him firmly on the threshold of a new world.

CHAPTER IV

The Coming and Spread
of Modern Man

EARLY UPPER PLEISTOCENE CLIMATIC CHANGE

ABOUT SEVENTY THOUSAND years ago, there began a world-wide lowering of temperature that heralded the onset of the Last Glaciation and the continental ice sheets advanced again in the higher-latitude belts. Twenty thousand years later, temperatures in the tropical and sub-tropical regions were already some 5° to 6° Centigrade lower than they are today and there is some indication of increased rainfall and greater availability of surface water supplies.

Now the northern and southern belts of Africa, which today are desert, became attractive country for occupation or re-occupation by man due, on the one hand, to the southward-fingering spread of the Mediterranean vegetation into the northern and central Sahara under pressure from the advancing polar front and, on the other hand, to the extension northwards into the Kalahari and Namib of the Cape and Karroo vegetation, under the influence of the spreading Antarctic ice cap.[1]

At the same time glaciers on the high mountains in east Africa were able to extend some three thousand feet lower down than their present-day position and the eastern part of the continent south of the Sahara appears to have experienced a general, though moderate, increase in rainfall. The lowered temperatures and decreased evaporation also permitted the evergreen montane forests to expand and move, together with their associated animal species, to lower elevations and to populate parts of the interior plateau now occupied by savanna and occasional relict forest patches in which lowland and higher-altitude species are mixed.[2]

In the western parts of the subcontinent, on the other hand, the drying effects of the subtropical anticyclones and of the winds blowing over the cold Benguela Current, that flows up the west coast, were extended further to the north under the more northerly influence of the Antarctic ice cap and now affected the equatorial regions. The drying effects of these winds, that now reached deep in to the basin of the Congo and into west Africa, brought about a drastic retreat of the lowland tropical forest. This was replaced by drier-loving woodland and grassland, if the few pollen counts we have are typical of general conditions at that time.[3]

At this time also there began a world-wide lowering of sea level by as much as two hundred and fifty to three hundred feet below the present shore line, caused by the locking up of huge masses of water in the ice sheets. This marine regression reached its maximum about twenty thousand years ago and sometimes exposed considerable areas of the continental shelf for human occupation and movement.

This period of lowered temperature lasted, with interstadial fluctuations toward warmer conditions, until about ten to twelve thousand years ago, when temperatures steadily rose again and the climate became more humid, which situation has continued with minor changes to the present day.

The end of the long Acheulian culture sequence at the Olduvai Gorge is coincident with a nearly desertic climate, indicated by its burial under a thick, wind-blown deposit of tuff or volcanic dust. The valley of the Vaal river in South Africa became clogged by many feet of calcified sands following an advanced stage of the Acheulian, and in the Congo basin the volume of water in the rivers and streams was lowered beyond that of the present day. In northwest Africa, also, there is at least one site (that of Sidi Zin) where the evolved Acheulian large cutting tool tradition is found associated with dwindling water resources. The Kalambo Falls radiocarbon dates suggest that the Upper Acheulian ended between sixty and fifty thousand years ago.

This trend towards desertification at the beginning of the Upper Pleistocene was probably the initial outcome of the general lowering of world temperature and the accompanying more powerful effect of the wind systems, since already, by sixty thousand years ago, there is evidence from both north Africa (Haua Fteah) and the Mediterranean basin generally as well as from tropical Africa (Kalambo Falls) for wetter as well as cooler conditions. At an estimate, this climatic adjustment from the warmer, humid Middle Pleistocene to the cooler and wetter conditions of the Upper Pleistocene took about ten thousand years or less to complete. Obviously, the readjustment by the main vegetation zones and their associated faunas, necessitated by these climatic changes, must have had an important effect upon the spread and distribution of the human populations in the regions concerned.

NEW HABITATS AND NEW INDUSTRIES

It was at about this time also that the various subspecies of *Homo sapiens* made their appearance in the archaeological record in Africa. As we have seen, *Homo erectus* was found in particular in a grassland and open savanna environment, together with the Lower Acheulian and Developed Oldowan tool traditions with which he is associated in east and northwest Africa, and this form may also be associated with many of the Upper Acheulian cultural assemblages dating to the later Middle Pleistocene. With the coming of *Homo sapiens*, however, there is now for the first time evidence for regular occupation of the equatorial forest on the one hand and, on the other, of what are today the desertic and semi-arid steppe lands of the Horn and northeast Africa. The earliest evidence of continuous occupation of regions such as the Congo forests, as of Somalia and the Nubian section of the Nile valley, dates from this time. This is not to say that nowhere in these areas are there any earlier sites. A few, certainly, are known but they are generally peripheral

Fig. 21

and serve to emphasize the discontinuity of occupation of the forest or desert habitats prior to this time.[4]

There can be little doubt that the climatic and vegetational shifts in the early Upper Pleistocene were an important influence on man's choice of new habitats, but it is equally certain that they were not the only reason for this spread. Intellectual and technological abilities were at this time undergoing rapid changes and, without the intellectual means of perceiving the advantages to be gained from exploiting new habitats, as well as the technical abilities and skills for so doing, the success with which the human populations adapted to meet the new conditions would have been severely impeded. The rapidity with which the tool traditions underwent change between sixty and thirty-five thousand years ago is of the greatest significance for attempting to understand the intellectual and technical level of the period. During these twenty-five thousand years, stone tools not only show the beginnings of regional specialization but also proliferation in the number of variable tool-kits within the regions and a notable increase in the number of standardized forms of tools. The rapidity with which these changes took place—during what has been called 'The First Intermediate Period'—is in marked contrast to the very slow development of the Acheulian tool tradition during the preceding half a million years or more.

Figs. 21, 30 At the same time the distribution maps show a definite increase in the number of sites in the continent as a whole and, by the beginning of 'Middle Stone Age' times, as they are called, about thirty-five thousand years ago, there were almost no parts or ecological niches that man had not occupied, except for the heart of the humid forests. This proliferation of sites and the regional specialization that is now apparent is interpreted as indicative of an equally rapid and over-all increase in the human populations of the continent, attendant upon their ability to exploit more thoroughly the resources of the varied habitats in which man was now capable of living.

The African situation is no different, and the time taken to complete the processes of culture change was neither faster nor slower than it was in the other parts of the inhabited world at this period, though the tool-kits whereby these changes were effected differ considerably.

Fig. 21 Distribution of Mousterian, 'Fauresmith' and Sangoan sites. (After J. D. Clark, 1967)

109

After about sixty thousand years ago, the Acheulian large cutting tool tradition is found in modified form only in those parts of the continent (in east and South Africa) where it is postulated that there was a persistence of the ecological conditions to which it had for so long been adapted. Elsewhere it underwent rapid change and, while the earliest tool-kits in those habitats now occupied for the first time clearly form part of the Acheulian Industrial Complex, they had already undergone some adjustment and were thereafter quickly replaced.

This evolved Acheulian large cutting tool tradition, sometimes known under the name of 'Fauresmith' from a town in the type area in the Orange Free State,[5] is found in those parts of the interior plateau that are today covered with an open grassland or steppe vegetation. This tradition continued to be used by peoples exploiting the montane grasslands, as in Basutoland or on the higher plateaux or mountains in Kenya and Ethiopia and by others who occupied the acacia grasslands and drier steppe of the Karroo and Highveld or the sandy and stony sclerophytic parklands of the Horn and Nubia. Since the tool-kits are an expression of activities, it may be presumed that these groups were using the same kinds of vegetable and animal resources and exploiting them in much the same traditional kind of way as had the earlier Acheulian people before them.

Besides the handaxes and cleavers, which are now often of quite small proportions, there are a number of retouched scraper forms made on flakes often struck from specially prepared cores giving either thin, broad, Levallois flakes or long, blade-like forms. Like those of the Middle Pleistocene, most of these assemblages are found on open sites adjacent to water sources but others are situated in caves which by now were regularly occupied places of settlement. At the Cave of Hearths in the Transvaal, for example, the evolved Acheulian is found throughout 30 feet of deposit.[6] At Montagu Cave[7] in the Cape there is a similar, but less thick, accumulation of occupation

Fig. 22

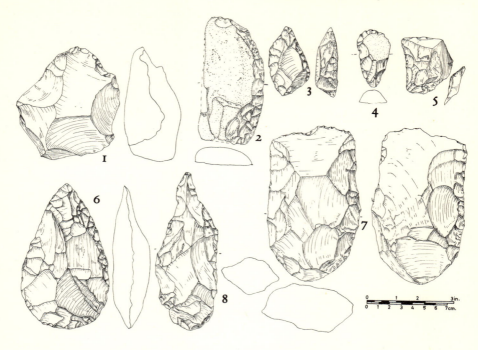

Fig. 22 'Fauresmith' tools from Rooidam, near Kimberley, northern Cape Province. The Archaeological Occurrence is contained in old pan deposits sealed under 5 ft of surface limestone. 1 radially prepared core; 2 side scraper; 3 convergent scraper; 4 side and end scraper; 5 concave side scraper; 6, 8 handaxes; 7 cleaver. 7 diabase, others indurated shale

débris and it is possible to trace idiosyncratic changes in the forms and composition of the tool-kits between the respective horizons.

In those parts of the continent south of the Sahara where climatic conditions favoured the spread of a more closed vegetation pattern—savanna woodland, forest and a mosaic of forest, grassland and savanna, for example—the old, large cutting tool tradition was rapidly replaced by one composed of a number

Fig. 23

of small scraping and cutting tools and certain heavy-duty equipment, notably steep scraping forms and crude pick-like tools. These latter, although superficially they resemble early Acheulian handaxe forms, are a very different kind of tool from the handaxe and cleaver and have been described as 'core-axes'. They are clearly artifacts to be used in the hand and often have been flaked so that the side edges converge to, so to speak, a rounded point at the distal end. The proximal end is generally unworked and, since the tools are often made from cobbles, the cortex that is left provides a smooth hand-hold as well as adding the necessary weight. The distal end not infrequently shows signs of use—bruising and battering and, sometimes, resharpening —the result of working some material that was hard but not as hard as stone.[8] With these are sometimes found convergent- or parallel-sided picks. Among the light-duty scraping equipment there is a high frequency of tools with denticulated and concave edges.

At first, prehistorians interpreted this apparent return to crudity in the stone tool equipment as a degeneration in ability and so, by implication, in the intelligence of the makers. Such an interpretation, however, cannot be entertained in the light of modern evolutionary theory and, indeed, cultural ability and intelligence cannot be measured by material products alone. If, however, this equipment represents the tools of the artisan, used for manufacturing others, not in stone but in materials that have not generally survived—most likely in wood and the by-products of wood— then it is very apparent that this tool-kit—Sangoan, as it is called —does not represent a falling-off in technical skills but rather an advance in that a more extensive range of raw materials was now being exploited and a more constant use was being made of these than ever before.

In some regions, notably in the Congo, Lake Victoria and part, at least, of the Lake Tanganyika basins, a new form of tool now makes its first appearance. This is a long, lanceolate point of

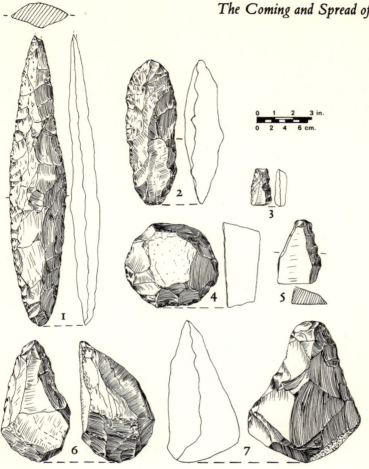

Fig. 23   Sangoan/Lower Lupemban tools from the Congo Basin (1, 2, 4, 6):
1 lanceolate; 2 core-axe; 4 core scraper from Camafufo, northeastern
Angola; 6 pick from Mussolegi. Polymorphic sandstone and quartz. Date >
36,000 BC. Sangoan tools from Kalambo Falls (3, 5, 7): 3 double-edged
serrated scraper; 5 notched end and side scraper; 7 core-axe. Ochreous Sands
Member, Site B2/59. (After J. D. Clark, 1964). 3 and 5 chert; 7 quartzite.
Dates: 38,600–44,150 BC

stone worked over both faces. Clearly, these were too carefully retouched to have been part of a jobbing carpenter's kit and were obviously an end-product in themselves. Many examples are found later with the regional 'Middle Stone Age'—the Lupemban—in the Congo basin and represent some of the finest Palaeolithic stone work in the continent. They are clearly related to a specific activity or activities to which we shall return later.

This specialized so-called Sangoan equipment type extends no further north than the fifteenth parallel of latitude which is roughly the northern boundary of the Sudan belt with the Sahel and Sahara vegetation. We have, however, no certain knowledge of the extent to which the Sahara was occupied between the end of the Acheulian and the appearance of the fully developed Aterian—the equivalent of the sub-Saharan 'Middle Stone Age' Industries—since few, if any, sites are known from this time.

In north Africa, however, the pattern is one that has most in common with the Mediterranean basin as a whole and various tool-kits that belong to the well-known Mousterian tradition make their appearance. At least three regional forms of this *Fig. 24* tradition are known—one or more Nubian forms with and with-*Fig. 32, 10–18* out bifaces,[9] a Cyrenaican[10] and a Maghrebian[11]—and they

Fig. 24 Mousterian and Libyan 'Pre-Aurignacian' tools (flint). 1–4 Mousterian from Jebel Irhoud, Morocco: 1, 2 unifaced points (1 with basal retouch) ; 3 double side scraper; 4 convergent scraper. (After L. Balout, 1966). 5–9 'Pre-Aurignacian' from Haua Fteah, Cyrenaica, Layers 69–176: 5 handaxe trimming flake; 6, 7 utilised and backed blades; 8 awl-burin; 9 proto-burin. (After C. B. M. McBurney, 1967). 10–13 Mousterian from Hajj Creiem, Cyrenaica: 10 point; 11 double side scraper; 13 single side scraper, made on Levallois flakes; 12 disc core. (After McBurney and R. W. Hey, 1955). The Libyan 'Pre-Aurignacian' represents an early blade tradition related to the Jabrudian and Amudian of the Levant and likewise is superseded by Mousterian industries.

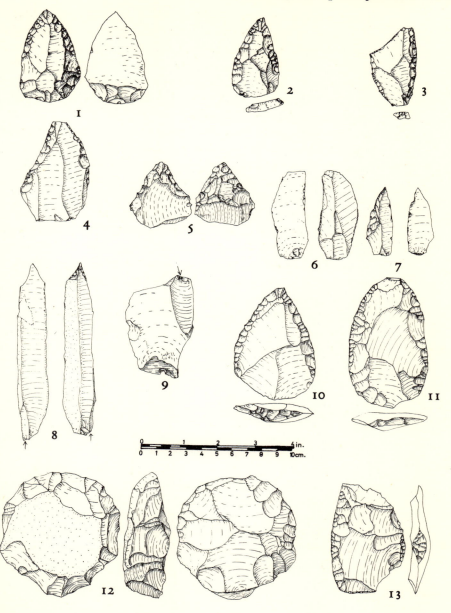

make varying use of the Levallois and disc core methods of flake production. The Levallois technique predominates so that these north African archaeological occurrences are sometimes described as 'Levallois-Mousterian'. This is all essentially light-duty equipment and consists of a number of standardized scraper and point forms and flake knives with evidence of edge damage and only minimal modification.

The Mousterian is found in one of the longest and most spectacular sequences in the whole of north Africa. At the Haua Fteah cave in Cyrenaica there are some forty-five feet of stratified occupation waste and cave earth, showing a long sequence of developing Mousterian overlying an industry made on long blades and blade-like flakes. The Mousterian here dates between at least forty-nine thousand and ?forty thousand years before the present. Several sites are known on the coast of Algeria where caves cut by the last interglacial high sea level were occupied by bands of Mousterian hunters. In the Maghreb, the Mousterian has been found from the northern border of the Sahara to Atlantic Morocco. The Mousterian folk were continual visitors to the spring site of El Guettar in southern Tunisia where many broken animal bones bear witness to their success in hunting and, in one layer at this site, there was found a pile of spherical stones, some intentionally shaped, but whether for use as missiles in hunting or as pounding stones for gathered foods is not known.[12]

Another especially interesting cave site in Morocco—Jebel Irhoud—may have been more continuously occupied, like the Haua Fteah, as it contains many feet of deposit full of artifacts and animal bones, together with hearths and two human crania.[13] The Mousterian appears to have stopped short at the Sahara, however, since no certain assemblages have yet been found there.

These Mousterian assemblages appear as an already fully developed tradition and there is as yet little evidence that they evolved out of the Acheulian in north Africa. This has suggested

Plate 18

Fig. 24, 5–9

Fig. 24, 1–4

the possibility that they may have been introduced by a migration or migrations from outside the continent. The Cyrenaican form shares a number of common characteristics with that from Palestine but both of these differ from that found in Nubia, where there are many denticulated artifacts, and the Maghrebian form, similarly, shows distinct regional differences. There did, however, enter north Africa at this time certain Euro-Asiatic animals— notably the bear, the European rhinoceros and a deer—and with them, possibly, came Neanderthal man, the maker of the Mousterian tool-kits.

THE COMING OF HOMO SAPIENS

For the first time in Africa we can now identify several contemporary and regionally distinct industries within the Sangoan, Mousterian and 'Fauresmith' cultural traditions. These can be seen as the outcome of minimally specialized adaptations to broadly different environmental conditions. Each of these regional specializations can be shown to be the work of *Homo sapiens neanderthalensis* or his more southerly African cousin *Homo sapiens rhodesiensis*.

Fig. 25

The earliest fossils that have been classified as *Homo sapiens* come from later Middle Pleistocene associations in Europe, from Steinheim in Germany and Swanscombe in England, where the skull bones are associated with a Middle Acheulian industry. These fossils date to the later part of the Middle Pleistocene, probably between two hundred and one hundred and fifty thousand years ago, and there are also some younger fossils from France. They postdate the known *Homo erectus* fossils by a considerable period of time and it is apparent that evolutionary trends during the later part of the Middle Pleistocene had led to the appearance of an early *sapiens* form of man with increased cranial capacity more equal to that of modern man (increased from about 1100 to 1300 cc.) but with a face and heavy brow ridges that reproduce the facial pattern of *Homo erectus*, though to a reduced degree (Steinheim). Whether or not this was a general evolutionary trend, or whether it was confined more specifically to Europe, we cannot yet say but, some one hundred thousand years later, a more specialized *sapiens* stock was spread widely over the inhabited more southerly parts of Europe, Asia and north Africa.

Considerable variability is shown by these populations but they all exhibit fairly massive bossing of the supra-orbital area of the skull to support the powerful chewing mechanism and heavily built jaws. These features are most pronounced in Rhodesian Man[14] and in the classic Neanderthalers from western Europe, but there is not a little regional variability shown as well, within a single site (for example, at Broken Hill), so that the variations shown by these populations justifies considering them as separate races. In most other respects Neanderthal man closely resembled modern man and the rest of the bony skeleton—the pelvis, limb bones, hand and foot—can scarcely be distinguished apart.

Neanderthal man is known from two jaw fragments with the Mousterian in the Haua Fteah cave and, as we have mentioned, by two skulls from the Jebel Irhoud cave (see page 116). A jaw fragment with characteristics described as Neanderthal comes also from a cave in eastern Ethiopia (Dire Dawa)[15] and, together with the Mousterian in Nubia, suggests a southward spread in the northeastern parts of the continent.

The Rhodesioid race was spread widely south of the Sahara from the tropics (Nyarasi by Lake Eyassi[16] and Broken Hill in central Zambia and, also perhaps, the fragmentary fossil from the site of VEK IV at the Olduvai Gorge),[17] to the winter rainfall area of the Cape (Elandsfontein),[18] a distance of more than 3,500 miles. The almost complete skull from the mine at Broken Hill is unusually massive as to the brow ridges and face but, in other respects, it and the pelvis and limb bones that belong with it are similar to those of modern man. The type fossil was found

Plate 33

Plate 33

with stone implements that are characteristic of the light-duty component[19] of the Sangoan Industrial Complex, including some of the first intentionally shaped bone tools from Africa. Spheroids are also associated but the other heavy duty elements are lacking.[20] The fauna comprises mostly woodland and some

Fig. 25   Upper and some Post-Pleistocene Fossil Man sites. (After J. D. Clark, 1967)

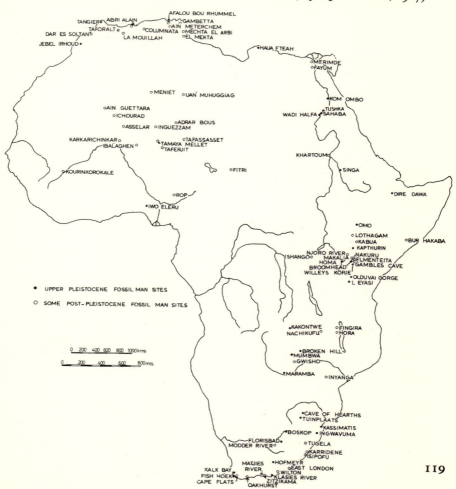

grassland species. On the other hand the skull cap from Elands-fontein near Saldanha Bay in the northern Cape is associated with an evolved Acheulian industry (?'Fauresmith') and a grass-land fauna.[21] These finds show that the Rhodesian physical type belongs near the beginning of the Upper Pleistocene, forty to sixty thousand years ago on the evidence of the Kalambo Falls dates, and was probably capable of occupying the full range of biotopes settled by man at this time south of the Sahara.

If isolating palaeo-geographical factors brought about, as we believe, biological as well as cultural adaptation, then selective pressures acting on the gene pool were responsible for the diver-gence that can be seen in the early *Homo sapiens* fossils from Africa. At the same time, however, the mobility necessary for the successful pursuit of hunting and gathering would, in favourable circumstances, have encouraged gene flow and the rapid trans-mission of selectively improved characteristics. It is believed that it was in this way that modern man replaced the Neanderthal races some forty to thirty thousand years ago.

This replacement was relatively sudden in Europe, southeast Asia and in most parts of Africa, which suggests that modern man evolved in some other part of the world. It is probable that the so-called mixed population showing a blending of Neander-thal and *sapiens* characteristics in caves at Mount Carmel, Israel, documents the emergence of an early *sapiens* form from an un-specialized Neanderthal one, but the dating of the fossils is crucial to their interpretation. Should later finds confirm the earlier emergence of modern man in southwest Asia, it might be expected, since these genetic changes must have taken place over a relatively wide region, that the replacement of the old Neander-thal and Rhodesian populations began to take place at much the same time both in northeast and in east Africa.

The oldest African fossils that belong to the modern species of man have been found in east Africa and are represented by fragmentary crania from Kanjera[22] on the Kavirondo Gulf of

Lake Victoria and by two recently discovered skulls, more complete but lacking the face, and fragments of a third, from late Middle or early Upper Pleistocene deposits in the lower Omo basin, north of Lake Rudolph.[23]

Fig. 26

Both the Omo crania belonged to adult individuals and an appreciable part of the post-cranial skeleton and fragments of the face are associated with the first. The Omo I cranium is more lightly built than the second, is higher and broader and well rounded behind, while a jaw fragment shows a well developed chin. Although the skull and limb bones are robust, they are essentially modern in appearance. The contemporary Omo II cranium is even more robust than Omo I but differs strikingly from it. The forehead is sloping and low and the back part of the skull more angular with a ridge and strong muscle impressions. While basically *sapiens* it is said to show features in common with the African fossils from Broken Hill and Kanjera and even with *Homo erectus*. The Kanjera crania, which are believed to be contemporary, and the Omo III fragments are again of modern appearance. Clearly, a considerable degree of variation was present in the population of east Africa at this time, therefore, and these early *sapiens* fossils probably represent the basic stock from

Fig. 26 Omo crania: right lateral view and left lateral view from Member I, Kibishi Formation, ? Ethiopia. (After M. H. Day, 1969)

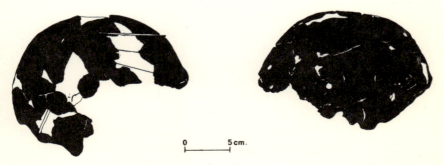

0   5 cm.

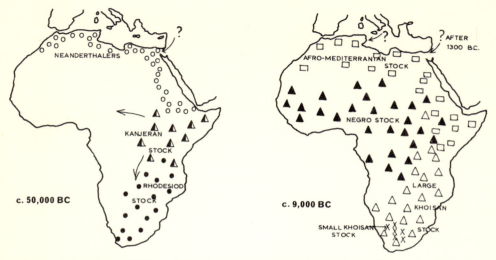

NEANDERTHALERS

KANJERAN
STOCK

RHODESIOD
STOCK

c. 50,000 BC

AFRO-MEDITERRANTAN
STOCK

? AFTER
1300 BC.

NEGRO STOCK

LARGE
KHOISAN

SMALL KHOISAN
STOCK

STOCK

c. 9,000 BC

Fig. 27   Possible scheme of population change in Africa. (After D. R. Brothwell, 1963)

which the modern African races developed. It has been suggested, indeed,[24] that this was the common ancestor of both the
large Bush and the Negro races and the diversification shown by
the African human fossils from the later half of the Upper Pleistocene can probably best be explained in terms of the natural
selection and adaptability within the different environments that
has taken place since that time. Thus, the populations of the drier
savanna and grassland of east and southern Africa, through a
process of both natural and social selection, mostly belong to the
large Bush (or the Khoisan) race, while the higher-rainfall regions
of Equatoria and west Africa may be seen as the place where the
African Negro evolved (cf. Fig. 27). A number of 'hybrid'
forms are known and this morphological differentiation took
between ten and twenty thousand years to complete, involving
initially interbreeding and rapid replacement of the Neanderthal
and Rhodesioid stock before twenty thousand BC, if the Singa
fossil from the Sudan has been correctly dated.[25]

It was likely that there was considerable fluidity in the structur-
ing of human societies at this time or gene flow would have been

slowed down. However, the comparative rapidity with which these changes took place also presupposes, not only superior intellectual ability, but also a more efficient and preferred pattern of behaviour and the technology that made this possible.

UPPER PLEISTOCENE TOOL-KITS

There can be no doubt of the superiority of the tool-kits associated with these early representatives of modern man wherever they occur in the Old World between thirty and forty thousand years ago. These are often associated with blades that have been produced by being struck from the core with the aid of a punch. From these 'blanks', as they may be called, a number of standard kinds of tool were manufactured—various forms of scrapers and awls, chisels (or burins), blunted backed knife blades and a number of other implements including broad and narrow, leaf-shaped and stemmed points. This is the general pattern in the Upper Palaeolithic tool-kits of western Europe, northern Asia and north Africa and, in the colder environments closer to the ice sheets, they are associated with a range of tools made from bone, ivory and antler and with magnificent and well-developed artistic traditions.

Fig. 28

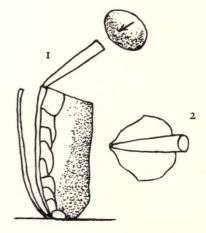

Fig. 28   Technique of removing blades by use of a punch: 1   side view, one blade only removed; 2   platform view. (After F. Bordes, 1967)

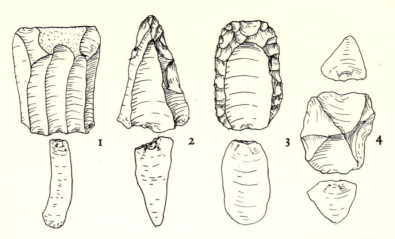

Fig. 29 Types of prepared cores and the derived 'blanks' found with 'Middle Stone Age' Industries. 1 blade; 2 convergent; 3 oval Levallois; 4 disc

In many parts of sub-Saharan Africa, however, the older, prepared core techniques for making flakes and blade-like forms continued to be used up to about ten thousand years ago and sometimes even later. In the past this fact has been construed to mean that, after the end of the Middle Pleistocene, Africa received more cultural stimulus from outside its boundaries than it transmitted. It has been interpreted also as showing the extreme conservatism of African culture and its populations. However, recent analytical studies of 'Middle Stone Age' collections from Montagu Cave at the Cape, from the Cave of Hearths in the Transvaal and from the Leopard's Hill Cave in Zambia,[26] show that blades made by the punch technique are an integral part of these industrial assemblages at much the same time as these forms occur in Europe and north Africa, though proportionally they are not usually as important an element as are the various flake types. It is becoming evident, therefore, that long persistence of the prepared core techniques is not due to any late survival of Neanderthal genes or innate conservatism, as had been inferred, but rather to a strong preference on the part of the people who made them for the various kinds of flakes and blades that can be struck from prepared cores and subsequently modified into the many sorts of scraper and point that are some of the commonest tools found with the African 'Middle Stone Age'. As many distinct and regionally specialized 'Middle Stone

Fig. 29

Fig. 30   Distribution of Upper Palaeolithic and 'Middle Stone Age' Industries. (After J. D. Clark, 1967)

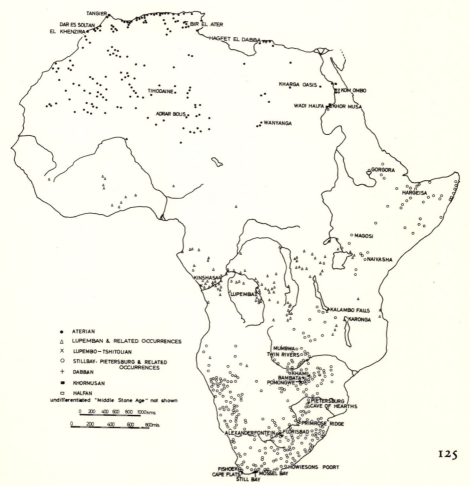

Age' tool-kits make their appearance in Africa as are to be found in the contemporaneous Upper Palaeolithic blade industries of other parts of the Old World and it can hardly be doubted that this variability reflects the more selective adaptation to different environments that was now possible. Thus, region by region, man developed equipment designed specifically for use with particular materials or for hunting certain animals in what the environment and his choice dictated as the most efficient way.

Fig. 30

In northwest Africa the Mousterian was replaced by an industry making use of the Levallois and disc core techniques, in which many of the trimmed forms have a stem or tang worked at

Fig. 31   Aterian tools from Aïn Fritissa, Middle Atlas, Morocco (1–7) (after J. Tixier, 1960) and from Adrar Bous, Ténéré, Niger (8) (after H. J. Hugot, 1962): 1   bifacial, foliate point; 2   angle burin; 3   Levallois flake; 4   double concave side scraper; 5   Levallois core; 6   tanged point; 7   tanged Levallois flake; 8   bifacial, tanged point. All flint

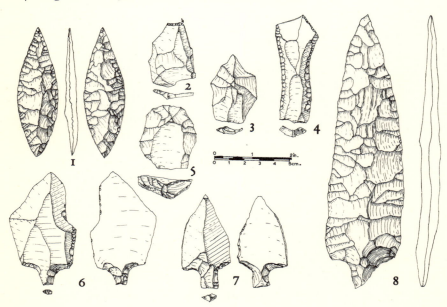

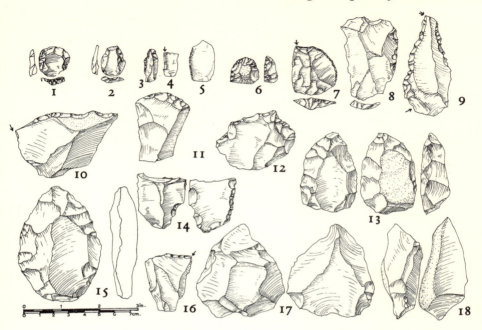

Fig. 32 Nubian Mousterian, Khormusan and Halfan tools from the Nile Valley (after F. Wendorf, 1965 and 1968, Vol. I). Halfan (1–5) : 1, 2 diminutive Levallois flakes ; 3 backed blade ; 4 burin ; 5 inverse side scraper. All chert. Khormusan (6–9) : 6 short end scraper (Late Khormusan) ; 7 side scraper and burin ; 8 utilised Levallois flake ; 9 denticulate with burin facets. Ferricrete-sandstone and chert. Nubian Mousterian, type A : (10–14, 16–18). 10 side scraper with burin facet ; 11 end scraper ; 12 borer ; 13 Levallois point core ; 14 denticulate ; 16 burin ; 17 Nubian core, type 1 ; 18 cortex backed knife. Type B (15) : biface. All ferricrete-sandstone

the lower end to facilitate hafting. This industry is called 'Aterian' from a site in eastern Algeria.[27] It is found from Morocco to Tripoli and southward into the Sahara as far as the fifteenth parallel and shows three main developmental stages. A late Aterian is also found as far east as Kharga Oasis[28] in the western desert of Egypt and spread perhaps also to the Nile in Nubia,

Fig. 31

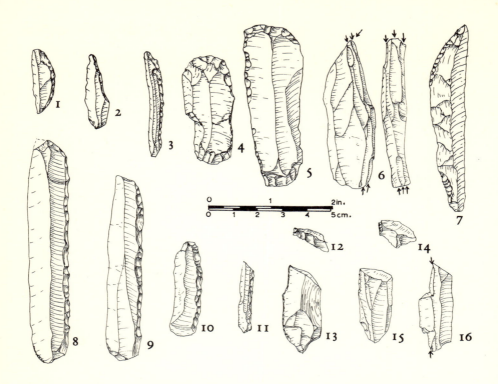

Fig. 33   Dabban tools from Hagfet ed Dabba Cave, Cyrenaica (after C. B. M. McBurney and R. W. Hey, 1955). 1–7   Late Dabban: 1   lunate; 2, 3   backed bladelets; 4, 5   end scrapers; 6   burin; 7   backed blade. 8–16   Early Dabban: 8–11   backed blades and bladelets; 12, 14   resharpening spalls from chamfered blades; 13, 15   chamfered blades; 16   angle burin. All flint

while the characteristic tanged tools are also present in northern Chad.[29] From its wide distribution throughout the Sahara, therefore, the Aterian may be considered as being specifically adapted there to the 'richer desert' environment of the Upper Pleistocene.

In the Nile valley, however, the local Mousterian tradition never adopted the tanged point and evolved into one—the Khormusan—that continued to be composed of light-duty flake equipment made by the Levallois method and with a high proportion of denticulate forms. A gradual diminution through time is noticeable in the over-all measurements of the tools and, in the next stage—the Halfan—very small Levallois flakes are associated with bladelets that decrease in size with the decreasing age of the site, reaching microlithic proportions at the end of the sequence about fifteen thousand BC. At the same time there is a corresponding increase in the importance of the blade element on the later sites.[30]

Fig. 32, 6–9

Fig. 32, 1–5

A sharp break with the prepared core tradition is seen at the Haua Fteah cave in Cyrenaica where the local Levallois-Mousterian is replaced by a punched-blade industry in the Upper Palaeolithic tradition. This industry, called the Dabban from the cave of Hagfet ed Dabba, has many straight, blunted backed blades and various scraper and chisel (or burin) forms. It lasted from about forty to about fifteen thousand years ago when it was replaced by another blade industry with an increasing emphasis on the microlithic element—known as the eastern Oranian.[31]

Fig. 33

As yet the Dabban is known from only these two cave sites and it is a matter for surprise that it never appears to have spread southwards into the Sahara or westwards into Tripolitania. Whereas the Aterian may be considered as a good adaptation to life in the desert, the Dabban appears to have remained confined to the coastal ranges of the Mediterranean.

South of the Sahara a number of more specialized equipment traditions make their appearance after about 35,000 BC. If radio-carbon dates recently obtained from Montagu Cave in the Cape and Bushman Rockshelter in the Transvaal are correct, some may be as much as 50,000 years old. That in the Horn, to begin with (described as 'Levalloisian'), shows connections with northeast Africa but this later gives place to an industry ('Somaliland Still-bay') with finely retouched leaf-shaped points and scraping equip-ment that shows associations with those of the east and South African savanna and grasslands where many variations on the

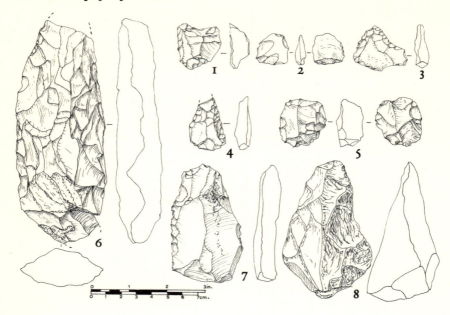

Fig. 34 'Middle Stone Age' Industry from Twin Rivers, Zambia: 1 angled scraper; 2 utilised flake from diminutive disc core; 3 convergent scraper; 4 convergent scraper with point missing; 5 diminutive side scraper; 8 handaxe. 3 chert, 8 dolerite, all others quartz. Dates between 32,000 and 22,000 years BP

Fig. 35 Bambatan and Pietersburg tools. Bambatan (= 'Rhodesian Stillbay') from Bambata Cave, Rhodesia, 2–4: 2 backed flake with concave marginal retouch on cutting edge, ?felsite; 3 borer, chalcedony; 4 bifacial point, quartz. Upper Pietersburg—from Cave of Hearths (5–10) and Mwulu's Cave, Transvaal (1): 1 bifacial point, felsite; 5 retouched bladelet, quartz; 6 (felsite) and 10 (indurated shale) double side scrapers; 7 single side scraper, chert; 8,9 unifaced points, indurated shale. Middle Pietersburg, from Cave of Hearths (11–15): 11 utilised, radially prepared flake, quartzite; 12, 13 marginally retouched, quadrilateral, Levallois flakes, quartzite and felsite respectively; 14 disc core, quartzite; 15 utilised, triangular flake from prepared core, indurated shale. Lower Pietersburg, Cave of Hearths (16–18): 16 (felsite) and 18 (indurated shale), minimally retouched blades with facetted platforms; 17 horizontally retouched Levallois flake, quartzite

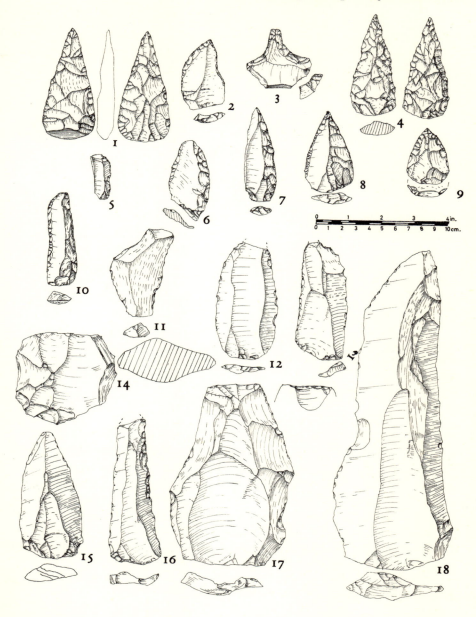

scraper and point forms are found.[32]. This is all predominantly light equipment—knife blades, projectile points, scrapers. Sometimes, as in Zambia, spheroids are associated—evidence, perhaps, for a stone-headed throwing club—and the amount of grinding and polishing equipment and some heavy-duty tools show a progressive increase at some savanna sites (for example at the Kalambo Falls and Twin Rivers). Raw material and the size in which it occurs is, of course, an important contributing factor to the form and attributes of the stone artifacts. Long, triangular flakes and blades with minimal retouch were preferred forms in hard quartzite or indurated shale, while the proportions and texture of quartz, obsidian or silcrete (fine-grained quartzite) were such that these were used to produce many bifacially trimmed artifacts, often smaller in size. Most of these 'industries' and 'phases' are known only from general descriptions and need to be precisely defined before they can be adequately compared and the differences they show better understood.

Fig. 34

In the Gregory Rift the Levallois and blade techniques are associated in the 'Kenya Stillbay' with rather stubby points, side and convergent scrapers made mostly in obsidian.[33] In Rhodesia cloudy quartz and chalcedony were generally used by the makers of the Bambata Industry and the unifacial and bifacial points and scrapers were made from irregular and triangular flakes struck often from disc cores.[34] In the Transvaal three stages of the Pietersburg Industry have been stratigraphically distinguished and described from the Cave of Hearths. These used blade, Levallois and disc core techniques—an early Phase characterized by large blades and Levallois flakes and minimal retouch; a middle Phase with more standardized forms and shorter mean dimensions but still not very much retouch; and a late Phase where the artifacts are again smaller in over-all proportions but are often carefully retouched.[35]

Fig. 35, 2–4

Fig. 35, 1, 5–18

In the middle reaches of the Orange river, recent work has established a threefold division of the 'Middle Stone Age' based

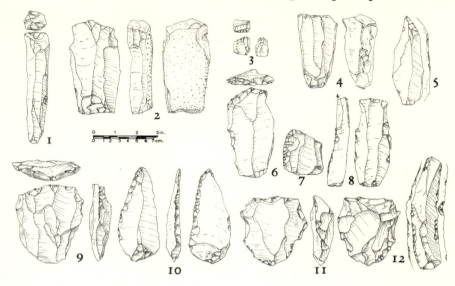

Fig. 36 'Middle Stone Age' of the Orange River (after C. G. Sampson, 1968). Phase 3 (1–5): 1 end (frontal) scraper; 2, 4 alternate and single-ended prismatic blade cores; 3 microblade core; 5 partly-backed and utilised blade. Phase 2 (6–12): 6 end (frontal) scraper; 7 convex side scraper; 8 burin; 9 single platform blade core; 10 trimmed point with reduced butt; 11 Levallois core; 12 trimmed/utilised blade. 3 jasper, all others indurated shale

on blades struck from cores of indurated shale.[35]

    Phase 1 is characterized by very large narrow blades and in this and the later Phases the blades generally show only interrupted marginal trimming and utilization. Some blades are backed and in Phase 2 burins and trimmed points are present but become rare again in Phase 3; small numbers of end scrapers occur in all three Phases. Of especial interest are the settlement sites associated with the two later Phases. At Orangia I a camp site with a Phase 2 assemblage preserves evidence of eight, mostly semi-circular, concentrations of stones such as would have formed the

Fig. 36

Fig. 37

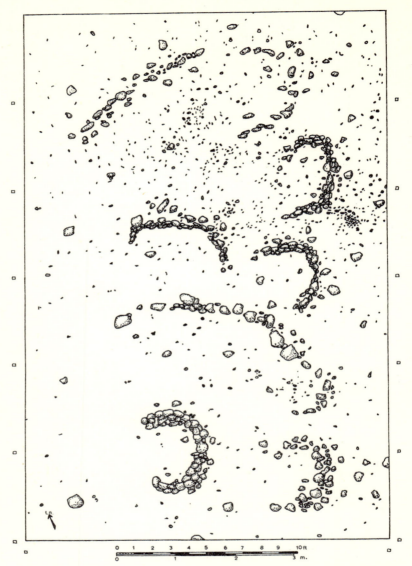

Fig. 37 The 'Middle Stone Age' settlement at Orangia 1 Site, van der Kloof Dam area, Middle Orange River, showing the cobble concentrations and distribution of untrimmed artifacts. (After C. G. Sampson, 1968)

foundations for screens or windbreaks, and in and around these were concentrations and scatters of tools and flaking waste. Evidence of a single large structure of this kind comes from another site, Zeekoegat 27, belonging to Phase 3 times. These are the only sites known as yet which show what 'Middle Stone Age' settlements were like and are, therefore, of very considerable interest.

In the southern part of the Cape Province it is possible to distinguish at least two subdivisions of the 'Middle Stone Age' on the evidence from Skildergat Cave, Fishhoek:[36] an earlier 'phase' based on hard quartzite in which denticulate (oak-leaf) forms of point and scraper abound, and a later 'phase' (more specifically identified with the classic Stillbay) in which silcrete was commonly used resulting in various unifacial and bifacial leaf-shaped tools. From Mossel Bay and other sites further east (for example Montagu Cave, Klaasies River, Geelhoutboom and others) another expression is found using hard quartzite with many minutely retouched triangular flakes and long blades, bifacial points and backed flakes.[37]

Fig. 38, 6–10

Fig. 38, 1–5

As we have said (see page 114), the Congo forest-mosaic environment has produced some of the most specialized Palaeolithic stone-work in the whole of the continent. Here again, the general trend from larger and cruder to smaller forms and an increased number of more sophisticated tools is clearly seen in the Lupemban Industrial Complex. The two commonest tool types in this region are a bifacially trimmed axe or adze, often with a gouge-like working end and a thin-sectioned, long lanceolate form with a point and cutting edges. The first type, the core-axe, reflects the importance of wood-working and the lanceolates were probably combination tools that did duty as a machete and projectile point. The Levallois technique is distinctly rare or quite absent from the earlier Lupemban Archaeological Occurrences but is well represented at the end. The raw material was a fine-grained quartzite or, where this was not available, quartz.[38]

Plate 20

Fig. 39

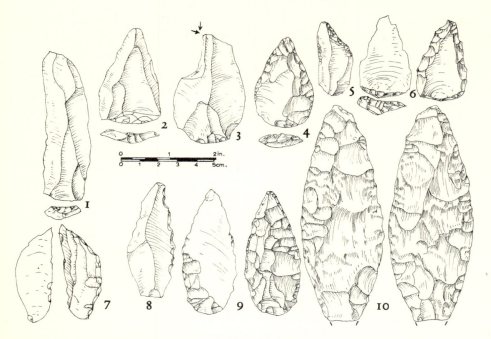

*Fig. 38 Mossel Bay Industry tools (1–5) from the type side (after C. M. Keller, 1969):
1 blade; 2 triangular flake; 3 dihedral burin; 4 unifacially trimmed point; 5 obliquely
truncated blade. All quartzite. Stillbay Industry tools from sites in the southwestern Cape (6–10)
(after A. J. H. Goodwin and C. van Riet Lowe, 1929; B. D. Malan and A. J. H. Goodwin,
1938): 6 'oak-leaf point' (convergent denticulate); 7 backed flake; 8 denticulate scraper; 9
parti-bifacial point; 10 bifacial foliate point. All silcrete*

These few examples—from the many that might be cited—
serve to show something of the diversity recognizable in the stone
tool equipment of this time. The chief significance of stone tools,
in themselves and in their context on a living floor, is for what
they can tell us about the way of life of the people who made them.
Regionally adapted traditions, such as these of the later Pleistocene, can show the direction and intensity of exploitation of the
resources of the environment by their makers and the preferred

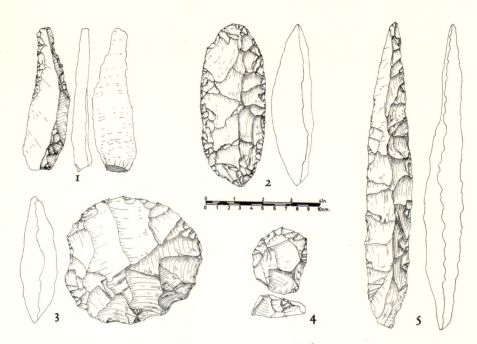

Fig. 39 Lupemban Industry tools from Kalina Point, Kinshasa, Congo Republic (after J. Nenquin, 1969): 1 trimmed and utilised blade; 2 double-ended core-axe; 3 disc; 4 end and side scraper; 5 bifacial lanceolate. Polymorphic sandstone

behaviour this induces. As yet, interpretative studies of this kind are in their infancy, by reason of the inadequacy or total lack of the right kind of data. It is, nevertheless, permissible to put forward hypotheses if these are considered as tentative only, to be modified as the evidence accumulates.

THE WAY OF LIFE OF UPPER PLEISTOCENE MAN

As has been mentioned, man now occupied all kinds of country from the sea coasts to the high mountain plateaux and from the forest fringes to what is now waterless desert and the number of sites located must, in fact, reflect an over-all increase in the density

137

of human population. The majority of sites are still near to permanent water supplies but there are now others that are related to temporary or intermittent sources of water as, for example, the Aterian sites associated in the Sahara with the interdune depressions of the Mauretanian Adrar or of South West Africa in the Namib Desert where swamps and seasonal pans or even *tsamma* melons were adequate for the needs of man and the game on which he lived.

Many caves and rock shelters were regularly occupied from this time onwards and it would appear from the wide range of tools contained in the deposits of the floor that they were camping places where a great variety of activities were carried on. From the depth of deposit at some of these sites—more than thirty feet, for example, at the Klaasies River Cave on the South African south coast—it would seem that they may have served as near-permanent quarters for the group, to which the products of gathering and the hunt were regularly brought back.

Studies of the bone waste from meals have as yet barely begun but they show that, not only is there more bone present in the later than in the earlier 'Middle Stone Age' levels, per unit value of worked stone, but that there is a general tendency to specialize in the hunting of certain, often fast-moving species. Thus, at Florisbad in the Orange Free State grassland, the groups specialized in hunting bovids, while at Twin Rivers in the Zambian savanna, warthog and zebra were the commonest forms represented in the food waste.[39] Few counts have been made of the numbers of individuals indicated by these assemblages or of the percentages of different parts of the skeleton that are preserved, but it would appear that only certain parts of the animals were carried back to the camp. This is in accordance with the practice of modern hunter/gatherers who will often butcher and eat a part of the animal at the place where it was killed.

The bone waste shows, moreover, that it was mostly medium-sized to small animals that were carried back since the large

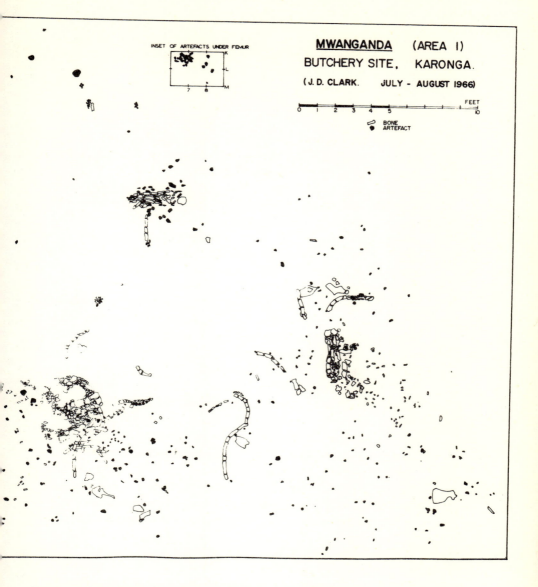

MWANGANDA (AREA I)
BUTCHERY SITE, KARONGA.
(J. D. CLARK. JULY - AUGUST 1966)

INSET OF ARTEFACTS UNDER FEMUR

FEET

BONE
ARTEFACT

Fig. 40 *Elephant butchery site at Mwanganda's, Karonga, Malawi, dating to the early Upper Pleistocene. Dismembered and broken elephant bones and associated artifacts (in black) by the bank of a shallow erosion gully.*

herbivores are generally represented by only rare or fragmentary material. Again, by analogy with modern practice, large animals, such as elephant and hippo, were butchered and eaten where they were killed, the whole group moving to the spot for this purpose.

A site of this kind, dating near the beginning of the 'Middle Stone Age', is situated at the northwest end of the Malawi Rift, near what was then the shore of the lake. Here were found the dismembered and broken remains of an elephant lying in three concentrations together with the stone tools—mostly flakes and small scrapers—that had been used to remove the meat. This site would seem to have been occupied only for as long as was necessary for the removal and disposal of the meat, and it may be concluded that the artifacts there are connected solely with butchering.[40]

Fig. 40

Fig. 41

The Mousterian hunters' camp at Hajj Creiem in the Wadi Derna in Cyrenaica was probably another of these temporary butchery camps, occupied at the most for a few days—or revisited for a few hours on several occasions—but to which a surprising number of animals was brought back.[41] It is estimated that the total number of individual beasts was five to ten Barbary sheep, three to four zebra, two or three buffalo and a gazelle. With these were about a thousand flake knives and scrapers—estimated to be about half of the original number before erosion had carried away part of the site. Since these tools were dispersed over a relatively small area, the inhabitants have been regarded as voracious eaters! The artifacts and food remains lay in an area of approximately 1,800 square feet and we might conclude, using the Bushman space requirement quoted previously of 140 square feet per person, that the group comprised some thirteen people.

At Kalkbank by the edge of a former pan in the Transvaal of South Africa, another hunting camp of the later 'Middle Stone Age has been excavated. Here the bones had been piled

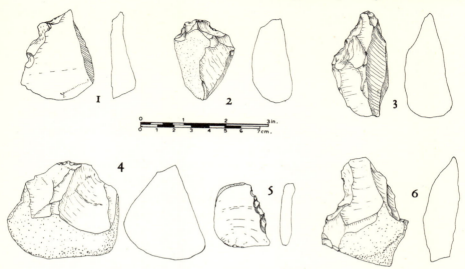

Fig. 41   Tools used for butchering the Mwanganda elephant: 1   notched scraper; 2   end scraper; 3   convergent scraper; 4   unifacially trimmed chopper; 5   denticulate scraper; 6 concave scraper. All quartzite

or stacked and some thirty-eight individual animals of thirteen different species are represented by nearly four thousand bone fragments, some of which, it has been suggested, had been made into tools. Except for two grindstones, the few stone implements (thirty-eight) associated resemble those from the Malawi site.[42]

Although there is undoubtedly greater selectivity in the species of animal eaten, the full range of those found at 'Middle Stone Age' sites is generally more extensive than at Acheulian sites. Thus, at six Acheulian sites in Africa the range of identifiable species lies between nineteen and eight, whereas at ten 'Middle Stone Age' sites it varies between forty-nine and twelve.[43] This certainly suggests that greater significance now attached to hunting and that more efficient and selective methods were used. Although little direct information is available on the techniques employed, the butchery camp of the Mousterian hunters in the gorge of the Wadi Derna and the many waterside sites suggest that the driving of game over cliffs or into water may have been regularly practised. Driving with the aid of fire may also have been common at this time.

By now it is certain that stone artifacts were hafted and the Aterian tang is probably one of the earliest and best indications. Projectile points—adding a cutting potential to the piercing quality of the pointed wooden spear—are most common in grassland and forest-mosaic country. Those found in the more open country are generally unifacial, lighter and shorter, being, it may be suggested, the points of throwing-spears. The long, bifacial types found most commonly in the forest-mosaic country resemble more closely the points of stabbing spears and knives.[44]

Plate 15   From the Florisbad mound spring comes part of a throwing-
Plate 16   stick dating to about thirty-five thousand years ago.[45] From the Kalambo Falls there is a short club with the Acheulian that is similar to those used today for throwing at game and we have already noted the possible stone-headed club from other central African sites.[46]

The late Acheulian occupation surfaces at the Kalambo Falls site have also produced some interesting additional information relating to behaviour during the early Upper Pleistocene. This documents the cultural changes whereby the Acheulian tool-kit was modified to meet the needs of groups exploiting both savanna and forest habitats. The camping-places are on sand and gravel banks adjacent to the water and fringing forest and, as the deposits in which they were found have remained water-logged since they were laid down, they have preserved much wood
Plates 12, 14   and other vegetable remains though, unfortunately, no bone has survived. The nature of the habitat is quite well known from the pollens and macroscopic vegetable remains that have survived and the edible fruits and nuts are of species still regularly eaten today. Since these fruits are ripe mostly towards the end of the

dry season, this was probably the time when the camps were occupied.

From the scatter of tools on these floors it is possible to recognize places where they were made and used. On one horizon a semi-circle of largish, natural stones was found enclosing an area about 8 feet by 3½ feet. Although there is no proof, these stones may have served to hold in position the branches of a wind-break. In two places, patches about 3 feet by 2 feet of compressed and carbonized grass stems and woody plants were found filling shallow depressions and these may, perhaps, represent sleeping hollows filled with bedding that had subsequently been burned.

There is much evidence for the use of fire in the form of charred logs and charcoals and reddened areas of sandy clays. There can, therefore, be no doubt that by this time—about sixty thousand years ago—man was regularly using fire in Africa and possessed the knowledge of how to make it. Some of the wood on the camping-places appears to have been shaped by the aid of fire and, besides the club mentioned earlier, there are several single- and double-pointed wooden implements and short, obliquely truncated sticks that could have served as digging-sticks.

Plate 13

Plate 16

Ethnography and experiment both show that wood can be shaped infinitely more easily by a controlled charring and scraping process than by directly working it with a stone tool. The possession of this knowledge must have been a very important factor in the evident success with which man occupying the forest savanna-mosaic country of Equatoria was able to exploit both these habitats.

There are now, therefore, a number of new lines of evidence which suggest that the Neanderthaloid and Rhodesioid populations, unlike the men of the Middle Pleistocene, were the possessors of a new self-awareness or concern for matters that had no immediate relationship to fulfilling such biological needs as, for example, hunting or mating. Variability is dependent upon individual invention and the ability, not only to transmit this knowledge, but to preserve and adapt it imaginatively through the act of memory. Moreover, it presupposes a degree of social cohesion strong and exclusive enough for distinctive cultural traditions to evolve but, at the same time, sufficiently flexible and receptive of the diffusion of new ideas, to accelerate the regular progress of adaptive behaviour.

There is evidence at this time from Europe and Asia for the intentional and careful burial of the dead, with food and weapons, in specially dug graves. It may be suggested that this argues, not only a concern for the future of the dead person, but also for the welfare of the group itself. Social sanctions are now of importance for the continued existence of the community and careful burial forms, as it were, an insurance for the continuance of group well-being as well as demonstrating concern both for the ancestors and for the living members. Even more pertinent in this connection is the find in the Monte Circeo cave in Italy of the Neanderthal skull set in the centre of a ring of stones which implies that social behaviour was now becoming controlled by ritual. Although these examples do not come from Africa, yet they provide evidence for an emerging social awareness that, read in conjunction with the biological and cultural evidence as a whole, can only have been world-wide.

At several cave sites in Africa, as well as in Europe and Asia, are found intentional collections of materials such as haematite, limonite or manganese, from which paint could be made and which also point in the same direction. The practice of art is founded on ritual. To quote Bernard Campbell, 'Ritual is a special form of language with a very high information content but, unlike language, the meaning of ritual depends upon its social context.'[47]

If ritual was one of the main ways of recording and transmitting cultural attainment, sanctions were also necessary to regulate the behaviour of the individual and ensure the stability of the social pattern. There must of necessity now have been rules controlling kinship structure, the division of labour between the sexes, the communal hunting practices of the men and the gathering activities of the women and children. At the same time, for the society to be an integrated and individual unit, legal strictures are needed to control relationships between the individuals of one society and those of neighbouring groups.

To restrict behaviour, especially that aimed at the fulfilment of immediate biological needs, is to produce conflict and it is precisely at this point in time that we become aware of conflict in the fossil record. One of the Neanderthalers buried at Mount Carmel died from a wooden spear that had penetrated his pelvis. Broken Hill Man had a circular hole in the side of his head such as could have been made by a simple, conical pointed, wooden spear, though he lived for a while afterwards. Another skull from Florisbad in the Orange Free State of South Africa shows a depressed fracture of the frontal bone.

In themselves, these injuries are, of course, open to other interpretations. They need not have been caused by individual or group fighting but, taken in context with the evidence as a whole, they point to the emergence of a 'social conscience and self-awareness', to quote Campbell again, that sublimated the demands of the individual to the needs of the community in which he lived.[48] Taken in conjunction with the greater regional specialization that is present from the African 'Middle Stone Age' onwards, therefore, this evidence perhaps points to the increasing concern of human society with a more limited territorial range.

On the other hand, from Iraq at this time there comes evidence, not of conflict but of tolerance and of care for the incapacitated. One of the Neanderthalers buried in the Shanidar Cave had suffered a serious injury to one arm that must have considerably handicapped his ability properly to fulfil his functions within the group. Nevertheless, he had continued to live for several years after the injury, implying that he was both tolerated and assisted by his fellows in spite of his incapacity.[49]

The achievement of awareness and integration, as with the transmission of knowledge, is, in the main, through speech. It is, therefore, probable that the first real advances in attempting to convey, not only knowledge of material things but also abstractions, took place at this time, since the evidence, slender as it may be, suggests that Neanderthal man was now governed by ritual and legal controls.

Speech, as distinct from communication by sound and gesture, may, it has been suggested, be related to the need for the naming of objects.[50] Initially, it is not necessary to postulate more than a simple, basic vocabulary relating to hunting and gathering practices or the transmission of information on tool manufacture or the preparation of food. The ability to communicate information—for example, that game, fruits, water or raw materials existed in certain places, or as to the knowledge of which materials or techniques were best for making specific pieces of equipment, to give instruction in the best uses of this equipment, such as hafting, perhaps, or, again, to convey a conception of time or numbers—this would be basic for closer integration and the developing of greater social awareness as well as for increasing the over-all economic efficiency of the group.

An ability to communicate by means of the spoken word most surely underlies the diversification of culture, the variability seen in the tool-kits, that characterizes the cultures of the Upper Pleistocene and the increasing number of ecological niches and sites that were now occupied. If the first experimental steps towards a structured and stable society were taken by the Neanderthalers, it was not until the appearance of modern man that this goal was fully attained.

The major cultural advances that were to be made in the next thirty-five thousand years and that are to be seen in the African 'Middle Stone Age' and the Upper Palaeolithic industries of Europe and Asia—the development of artistic and technical skills, ornamentation, painting, engraving and music; an aesthetic appreciation and codes of ethical behaviour—are so far in advance of what had gone before, that there is little room to doubt that it was the ability to speak and the possession of a fully developed language communication system that lay behind the success of *Homo sapiens*.

The rapidity with which all earlier forms of man were replaced is more easily accounted for if the ability to use language as we know it was a characteristic unique to modern man. It imparted to the individual the ability to reason and discriminate and to the group the means of stabilizing society so that culture could continue to develop along established traditional lines.

CHAPTER V

Specialized Hunting and Gathering Societies

THE SPREAD OF *Homo sapiens* some thirty-five thousand years ago means that, after that time, the archaeologist is concerned with the rational mind of modern man and the behavioural diversity and beliefs made possible through the medium of speech and language. There is now, therefore, a firmer basis for understanding the way of life of the varied and specialized hunting and gathering societies of the later part of the Upper Pleistocene and more meaningful comparisons can now be made between *their* behaviour and that of recently existing populations at similar organizational levels.

The increasing amount of cultural and fossil data for late Pleistocene and early Holocene times makes possible, also, a more precise knowledge of the prehistoric antecedents underlying the genetic and cultural diversity exhibited by the present-day African populations and, as we advance through time towards the present, a growing body of evidence becomes available. There are many more buried skeletal remains; larger numbers of living-sites, now spread over the full range of available habitats; and a generally greater diversity of cultural evidence such as, for example, the rich record of the cave art. All these provide the prehistorian with a more exact basis for his reconstruction of culture history.

These data are, of course, still seriously deficient in many respects and they are never likely to be complete enough to allow the kind of precision possible at the level of historic archaeology. It must, however, be apparent by now that prehistoric archaeology is essentially concerned with the broad processes of culture change through time, rather than with sequences of specific events or with individuals. For later prehistoric times we can now begin to have a greater confidence in the reliability of archaeological reconstruction on account of the connections being brought to light between the more recent past and the present-day populations and we are able to speak with ever greater assurance the nearer we approach to modern times and the greater the use that can be made of ethnographic, linguistic and ethno-historic data.

CLIMATE IN THE EARLY HOLOCENE

During the later part of the Upper Pleistocene and early Holocene, the environment again underwent considerable modification. Some of these changes can be shown to be coincident with comparable fluctuations in the temperate belts, although, in the tropics and sub-tropics, these were not as marked as were those, for example, from Glacial to post-Glacial in Europe. Nevertheless, environmental changes in Africa at this time must have had an important effect upon the way of life of a large part of the population. The Late Pleistocene, some fifteen thousand to ten thousand years ago, was a time of cooler temperatures and lower evaporation throughout the continent.[1] In some parts of tropical Africa, rainfall and humidity were still above that of the present day but, in other parts, south of the Sahara and at lower elevations, there is evidence for the onset of more arid conditions.[2] By about eight thousand BC there is general evidence for a warmer and more humid climate that terminated about two thousand five hundred BC.[3] This period coincides with the Boreal and Atlantic in Europe. The east African lakes at this time contained a lot of water though, about four thousand years later, they began to shrink.[4]

Similar changes took place in north Africa and the Sahara. In the Nile valley, some eleven thousand years ago, there is continued evidence for moister conditions but, by the middle of the eighth millennium, the climate in Nubia had become arid and there was a significant diminution in the floodwater being carried down the Nile. Further fluctuations of climate took place, the last of the moister periods dating to about three thousand BC at which time there was much big game and vegetation in the wadis, as can be seen from the *bas reliefs* and other representations during early Dynastic times, as well as from the finds at living-sites. However, five hundred years later the game and vegetation had both disappeared and the extreme aridity had set in that has continued to the present day.[5]

During probably much of the Upper Pleistocene the northern and southern boundaries of the Sahara desert were between 60 and 125 miles nearer the centre than they are today and rainfall which is now between one quarter of an inch and three inches rose to as much as two to eight inches or more.[6] In the southern Fezzan at the eastern end of the Tassili range, one of the richest storehouses of prehistoric art in the world, a sequence of two moister periods (about 5600–4000 BC and 3500–2500 BC) separated and followed by aridity is broadly contemporary with similar events in Egypt and is found repeated at other localities in the Sahara.[7]

In final Pleistocene and early Holocene times the Sahara must have been a highly favourable environment for hunters, fishers and pastoralists. Freshwater lakes existed between the dunes in what is now the Ténéré desert,[8] Lake Chad covered roughly eight times its present area, in and around the highlands there grew stands of Mediterranean forest trees, and the large animal fauna was spread throughout the desert.[9] The slow drying-out process which began after about five thousand BC seems to have resulted in the present-day demarcation of the Sahara being reached about the middle of the third millennium.

These climatic changes would have been felt, not so much in the high-rainfall areas, but in the more arid regions where even minor fluctuations in rainfall, humidity and temperature may make all the difference between whether a habitat is favourable, marginal or unfavourable. Behaviour studies show that aridity can be expected to encourage greater mobility on the part of the animal and human populations. It may also, therefore, be expected to have militated in favour of more rapid and more widespread transmission of significant inventions and techniques affecting the livelihood of a group. It would, thus, have stimulated the adaptations and adjustments necessary in the social and economic structures of those societies most affected.

THE GENERAL PATTERN OF EARLY HOLOCENE INDUSTRIES

Ecological change thus lies behind the multi-variant patterns *Fig. 42* of the stone industries of terminal Pleistocene and earlier Holocene times. The main stimuli leading to the more rigid social and economic patterning that this lithic differentiation implies must, however, surely derive from culture contact, diffusion and population movement. Broad similarities that permit the regional grouping of archaeological occurrences into industries are, as we have already seen, most probably the outcome of adaptation to broadly similar environmental conditions. In the same way the changes that can be seen to pertain through time can be looked upon as the long-term outcome of more efficient ways of exploiting the resources of the habitat. However, the synchronic, minor variations that distinguish, for example, a particular contemporary 'Later Stone Age' Nachikufan assemblage on the Zambian Copperbelt from one using the same raw material in the Muchinga Escarpment, some four hundred miles to the northwest, can probably best be seen as the outcome of group preference. They also emphasize the individuality as well, perhaps, as the relative isolation of the hunting communities that occupied the sparsely populated central African savannas at that time.

Basic differences in technique or in tool types *must* go beyond mere idiosyncratic differences, however. Sometimes, as in the Nile valley in the terminal Pleistocene, differences in tool types which can be shown not to have been due to the raw material used suggest the contemporary existence of several mutually exclusive traditions, though whether or not the populations that practised them were also different, physically or in other signifi‑ cant respects, is at present unknown.

Fig. 42   Distribution of Late Pleistocene and Holocene Industries. (After J. D. Clark, 1967)

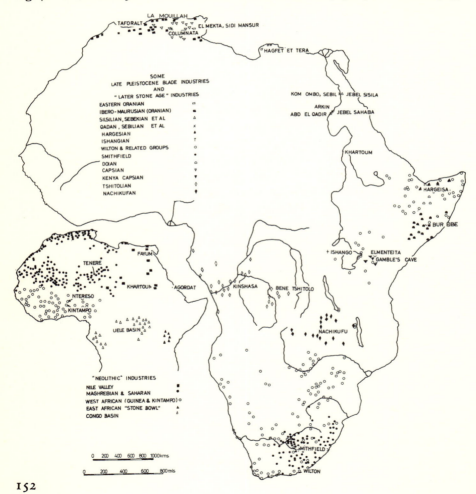

The later prehistory of Africa, as that of many other parts of the world, used to be viewed in the light of a series of invasions by immigrant peoples. In Africa the invaders were thought to have passed south of the Sahara and to have brought with them new techniques and tool-kits which were later disseminated throughout large parts of the subcontinent. These waves of melanoderm and leukoderm migrants that were believed to have swept through Africa, as did the Huns through Europe, were thought of as either killing-off the older populations or inter-marrying with them. The differences apparent from a study of the various fossil human remains known from sub-Saharan Africa have been cited as evidence for this migration theory and, indeed, when we look at the historic data there are numerous examples that can be used to demonstrate large-scale population movements in later times.

The growing quantity of cultural and fossil material for times before the spread of food production and the over-all population increases which domestication permitted, now show, however, the drawing of analogies from historic times to be not only un-wise but misleading. A better understanding of the manner in which much of the Bantu migration has taken place since the beginning of the present era also makes it most unlikely that there were any population movements in earlier prehistoric times of the magnitude that was originally thought.

Of course, it is not intended to imply that all changes to be seen in post-Pleistocene Stone Age industries can be explained in terms of autochthonous development. Migration and popula-tion movement undoubtedly did take place, as we have seen for example in regard to the spread of the Aterian Industrial Com-plex throughout what appears to have been at that time an empty Sahara (see page 127). Since, however, there are a number of additional factors, other than population movement, that can produce changes in cultures we need to be very sure of the evidence before we ascribe such changes to migration.

Among semi-isolated but highly mobile bands of hunters and gatherers who were not in competition for territory and water to the same degree as were the agricultural populations of later times, the most significant agency for change is likely to have been diffusion through culture contact. It can be observed in Africa, as in many other parts of the world, that if an idea, invention or technique is one that affects for the better the kind or quality of food sources or the ease with which these are exploited, or if it has prestige value, then there is no doubt that it will be adopted, even though traditional conservatism or prejudice may delay it for a while. Where prehistoric hunters and gatherers are concerned, therefore, it is probably nearer the truth to suggest that it was not so much large groups of people but *ideas* that moved and this cannot be better seen than in the spread of the microlithic technique throughout the African continent after about fifteen thousand BC.

MICROLITHIC TECHNOLOGY

Microliths are small bladelets or segments of blades and flakes often, but not always, geometric in shape that have been blunted by retouch along one or more edges, the blunted part being opposed to a sharp cutting edge. The blunting facilitates hafting and several of the segments might be mounted by setting them in mastic to form a composite tool or weapon. Various vegetable mastics or gums would have been available, as today, and what was used depended on what grew in any particular region. When heated, such gums are malleable and when cold they set hard and provide a fairly rigid and durable adhesive.

Fig. 43

The microliths were used in various combinations such as for the barbs on a multi-barbed spear, the heads of arrows, knife-, sickle- or saw-blades and so on. The stone working-parts of other implements were also tending to smaller dimensions at this time, as is indicated by, for example, the various forms of axe and adze blades and scrapers.

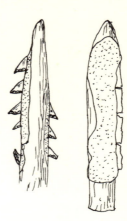

Fig. 43 *Bladelets and microliths set in grooved hafts and mounted with mastic to form the barbs of a projectile and the blade of a knife*

The finest and most suitable stone could be used to make microliths since only small pieces were needed. Chalcedony now replaced quartzite in the Congo basin and in the south-western Cape. Crystalline quartz was preferred to the cloudy, vein quartz in much of the central African savanna. Agates, chalcedonies and cherts were also used, side by side with indurated shale, for microliths on the South African Highveld and the small pebbles of Nile chert were exclusively preferred by some of the later industries in the Nubian section of the Nile valley.

At this time also there is evidence that some groups were utilizing bone and sometimes ivory to make simple points and ornaments. Although these materials had been used sporadically for a long time (for example, the boring and spatulate tools from Broken Hill Cave, and those with a late stage [about 15,800 BC] of the Khormusan in Nubia), it is not until the end of the Pleistocene that any more extensive and careful shaping of bone into tools occurred. Mostly bone was made into borers and simple points, for example in the Qadan Industry[10] in Nubia (about 10,600–9500 BC), in the eastern Oranian at Haua Fteah (about 13,000–7000 BC) by the Oranian and Capsian peoples of the Maghreb and in Rhodesia by the makers of the Pomongwan Industry (about 7450–5740 BC). Particularly in the later stages bone was used for the points and foreshafts of arrows, hafted, no

Fig. 44

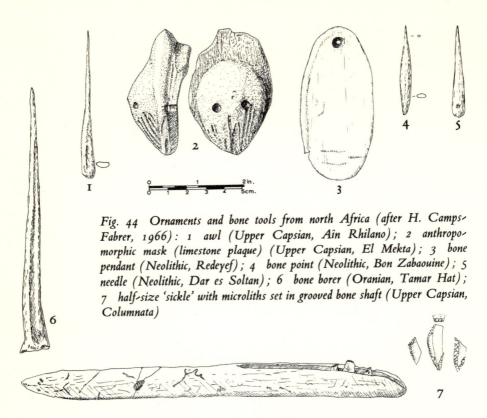

Fig. 44 Ornaments and bone tools from north Africa (after H. Camps-Fabrer, 1966): 1 awl (Upper Capsian, Aïn Rhilano); 2 anthropomorphic mask (limestone plaque) (Upper Capsian, El Mekta); 3 bone pendant (Neolithic, Redeyef); 4 bone point (Neolithic, Bon Zabaouine); 5 needle (Neolithic, Dar es Soltan); 6 bone borer (Oranian, Tamar Hat); 7 half-size 'sickle' with microliths set in grooved bone shaft (Upper Capsian, Columnata)

doubt, in a similar manner to those of the Kalahari Bushmen today.

The new composite tools clearly had advantages not possessed by the older, macrolithic tools. They were more versatile, the working parts could be hafted in the most advantageous manner and the implements were light and easily transported. In the case of the arrows, they might perhaps be considered rather flimsy, ineffectual items of equipment against a large animal such as an eland or a buffalo, but if the heads were poisoned they became formidable weapons.

Where and at what time the bow and arrow was invented we have no certain knowledge. It cannot be doubted that such a

Fig. 45

Fig. 45   Crescent adze-flake in chert, mounted in mastic, with rhino horn handle, from a cave at Plettenberg Bay, eastern Cape Province. (After J. D. Clark, 1959)

significant invention would have diffused very rapidly from its point of origin, wherever that may have been. The oldest unquestionable evidence comes from the north German plain in the ninth millennium BC. It seems more likely, however, that earlier than this, some of the later Aterian small tanged and barbed points from north Africa may have served as the heads of arrows and there is reason to suppose that this weapon was also known (though it may not always have been adopted) by the ninth millennium BC in sub-Saharan Africa where microlithic assemblages of that age occur in Zambia and the Congo basin. The rock engravings and paintings in the Sahara are tangible proof of its use in the desert from about the sixth millennium onwards and we possess an actual fragment of a bowstave from a mid-third-millennium site in Zambia.[11] Incidentally, this site—Gwisho Springs—on the edge of the extensive grasslands known as the Kafue Flats, has also produced interesting evidence for the probable use of poison at that time in the form of numerous pods of the shrub *Swartzia*, commonly used for arrow poison by the Kalahari Bushmen. This is all the more significant in the light of the fact that all the other plant remains that occurred in any quantity at the site were from edible species and had clearly been carried in for food.[12]

Microliths are generally produced from blades that are struck from cores by the aid of a punch. This method is particularly advantageous for making long and narrow blanks that could be worked into many different kinds of tool. Where the material occurs in large sizes, as with the Eocene chert or flint on the Tunisian plateau, the blades have sometimes to be broken down into convenient lengths for making into microliths. Generally, however, the cores were of small dimensions so that the bladelets and flakes were produced of the desired length.

POINTS OF PERCUSSION

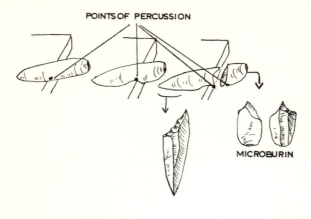

MICROBURIN

Fig. 46 One interpretation of the microburin technique for sectioning a blade. The blade is broken by resting it on an anvil and working a notch on one edge with a stone hammer. When the notch is sufficiently deep the blade snaps into two— the butt end with the microburin scar is discarded and the upper end further retouched to form a microlith, often of geometric shape. (After J. Tixier, 1963)

It used to be thought (and, no doubt, often still is) that the special notching and snapping method—the microburin technique, as it is called—used to break down the long blades was specifically connected with certain cultural and genetic affiliations. Thus, the fact that this technique, or modifications of it, occurs widely dispersed in certain parts of the continent would, at one time, have been interpreted as evidence of population movement carrying the technique with it. Such an explanation cannot be ruled out where other associated evidence exists—as in the Kenya Rift, for example—but elsewhere, such as at the Kalambo Falls and in the Orange River basin, there is no reason to suppose that the explanation lies in anything more complicated than that the technique represents the most practical way of breaking a longish blade at a particular place along its length.

Fig. 46

Blades struck by direct percussion have been used in north Africa from the end of the Middle Pleistocene and in sub-Saharan Africa from 'First Intermediate' times while a typical Upper Palaeolithic industry—the Dabban—using punch-struck blades, was present in Cyrenaica (see page 129) beginning about forty thousand years ago. If the Upper Palaeolithic tool-kit was so far in advance of that based upon the prepared core, it is not clear why the Dabban should not have spread rapidly throughout northern and southern Africa as this type of industry did in Europe and Asia. Evidently it does not appear to have been particularly advantageous in the African environment and it is not until about fifteen thousand BC that we begin to find any wide distribution of the punched-blade technique in north Africa. At this time the Oranian tradition using bladelets began to spread widely into northwest Africa, superseding the Dabban in Cyrenaica,[14] and the believed related assemblages in the Nile valley also show an over-all diminution in the size of the backed blades, many of which are now of microlithic proportions; the microburin technique also makes its appearance in Africa at this time. It may, therefore, be suggested that it was the need for very small flakes and blades for the working-parts of composite tools that triggered-off the spread throughout the continent of micro-lithic technology based upon the punched flake and bladelet.

Fig. 47

Fig. 47   Oranian (Ibero-Maurusian) Industry tools from Layer VII, Taforalt Cave, Morocco (after J. Roche, 1963): 1   microburin; 2–5   backed bladelets; 6   double backed blade; 7 bone point; 8   alternate ended micro-blade core; 9, 10   short end scrapers; 11   burin; 12 backed bladelet with basal retouch. Flint and chert

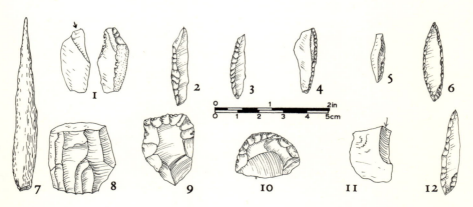

Whether from the start this was associated with the diffusion of the bow and arrow is not known but it seems not unlikely that it may have been connected. In a Late Pleistocene graveyard at Jebel Sahaba, a little north of Wadi Halfa in Sudanese Nubia, dated to between twelve thousand and ten thousand BC, were

Plate 35

buried many persons who had died a violent death.[15] The bodies show that they had been killed by weapons pointed with micro-liths or other small stone insets. One man had as many as one hundred and ten such artifacts associated in such a way as to suggest that they had entered his body as the barbs or points of projectiles and two of them were still embedded in his skull. Impacted stone artifacts were similarly found sticking in the bones of five other burials and, although it is not possible to be certain, of course, it would seem more probable that these were the points and barbs of arrows rather than of spears. If they had been mounted on spears the spearhead might be expected to have made a deeper wound where the conical point of the weapon had penetrated.

The Oranian Industrial Complex and the punched-blade assemblages in the Nile valley present an interesting problem since it does not seem likely that they could have evolved from the Dabban or the Aterian with their very different blade and flake technologies. The Oranian appears suddenly both in Cyrenaica and, though somewhat later, in the Maghreb and it is possible that it may be intrusive, perhaps from southwest Asia where there are late Upper Palaeolithic blade industries with which it may be related. Alternatively, it is not impossible that it may have crossed the Mediterranean from the Iberian peninsula. Perhaps, however, in view of the little that is known of the archaeology of the Red Sea hills region, it is unwise to speculate too widely on the intrusive nature of the Oranian which must, as yet, remain unproven. A somewhat similar problem is raised by the Capsian Industry and the Libyco-Capsian at Haua Fteah; these succeed the Oranian at some sites and are con-temporaneous with its later stages. There is a certain resemblance

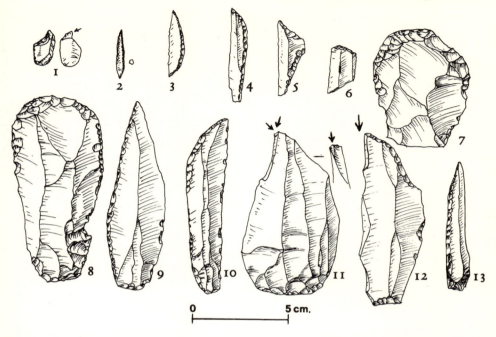

Fig. 48 Tools of the typical Capsian Industry from El Mekta, Tunisia (after R. Vaufrey, 1955): 1 microburin; 2 awl; 3–6 microliths; 7, 8 end scrapers; 9, 10, 13 backed blades; 11, 12 burins. Flint

between the Upper Palaeolithic cave art of Sicily and the earliest engravings in the northern Sahara which suggests the possibility of connections with southern Italy at this time. The Capsian is almost universally associated with huge shell mounds, the *Helix* (*escargots*) having formed for these populations a staple source of food on the Tunisian and eastern Algerian plateau.[16] Again, it is only possible to speculate on the origins of these industries but at present it seems more realistic to look for their antecedents inside northern Africa rather than outside the continent.

Fig. 48

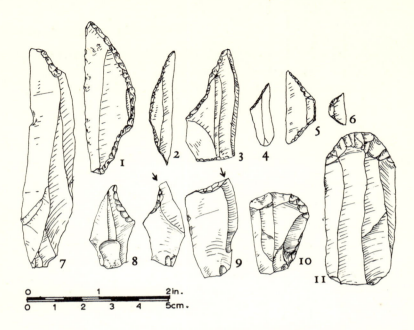

Fig. 49   Tools of the Kenya Capsian Industry (Phase A) from Gamble's Cave, Kenya (after L. S. B. Leakey, 1931): 1–3, 7   truncated and backed blades and bladelets; 4–6   microliths; 8   microburin; 9   angle burin; 10, 11 end scrapers. Obsidian

In the Gregory Rift a somewhat similar industry, which has been named the Kenya Capsian, is known from lakeside sites, its earlier stages dating to between six thousand and perhaps as early as eight thousand BC.[17] It is based on the use of long blades of obsidian in the same way as the north African Capsian used fine Eocene flint and the form taken may in both cases derive in some measure from the raw material. Certainly, there is little other than typology to connect the two, but it must be remembered that much of northeast Africa is unknown, prehistorically speaking, so that the Kenya Capsian, as also the little-known blade industry—the Hargeisan—in the Horn[18] *may* have north African connections via the Ethiopian plateau.

Fig. 49

It is from about fifteen thousand BC that the punched-blade technique begins to be found in many parts of sub-Saharan Africa, associated with what have been called 'Magosian' industries.[19] These combine an evolved expression of the 'Middle Stone Age' technique making use of the Levallois and disc core with a 'Later Stone Age' technology for the manufacture of microliths based on the punch-struck blade. The artifacts

Fig. 50   Tools of the Howieson's Poort Industry (1–9) from near Grahamstown, eastern Cape (courtesy of and after J. Deacon) : 1   parti-bifacial point ; 2   Kasouga flake ; 3   unifaced point ; 4   burin ; 5   truncated blade ; 6   trapezoid ; 7   diminutive convex scraper ; 8, 9   lunates. 7   quartz crystal, others silcrete. Tools of the Lupembo-Tshitolian Industry (10–18) from Mbalambala, Dundo, Angola (after J. D. Clark, 1961) : 10   bifacial, tanged point ; 11   unifaced tranchet ; 12, 13   backed blades ; 14   bifacial core-axe ; 15   backed flake ; 16   bifacially worked tranchet ; 17, 18   bifacial points. Polymorphic sandstone and chalcedony

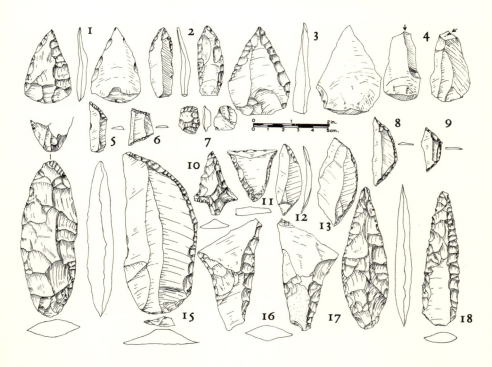

from this time present a degree of refinement and use of pressure technique for making the foliate and triangular projectile points not previously seen in the southern part of the continent. The small cores from which the blades were struck were probably held between the heels, as can still be seen today for the manu-

Plate 25 facture of gunflints in northeastern Angola and northwestern Zambia, and this is one of the more characteristic and significant ethnographic survivals, the prehistoric punch having perhaps been of horn and the hammer of hard wood.[20]

One such assemblage comes from a rock shelter at Howieson's

Fig. 50, 1–9 Poort in the eastern Cape and dates to c. 18,000 BC. The equiva-lent cultural stage in the Congo basin is known as Lupembo-Tshitolian and combines a refined bifacial technology with new

Fig. 50, 10–18 forms—tranchets and backed tools—made on blades and flake fragments.

THE ORIGINS OF AFRICAN RACES

It is from the closing part of the Pleistocene that we can begin to document the emergence of the various indigenous African races—the Mediterranean, the Negro and the Bushman-Hotten-tot. Most of the fossil remains belong to the closing stages of the Pleistocene or the early Holocene, but some are older. A number of fossils provide ample evidence for the antiquity and wide distribution of the large Khoisan stock, notably the robust man from Florisbad in the Orange Free State,[21] perhaps dating to forty thousand years ago; the Singa skull[22] from the area of Khartoum, dating to about seventeen thousand years ago, and a number of others which are mostly later. These large-brained Khoisan fossils are thought-of by some as representing a 'Boskop race' (named after the place in the Transvaal where the first fossil of this type was found), though the observable differences and the incompleteness of the fossils themselves make such an assump-tion premature if not misleading at the present time. It is not until approximately eleven thousand years ago that the first of the small Khoisan, or Bushman, fossils appear in South Africa—from the lower levels in the Matjies River cave on the south coast.[23] There can be little doubt, therefore, that it was about this time that what have been, somewhat loosely, termed Bushmen and Hottentots became differentiated in the southern parts of the continent, both evolving from the same gene pool during the relatively long period of isolation represented by the Upper Pleistocene. Another fossil from South Africa—the Tuin Plaats man, from a late Pleistocene site in the northern Transvaal —shows what have been described as a mixture of Negro and Bushman features.[24]

As yet we know little of the origin of the Negro. By some he is considered a recent immigrant to Africa. For others there is good reason to believe that he, like the Bushman, is derived from the ancestral African stock represented by the fossils from Kanjera. Of course this had undergone considerable modification caused by selection, genetic drift, human mobility, the direct influence of the environment on the phenotype and of hybridization and interbreeding. Proof of the identity of the antecedents of the Negro is difficult to come by because the homeland, or what is thought of as the homeland, of the Negro lies in west Africa and Equatoria, which do not preserve fossils. It is, therefore, generally only on the periphery of the forest lands that the fossil evidence is found and most of this is comparatively late in time.

The discovery in 1965 of a burial in a cave at Iwo Eleru not far from Benin in the Nigerian rainforest is, therefore, of the greatest interest, especially since it is dated by radiocarbon to about eleven thousand years ago (9,250 $\pm$ 200 BC). The burial is associated with a microlithic industry and, although no detailed report has yet been released, preliminary examination suggests that it is negroid in character though preserving certain robust archaic features.[25]

Other pertinent human fossils are associated with a lakeside fishing camp at Ishango on Lake Edward, dating probably to the seventh millennium BC. While the cranial features have little in common with those of the Negro and still possess the robustness of the undifferentiated stock, the limb bones do display the general slenderness of the classic west African Negro.[26]

A number of finds, dating mostly between about 5400 and about 1300 BC, are now known from the Sahara and they have been morphologically classified into three groups: those that show typical features of the classic west African Negro (for example, Ibalaghen, Tin Lalou and Asselar dated now to about 4440 BC); those of a more robust build with some archaic features but showing likenesses to the Sudanese Negro (as the fossils from Tamaya Mellet, El Guettar and Tamanrasset), and a tall, slender, long-headed and long-faced, non-Negro form (El Guettara No. 1). These are not regionally differentiated but it is apparent that peoples exhibiting several racial or sub-racial characteristics occupied the Sahara in post-Pleistocene times.[27]

The Sudanese Negro stock is also seen again at the fishing camp of 'Early Khartoum' on the Nile which dates probably in the fifth millennium or before.[28] That the Negro has for long been established on the Upper Nile there can be no doubt and it might be thought that the remains from the late Pleistocene Qadan microlithic blade industry cemeteries near Jebel Sahaba would help to throw light on this. However, the morphological status of this material is unfortunately as yet far from clear and authorities differ as to whether these people should be grouped with the Sudanese Negro race or with another tall, robust population named from two sites in the Maghreb 'the Mechta-Afalou race', which is that associated with the Oranian industry in northwest Africa.[29] However, one or two of the southeastern Sahara fossils also show features in common with the Mechta-Afalou populations, so that if, as all are agreed, there is no direct connection between the two such as would result from population movement, it is not impossible that the northwest African race and the populations on the Upper Nile associated with a rather similar kind of tool-kit (the Qadan) might derive from a common ancestral stock somewhere in north Africa or, perhaps, in southwest Asia.

The non-Negro stock recognized in the Sahara is certainly not related to the Mechta-Afalou race, but another race has been distinguished in northwest Africa and here the resemblances are said to be close. This second type is less well known than the first, makes its appearance somewhat later, and is associated in shell mounds with the Capsian Industry. It is appreciably less rugged than the Mechta-Afalou race; is long-headed; long-faced; of slender build and approaches a primitive Mediterranean type.[30]

Now, it is particularly interesting that the human remains associated with the Kenya Capsian and later related industries in east Africa also belong to a long-headed, tall race and this has led to their being described as Afro-Mediterranean.[31] Skeletal remains associated with the Wilton levels ($\pm$ 3000 BC) at the Matjies River Rockshelter on the south coast of South Africa have also been described as non-Bushman and compared with the long-headed Kenya fossils. However, before suggesting any southward penetration of an early Mediterranean stock it is necessary to be certain that these fossils are sufficiently distinct from the present-day populations of east Africa and the Upper Nile to preclude their being ancestral to any of them, in particular to the Nilotes, and so their having become genetically differentiated there.

Appreciably more research and more material are needed before it will be possible to document at all clearly the origins of the indigenous African peoples but a general picture is now beginning to take shape of two main races—the Negro and the Khoisan—with several sub-races. The Khoisan type was distributed widely in eastern and southern Africa in the savanna and grasslands where later the small Bushman and large Hottentot attained genetic distinction. The Negro evolved in the forested and savanna regions of western Africa where two further sub-races became differentiated. Serological and other genetic resemblances between the Bushman, Hottentot and Negro show beyond doubt that they belong to the same major gene constellation, though morphological and genetic markers point to a lengthy period of differentiation in relative isolation, each evolving independently by adaptive selection, mutation and extensive additions to the gene pool following hybridization.[32]

The extent to which environment can bring about morphological change can be well seen in the Pygmies of the Congo forests. The earliest archaeological remains from the primary forest region are surprisingly late, dating to the later half of the 'Middle Stone Age' and it would seem that it was not until this late date that man was living permanently within the forest zone. That genetic adaptation to the new environment, rather than hybridization, has been chiefly responsible for the development of the Pygmy stock during the past twenty thousand years or less is confirmed by the way in which Bantu groups that entered the forest only a few centuries back have now become morphologically closer to the Pygmies and different from the savanna groups from which they separated, showing that convergent morphological evolution in the equatorial forest was the main cause of the observed similarities.[33]

The genetic origins of the old north African races still seem unclear but before looking for these outside the continent it would be wise to consider whether these groups might similarly not be differentiated by selection, mutation and drift from the early Upper Pleistocene ancestral stock. For heat, dryness and sun do select for tall stature, slenderness and weight reduction.

In the Sahara and south of it the geographical distribution of the African races, with the exception of that of the Bantu-speaking peoples, is beginning to show as a very ancient one stretching some ten thousand years or more into the past—the large and small Bush type, the Negro and the Afro-Mediterranean stock were all present in much the same places as they are found today though, of course, with some, their present-day distribution does not accurately reflect the former extent of their dispersal.

INTENSIVE COLLECTING PEOPLES OF THE NILE VALLEY

Between the close of the Pleistocene and the introduction of domestication, somewhere between about five thousand and three thousand two hundred BC, an extremely interesting situation existed in the Nile valley. We find here a mosaic of cultural traditions which preserved their individuality in the face of the opportunity for interaction and free exchange of ideas. The climatic deterioration in the terminal and early post-Pleistocene is likely to have thrown these populations into closer juxtaposition than before and the dwindling resources available in the desert must have emphasized the importance of those in the valley of the Nile itself, with a resulting concentration of population there.[34]

Fig. 51

The Sebilian (*c.* 13,000–9,000 BC) is based upon a continuing Middle Palaeolithic tradition that evolved into the production of geometric microliths. The Qadan (*c.* 12,500–4,500 BC) is a microlithic industry made on diminutive, radially prepared flakes and blades. The Silsilian (*c.* 13,000 BC) is another microlithic industry but using the microburin technique for the production of small tools or blades and with resemblances to the Oranian of northwest Africa. The Sebekian (*c.* 13,000–12,000 BC), on the other hand, used mostly longer blades but the microburin technique is not found.

Economically, these groups lived by hunting the large savanna animals—the buffalo, hartebeeste, gazelle or hippo—that abounded. They also exploited the fishing and, from about twelve thousand years ago onwards in some localities they gathered and ground the wild grain.[35] The quantity of upper and lower

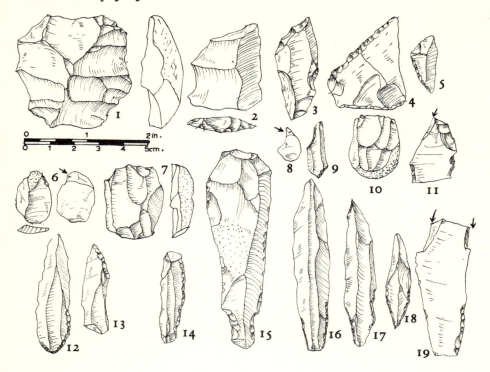

grindstones on some sites points to the greater emphasis now being placed on cereal grasses and it is just such a situation as this that can be expected to have anticipated the intentional planting of grain, so leading to agriculture and eventually to the beginnings of Dynastic civilization under the Pharaohs.

The Jebal Sahaba cemetery and an adjacent and similar one on the other side of the Nile, indicate the long-standing existence of social groupings larger than those suggested by the small individual settlement areas that occur spaced out overlooking the river and which occupied, it would seem, a closely defined and defended territory. Indeed, if the number of individuals, men,

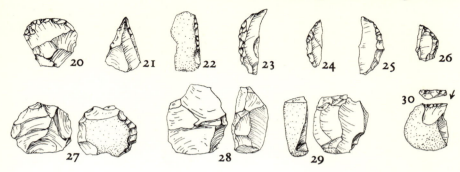

Fig. 51   Terminal Pleistocene Industries of the Nile Valley (after P. E. L. Smith, 1966 and 1968) Sebilian Industry tools (Middle and Upper Phases) from Kom Ombo, Egypt (1–7) c. 13,000–9000 BC: 1   disc core; 2–4   flakes with basal and oblique truncation; 5   backed bladelet; 6   microburin; 7   double ended micro-blade core. Chert. Silsilian Industry tools from Jebel Silsileh, Locality III (8–13) c. 13,000 BC: 8   microburin; 9, 13   basal and obliquely truncated bladelets; 10   micro-blade core; 11   burin; 12   blade with basal retouch. Flint and chert. Sebekian Industry tools from Jebel Silsileh (14–19), stratified above the Silsilian, c. 13–12,000 BC; 14   backet bladelet; 15   end scraper; 16–18   Ouchtata retouch, mostly basal; 19   burin. Flint. Tools of Industry named from Abd el Qadir (Qadan), Wadi Halfa (20–30) c. 12,000–4500 BC: 20   end scraper; 21   point; 22   side scraper; 23–26   lunates; 27, 28   micro-disc cores; 29   micro-blade core; 30   burin. Chert

women and children, (twenty-four out of fifty-nine, representing over 40% of the burials) that died of wounds is typical, then there must have been by this time continual competition for hunting and collecting rights and good fishing sites along the river.[36]

Plate 35

THE USE OF SEA AND FRESHWATER FOODS

Fish is an especially important source of protein and from about six thousand BC and perhaps earlier, we can see an emphasis on fishing and the use of other animal and vegetable sources of food in the lakes and rivers. In particular in the Nile valley and round the former lakes in the southern and central Sahara, there is

Plate 40

Fig. 52

ample evidence for waterside communities of fishers who used harpoons and fishhooks of bone and, in addition, hunted and ate hippo and crocodile.[37] Similar communities are known south of the Sahara also—round the shores of Lake Rudolph about five thousand BC,[38] at Gambles Cave by the side of Lake Nakuru in the Gregory Rift,[39] and in the Western Rift at Ishango on the shore of Lake Edward in the seventh millennium where they may have lived on off-shore sudd islands.[40] These groups hunted also but the use of water foods must have made them considerably more sedentary and more independent of seasonal food sources than would have been the case otherwise.

From the end of the Pleistocene also regular use begins to be made of sea foods, and numerous middens both in the open and in caves are known from the coasts of Africa from this time onwards. We have already noted the use of molluscs by the Capsian people at the eastern end of the Atlas range (see page 161) and extensive use was made of shellfish by the coastal Oranians and the 'Later Stone Age' populations of the south coast of South Africa, among others. At one cave site, Matjies River, more than 30 feet of shell and occupation midden had accumulated in about eight thousand years.[41] The successive occupation layers in this and other South African caves show a gradual shift from hunting as well as shellfish-collecting to more and more dependence upon sea foods and a rather sudden appearance of fish bones in quantity about three thousand BC.[42] The fish is most likely to have been trapped in tidal fish-weirs such as can still be seen in some parts, or speared from rocks or rafts near the shore, rather than caught with rod and line. Some of these pursuits are depicted in the rock paintings.[43]

The sixteenth- and seventeenth-century Portuguese and Dutch chroniclers tell us that the strandloopers, as these people were called, used to feed also off stranded whales and seals, the group camping round them until they were consumed. In fact, this source of meat was so plentiful that the groups on the southwest

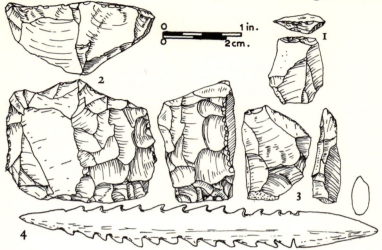

Fig. 52   Tools from the Ishangian Industry from the main fossiliferous horizon of the 10 m. terrace at Ishango, Lake Edward (after J. de Heinzelin, 1957) c. 6500–6000 BC : 1   end scraper, 2   core scraper, 3   utilised flake, quartz ; 4   bone harpoon head

coast used to construct their wind-breaks of whale ribs. Most of these 'Later Stone Age' populations lived also by hunting and, no doubt, the techniques and devices used varied as greatly as did their equipment.

THE 'LATER STONE AGE'

After five thousand BC, certainly in north Africa and the Sahara, the emphasis appears to have been on light projectiles—the bow and arrow and the throwing-stick—as well as on traps, if we believe the evidence of the rock art. Little is known of the hunting communities in the Sahara immediately before that time, but it is probable that they used arrow- or dart-heads in the Aterian tradi-tion and so their camping-places and stone equipment have not been adequately distinguished from those of the so-called 'Neolithic' communities that are so widely spread there after five thousand BC. The occupation layer at Fozzigarien dated to about 6010 BC belongs to this time. They specialized in hunting big game—elephant, rhino, hippo, giant buffalo and many of the larger antelope and gazelle—of the rich Ethiopian fauna extending throughout the Sahara and northern Africa at this time.

Recent work has shown that the first predominantly micro-lithic Archaeological Occurrences, characteristic of the 'Later Stone Age', appear in south central Africa about twelve thou-sand BC, appreciably earlier than had previously been thought, though they do not become common farther south until later.[44] In Rhodesia, the Orange Free State and on the south coast of South Africa are found contemporary industries with large side, end and core scrapers as the most characteristic tools. These are dated to *c.* 8000–10,000 BC in Rhodesia and *c.* 9000 BC at Matjies River. This is the tradition that in the Free State has been called Smithfield A. Tool-kits of the 'Later Stone Age' show more variability and specialization than at any time previously. This would seem to be the result of a more closely integrated social structure and a greater ability to select and to extract more from the resources available within the territorial boundaries.

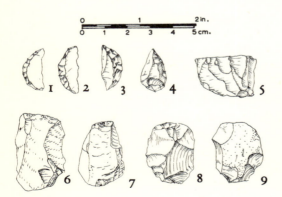

Fig. 53 Microlithic tools from 'Later Stone Age' Archaeological Occurrence at Old Oyo, Nigeria (after F. Willett, 1962): 1–4 lunates and backed bladelets; 5 micro-blade core; 6, 7 pieces with splintered ends (pièces esquillées); 8 micro-disc core. Quartz

The groups living in the Equatorial and moist forests of west Africa must have differed markedly in their way of life from those in the open and woodland savannas. Unfortunately, the scarcity of preserved bone makes it difficult to obtain any accurate idea of the basic economy, though knowledge of the present forest biome can provide the basis. The stone equipment consisted mostly of microliths, forming arrow barbs and perhaps hafted transversely, and small adze blades and scrapers.[45] If we can draw analogy from the Pygmies and other pygmoid forest dwellers, much of the meat supply would have been in the trees. Some groups may have hunted antelope and forest pig with the aid of nets and spears; others used bows and arrows. All groups would have especially sought the meat of elephant and hippo. Since game is generally scarcer in the forests, it can be expected that there would have been a corresponding increase in the importance of vegetable foods in those habitats.

Fig. 53

In the southern and western parts of the Congo basin the situation was rather different from that in west Africa and the Tshitolian hunting populations there made use both of the open grassland on the Kalahari sands and of the gallery forests along the rivers. The different ways of obtaining food and its varied sources resulted in emphasis on several kinds of equipment. [46] Thus, on the plateau, many leaf-shaped and tanged projectile points are found while in the valleys the emphasis is more on large trapeze- and triangular-shaped artifacts that could have been hafted as transverse arrowheads or used as equipment for working wood. Such arrows, though of metal, are still used by the people in these regions today.

Fig. 54

In the woodland savannas of Zambia and Malawi in south central Africa, the populations manufacturing the Nachikufan Industry, of which the intitial Phase is among the earliest 'Later Stone Age' industries known in southern Africa,[47] appear to have laid equal emphasis on hunting and on gathering. Microlithic lunates and semicircles attest to the use of projectiles with

Fig. 55

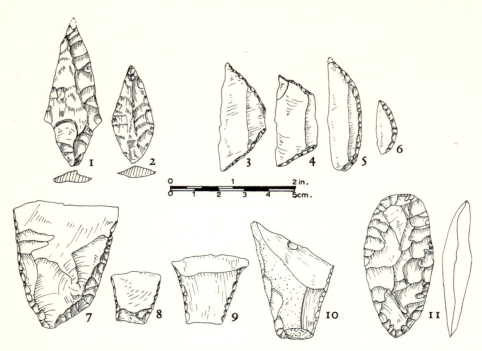

Fig. 54   Tshitolian tools from the Lower Congo and northeast Angola, c. 11,000–0 BC : 1 tanged and bifacial point ; 2   foliate point, from Plain of Kinshasa (after H. van Moorsel, 1968). 3, 4   trapeziums ; 5   backed blade ; 6   lunate ; 7–10   tranchets ; 11   bifacial core-axe, from Cauma, Iondi and Lussaca, Angola (after J. D. Clark, 1963). Polymorphic sandstone and chalcedony

Fig. 55   Nachikufan Industry tools from Nachikufu Cave, northern Zambia (after J. D. Clark, 1950) c. 8000 BC–AD 1600. Nachikufan III (1–13) (Layer C) : 1   polished axe ; 2 bored stone ; 3, 4   potsherds ; 5   double concave scraper with nose ; 6   ground quartz cylinder ; 7   micro-disc core ; 8   polished bone object (? lip plug) ; 9–12   lunates ; 13   double backed microlith. 1   diorite ; 2   schist ; 5, 13   chert ; 7, 9–12   quartz. Nachikufan IIB (14–26) (Layer D) : 14   polished axe, diorite ; 15   bored stone, soapstone ; 16   core scraper, side, quartzite ; 17   end scraper, quartzite ; 18   multi-notched scraper, chert ; 19   bone awl ; 20 concave scraper, quartzite ; 21–25   deep crescents and trapeziums, quartz ; 26   drill, chert. Nachikufan I (27–37) : 27   bored stone, schist ; 28   side and end scraper, quartz ; 29   double side scraper, quartzite ; 30   scaled piece (outil écaillé) quartz ; 31–35, 37   microliths, quartz ; 36 drill, chert

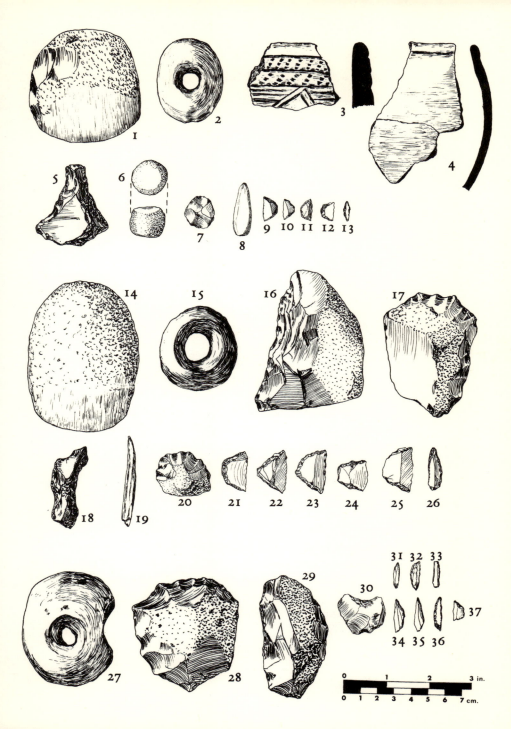

both pointed and transverse heads and the many heavy kinds of scrapers suggest extensive use of wood and its by-products, no doubt for making game fences, game stakes and traps of various kinds. Also probably associated with trapping are some of the numerous stones, usually flat, that have a hole bored through the centre and vary considerably in size. These may have formed part of the mechanism of a spring trap such as are still in use today. No doubt these bored stones served several purposes, one of the better attested being to weight a digging-stick for use in stony ground, as the Bushwomen in the southern Kalahari still did at the turn of the century.

Plate 42

Another interesting tool from this time is the edge-ground axe which is probably a very different implement from the Neolithic axe. One of these (from Mwela Rocks in northern Zambia) is as much as ten thousand years old.[48] Many of them are not very suitable for wood-cutting but, hafted, they may have been important aids to hacking out a bees' nest to remove the honey from a hollow tree and they may also have been used to strip and prepare bark for clothing, containers and rope.

The Nachikufan is also characterized by the large number of upper and lower grindstones. At least two different foods were prepared with these, as some of the lower stones have oval, dish-shaped groovings while others have circular, cup-shaped hollows. The upper stones combine a pounding face round the circumference with a smooth, flat, grinding or rubbing surface. Often in the centre of these stones is a dimpled hollow which was for catching the seeds and preventing them from being pushed off the under-stone before they were ground. There were many wild savanna fruits, nuts and plants available to these woodland populations and some of them, such as the fruits of the *mubuyu* and *musuku*, are still regularly collected and eaten by the Bantu-speaking peoples today.

In the more open parklands and bushlands of eastern and southern Africa are found various stone and bone tool-kits

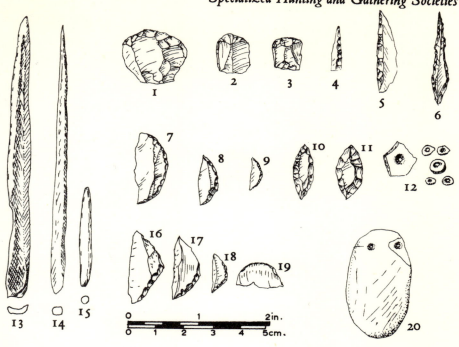

Fig. 56 *Wilton Industry tools (1–12) from the Cape Province, South Africa (after M. C. Burkitt, 1928): 1–3 short end scrapers; 4, 5 straight backed microliths; 6 awl; 7–9 lunates; 10, 11 'double crescents'; 12 ostrich eggshell beads. 3, 4, 12 from Wilton Rock-shelter, others from the Cape Flats. Chert and chalcedony. Matopan (= 'Rhodesian Wilton') Industry tools (13–20) from Amadzimba Cave, Matopos Hills, Rhodesia (after C. K. Cooke and K. R. Robinson, 1954); 13 spatulate bone awl; 14 bone point with bevelled butt; 15 link shaft; 16–19 lunates and deep crescents, quartz; 20 slate pendant*

that emphasize the use of very different kinds of microliths and small scraping tools—probably hafted as handadzes and of thumbnail size. These have usually been described as belonging to different regional traditions of the Wilton Industrial Complex

Fig. 56

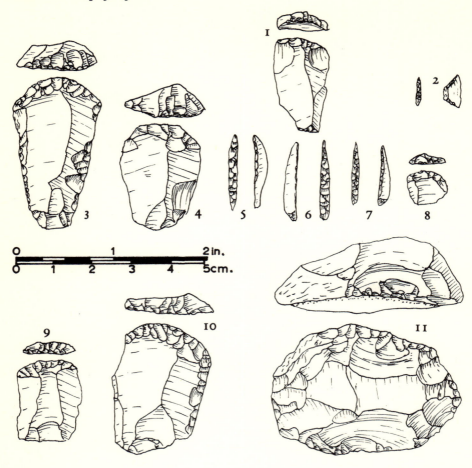

though, today, few prehistorians would wish to imply that there was any closer connection between them than a very general parallel course of development of lithic technology.[49] Where the predominant material used for tools was indurated shale, as on the Highveld in the Transvaal, Orange Free State and north-eastern Cape, there are, in addition to the microliths, a number of

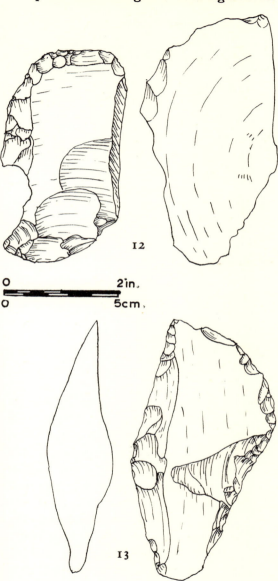

Fig. 57 Tools from the 'Later Stone Age' of the Middle Orange River (after C. G. Sampson, 1967). Phase 1 (= Smithfield A) from Zeekoegat 13 Site: 12, 13 large convex scrapers, indurated shale, c. 9000 BC. Phase 3 and Transitional 3/4 (= Smithfield C) from Glen Elliott Rockshelter (1, 2, 5–11) c. 600–300 BC: 1 splintered piece (pièce esquillée); 2 lunate; 5 backed blade; 6, 7 straight backed points; 8 small convex scraper; 9 small end scraper; 10 side and end scraper; 11 core scraper (pebble adze). Agate and chalcedony. Phase 6 (= Smithfield B): 3, 4 end scrapers, associated with pottery and bone tools, indurated shale. After AD 1200

larger scraper forms many of which resemble the Upper Pleisto-cene end-scraper. Recent work in the Free State has distinguished six lithic Phases showing that the cultural sequence is more complex than had previously been supposed and the idea of a single developing industrial complex, named the Smithfield, now has to be modified. The earliest Phase (= Smithfield A) is suc-ceeded by Phases having a predominantly microlithic compo-nent based on the use of agate and chalcedony pebbles (= a regional Wilton). These are followed by a phase without micro-liths (= Smithfield C) and the final Phase again emphasizes the larger scraper forms made from indurated shale as well as the bone

Fig. 57

tool element and pottery to the virtual exclusion of microliths.[50] In the earlier part of this century Bushmen were still living who could demonstrate how these *kuin* stones were made and used, for scraping, cutting, cleaning skins, preparing skin blankets, clean-ing the meat off bones and in the making of wooden clubs, bows and arrows. A number of regional 'industries' have been dis-tinguished within the Smithfield Industrial Complex.

ROCK ART

It is the later stages of these 'Wilton' and 'Smithfield' traditions in central Tanzania, Rhodesia, South and South West Africa that have left behind them such a wealth of art—paintings on

Plates 3, 46
Plate 2

the rocks or in caves and rock shelters and engravings on flat rocks in the open. Although none of these is probably much more than two thousand years old, except, perhaps, the oldest en-gravings, they, nevertheless, show by the sophisticated and fully developed nature of the earliest surviving examples, that the beginnings of this art must go back at least to the beginning of Holocene times.[51]

It is from their art that we obtain so many insights into the life of these 'Later Stone Age' peoples. Some of the art was, no doubt, inspired by magical or ritual considerations—sympathetic magic to ensure success in the hunt, rain magic, or ritual to instruct

Fig. 58 Incised, natural-istic engraving of a white rhino from an outcrop of dolerite at Bosfontein Farm No. 607, Krugersdorp dis-trict, Transvaal

initiates or to ensure passage for the spirit of the dead. Most of it, however, appears to be representational and to be inspired by the desire to record events in the daily life of the group—a suc-cessful hunt and the uses of the many animal-head disguises; a bestiary of the animals that abounded in the locality and those that provided the most favoured meat; fights; dances; honey- and plant-collecting and many other domestic scenes.

This work is generally of such a high order that it presupposes the presence of consummate artists whose mastery of line and skill with colour place this art among the most vital and most pleasing the world has ever seen. The pigment was obtained from grinding various kinds of mineral rock—haematite, manganese, kaolin—and mixing the powder with some fatty or resinous medium. It was sometimes stored in little horn containers and was applied with the aid of a feather brush or a wooden or bone spatula. The magnificent polychrome work of the later Basutoland Bushmen may have been painted by using the mouth as a blow-gun to spray the paint onto the wall or by using a fine-bristled brush such as could be obtained by teasing out a section of *Velosia* stem.[52]

Plate 46

Of equally superb naturalistic portrayal are the engravings done by direct incision or pecking in the hard rocks on the top of some kopje from which the hunters could observe the game grazing on the plain below. Pecking could be done with any

Fig. 58

convenient hard and pointed rock fragment but for a long time the technique used for making the line engravings on hard dolerite remained unknown. It was even suggested that diamonds had been employed but, if so, the artists have been very careful to carry them away when they moved on! The answer, provided recently, is that the engraving was made with a convenient sharp flake of the country rock which cut through the yellow-brown, comparatively soft and generally thick, weathered skin that forms on dolerite under humid conditions, to expose the purple, un-weathered rock within. Over the centuries acid ground-water standing in the incisions etched them deeper into the virgin rock so that when the outer crust weathered away, the engraving was still, though faintly, preserved.[53]

GENERAL WAY OF LIFE

Many of these hunting communities made beads, pendants and other objects of shell, bone or ivory with which to adorn their persons. Wherever it could be obtained, the shell of the ostrich egg was used for beads which were made into long strings and wrapped round the body or sewn onto leather aprons. Where ostrich egg-shell was unobtainable, various sea and freshwater shells, nacre and others were used. The woodland peoples, no doubt, wore clothing of bark cloth; those in the savannas used skins, often skilfully sewn together. The body was often decorated with red, black or white paint and the hair was sometimes dusted with specularite to give a silvery lustre.

The size of the camp would have depended on the availability and abundance of the food resources. Sometimes, especially in waterside camps, there may be expected to have been as many as fifty or more individuals in the multi-family band. Usually, however, the camps must have been smaller and would probably have been unlikely to contain more than fifteen to twenty-five persons living in six or less nuclear family groups. They would have lived in wind-breaks constructed of branches, thatch or matting—the remains of one such collapsed wind-break was found at Gwisho Springs dating to the mid-third millennium BC[54]—and the scatter on a nuclear family's living-site might be expected to look not unlike the one in Fig. 37 from Orangia I after more than four thousand years had gone by.[55]

If the 'Later Stone Age' hunting and gathering way of life can now be shown to have begun much earlier (about twelve thousand years ago) than had at one time been thought possible, it can also be seen to have persisted much later in some parts, in spite of long contact with food producers, especially in the desert country of southern Africa and in the Congo forests. Indeed, in the Baines Mountains of South West Africa, groups of OvaTjimba still use stone for tools.[56] From about five thousand BC onwards, therefore, there were African communities living at several different economic levels. Agriculturists and pastoralists existed, to begin with, mostly in the north; then the methods of the farmer and a knowledge of metallurgy spread south of the Sahara, penetrating the savanna belts and west African forests, and wholesale economic changes began to take place. As time went on, these affected most of the subcontinent also. But—such is the attraction of the hunting way of life—hunting and gathering societies have continued in some parts until the present day and now provide the ethnographer and archaeologist with some of the most valuable evidence for reconstructing the way of life of the 'Later Stone Age' populations.

Plates 23, 24

Plates 36, 37, 39

The many scenes of daily life preserved in the rock art make it hard to think of the 'Later Stone Age' hunter as a miserable, starving savage. Rather is one led to envisage him as enjoying somewhat more than his share of the 'good life'. The natural richness of the African tropical environment for Bushman and Negro alike; the possession of an intimate knowledge of the country in which he lived and of the habits of the various plants and animals that shared it with him; the general simplicity of his needs, the possession of a rude but efficient technology with which to satisfy them and the leisure to record it all; as well as the absence of competitors; all these go a long way towards confirming the contention that hunting is not merely a 'subsistence technique' but for some, certainly, was indeed 'the master behaviour pattern of the human species'.[57]

CHAPTER VI

Farmers and Present-Day People

INITIAL STAGES OF FOOD PRODUCTION

THE HUNTING WAY of life may have had much to commend it for many of Africa's 'Later Stone Age' populations in the rich savanna lands south of the Sahara, where they were able to enjoy liberal quantities of 'berries, locusts, snakes, roasted willow tree caterpillars, eland meat and marrow bones'. On the other hand, for those in the more arid and impoverished lands, the 'lenten fare' these provided cannot, to mix a metaphor, have been everyone's 'cup of tea'. It is, therefore, hardly a matter for surprise that, when circumstances made possible—perhaps even necessitated—a fundamental change in the economic basis in the more arid northern parts of the continent, the hunting/gathering communities there turned to producing their own staple sources of meat and meal, instead of simply exploiting the supply of wild foods.

The change to cultivating crops and herding stock did not come about overnight, however, and the process covered several millennia. In southwest Asia, the evidence from sites in the Levant at one end of the Fertile Crescent, or in southwestern Iran at the other, shows, first, intensification in the use of wild cereal grasses by the hunters of onager, gazelle, or wild ox and then their incipient cultivation, accompanied by domestication of the goat and sheep before seven thousand BC. The wheats, barley, goats and sheep that were the earliest domesticates are indigenous to southwest Asia and bear out the archaeological evidence that it was here that cereal cultivation and stock herding were first developed by such specialized hunting and gathering societies as those of the Natufians in Palestine after nine thousand BC.

The obvious advantages of producing a surplus of grain that could be stored and an ever-present source of meat on the hoof,

might, one would think, have led to a rapid adoption of domesticated plants and animals. That, within this nuclear centre, it
took, in fact, at least two millennia to bring about the change
must in large part have been due to the need to evolve satisfactory
domestic strains by people having no knowledge of selective
breeding and no very certain idea of the ultimate advantages. By
about five thousand BC, however, which is the time when the
first evidence of domestication appears in Africa, this had been
achieved in respect of a number of plants as well as goats, sheep,
pigs and cattle, of which, with the exception of cattle, no wild
progenitors occurred in the continent.

The now assured and surplus food supplies resulted in more
rigidly structured social groupings and in a considerable over-all
increase in population density, while the maximum size of a
community no longer depended on the number that could be
supported by wild sources through the leanest season of the year.
Cultivators, moreover, are less exacting in the amount of territory
they require.

The mobility of ideas and of trade articles in the Middle East
from the end of the Palaeolithic onwards is well illustrated by
the extent, both in time and space, of the trade in obsidian,
mostly from sources in Anatolia.[1] This is very impressive,
reaching to all parts of the Fertile Crescent, and clearly demonstrates that mobility and free exchange must have ensured that
progress towards efficient food production would be a widespread
process throughout southwest Asia rather than the invention of
one region alone. It is all the more surprising, therefore, that the
appearance of food production in north Africa is relatively
sudden and we have as yet no evidence of the intitial stages
towards incipient cultivation there that we know in the Levant
and Mesopotamia.

Since the fertile agricultural lands of the Nile delta are only
some three hundred miles to the southwest across the isthmus
of Suez from the early centres in Palestine, it might be thought

that Egypt would have experienced a similar history of initial experimentation with potential local domesticates. As yet, however, we have no evidence that this was so, in spite of the increased use made in the terminal Pleistocene of wild grasses now known from recent work in Nubia and Upper Egypt (Kom Ombo).[2] These communities do not appear to have succeeded in domesticating any of them. This could have been because none of these grasses and plants were particularly suitable cultigens, or it may have been that the waterside Nile habitat was so rich in early post-Pleistocene times that there was not the incentive to develop efficient domesticates and, indeed, Herodotus speaks of certain water plants that were extensively used by the Delta peoples in his time.[3]

If the drier conditions for which there is evidence both in the Middle East and in Africa at the end of the Pleistocene and the beginning of Holocene times were responsible for the concentration of settlements and the hostility apparent among groups in the Nile valley at that time, then the warmer and more humid conditions reflected there between seven thousand and three thousand BC must have been optimum for the highly specialized societies of those times. Where, therefore, the challenge is lacking the expected response may also be absent and this was certainly the case in later times in sub-Saharan Africa.

Since there is a gap in our knowledge of the cultural succession in Upper Egypt and the Delta between the microlithic ('epi-Levalloisian') industries of the terminal Pleistocene and the oldest Neolithic, agricultural communities in the Fayum, it may be that the crucial evidence will later be found to exist there, after all. One undated assemblage from a site at Helwan, near Cairo, certainly recalls the Palestinian Natufian. Also, between eight thousand and five thousand BC the Nile floods were lower so that it is probable that the occupation sites, which in Nubia by this time are confined to the flood plain, lie buried under many feet of later alluvial deposition.[4] Higher up the river, in Nubia, the

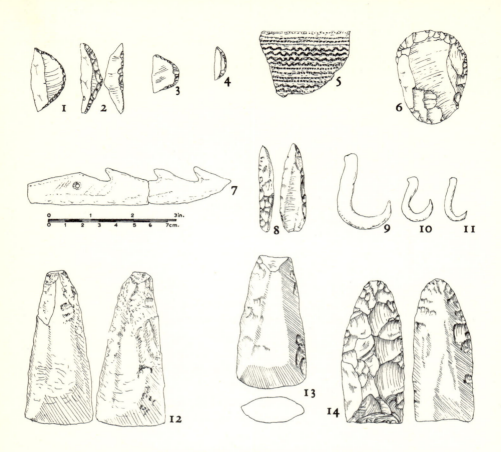

Fig. 59 Neolithic tools from Es Shaheinab, Khartoum, Sudan (after A. J. Arkell, 1953):
1, 3 deep crescents; 2 backed blade; 4 lunate; 5 sherd with 'dotted wavy line' decoration;
6 end scraper; 7 bone harpoon head; 8 drill; 9–11 shell fishhooks; 12 polished bone
celt; 13 polished stone celt; 14 gouge with vertical polishing. 1–5, 6, 8 quartz and fossil
wood; 13, 14 rhyolite

Fig. 60 Wooden sickle holder with flint blades from Site 51, Fayum A, peasant Neolithic
village, Fayum Depression, Egypt. Length: 50 cm. (After G. Caton Thompson, 1934)

microlithic hunting communities still regularly occupied small camping-sites along the levées or by seasonal ponds back from the main channel of the Nile.[5] These continued into the fourth millennium and the first clear evidence for domestication in the upper reaches of the river is a dwarf goat associated with a 'Neolithic' tool-kit from the site of Es Shaheinab near Khartoum (about 3200 BC).[6]

Fig. 59

Even though communities in the upper reaches of the Nile may have been late in abandoning the hunting/gathering way of life, there is no indication that this was necessarily the case also in the lower reaches. That it was not so, in fact, is shown by the existence of farming communities in Lower Egypt by the middle of the fifth millennium. The Neolithic Fayum A subsistence farmers cultivating emmer wheat and flax for cloth on the shores of the lake in the Fayum depression represent to date the oldest evidence of food production from the Nile (about 4400 BC). Their stone industry with its many bifacial tools suggests a fairly long-established tradition of African origin and there is little in the material culture, except for the domesticates, that suggests an origin in Asia.[7]

Fig. 60

Bones of goat, sheep, pig and cattle have been recognized, but whether domesticated or not has yet to be determined. Certainly, if the first two have been identified correctly, they must clearly have been diffused, since no wild Caprini, except for the Barbary sheep, occur in Africa. The Fayum people may have been rather marginal, incipient cultivators, moving seasonally with their herds. Their living-places and dwellings, which have left no trace, were situated some distance away from the coiled basketry silos in which the grain was stored and may have been made of matting or skins spread over a withy frame. Probably more typical of this time is the large village community somewhat to the north at Merimde on the edge of the Delta, the earliest levels of which go back to the fifth millennium. This was a permanent village of wattle-and-daub houses and the typically

Egyptian flint implements (ground stone axes, sickle blades, knives and hollow-based arrowheads) are associated with other traits and equipment that support the view that they are derived from Asian forms.[8]

Fig. 61 Pre-Dynastic Egyptians and their weapons—bow and arrow with transverse head, spear, throwing stick and knives. (After British Museum Guide to Egyptian Collections, 1930)

ANCIENT EGYPT

The archaeological sequence in Upper Egypt, starting with the Neolithic settlement and cemeteries at Badari, is much better known, though almost as insecurely dated.[9] More has probably been written about the pros and cons for a local or an exotic origin for Egyptian Dynastic civilization, than has been published on the whole of the rest of the continent put together, but the question is unlikely to be resolved until new and systematic studies of the earlier Neolithic and Predynastic occupation sites and cemeteries are carried out. It is not, however, with Egyptian civilization and its extraordinarily conservative cultural continuum that we are now concerned and, unfortunately, a book of this size does not permit of more than a passing reference to the sequence of events that led to the unification of Upper and Lower Egypt under Narmer or Menes, ruler of Upper Egypt, about three thousand two hundred BC.

The Predynastic can be divided into an earlier and a later stage (Naqada I, about 3800–3600 BC and Naqada II, about 3600–3200 BC) and appears to follow directly out of the earlier 'Neolithic' communities such as those of Fayum A, Merimde and Badari. It exhibits an essentially African flavour and origin, onto which have sometimes been grafted certain non-African elements that never amount to anything very definite until the closing stages of the later Predynastic.[10] Rather do they indicate interchange of ideas and trade objects, and suggestions of any large-scale influx of foreign invaders are quite without foundation. The hypothetical 'Dynastic Race' said by some to have established the First Dynasty still has to be given substance in fact and the latest assessments of the physical nature of the population show that it underwent remarkably little change from the beginning of the Predynastic to the end of Dynastic times.[11]

Similarly, the Ancient Egyptian language is considered by Greenberg not to be derived from Semitic, as was previously assumed but rather to share a common ancestor with it. Together they form two of the five co-ordinate branches of an Afro-Asiatic language family—with Cushitic, Berber and Chadic.[12]

The growth of urban civilization, the appearance of class distinction, writing, fine craftsmanship and monumental architecture can be seen as the outcome of increasingly regular interaction with Mesopotamia and the Levant through trade, movements of professionals and especially the exchange of ideas and knowledge of political and social developments.[13] The particular form of civilized government established under the rule of the Pharaohs is, nevertheless, an essentially African one, very reminiscent of that of the despotic and divine rulers of later times on the Upper Nile and in west Africa. Indeed, in Egypt, unlike

Fig. 61

Mesopotamia, the genius behind the unification of the two kingdoms would seem to have been that of a single individual or family—'King Scorpion', Narmer, Menes?—a man, or men possessed of the outstanding ability to lead, organize for conquest and to consolidate as did Tshaka, Moshesh or Lewanika in later times.

Although Egyptian dynastic rule lasted for two thousand five hundred years and the Meroitic Kingdom on the Upper Nile continued Egyptian civilization for another thousand years more, it is hard to gauge its influence on the rest of Africa since the scholarly emphasis has always been focussed upon Egypt's relations with neighbouring civilizations of the Middle East, a focus that was as all-important then as it is today. Its effect upon the populations of the Ethiopian highlands or on those of the savannas of the Sudan belt remains unknown, since practically no research has been done in this direction. We read of trading expeditions to the Land of Punt from the time of the Fourth Dynasty and Meroe received a full share of the Indian Ocean trade.[14] If we could read the Meroitic script the situation might appear very different but at the present time it seems that the civilization of the Nile had little direct effect upon sub-Saharan Africa, due partly, no doubt to the geographical barriers of the desert and the Nile sudd. Attempts to show the Egyptian derivation of certain traits—divine kingship, for example—found in the cultures of the Upper Nile and west Africa would be more convincing if a clearer relationship between the traits themselves could be demonstrated.

THE SPREAD OF DOMESTICATION

Further westward along the Mediterranean coast, the sequence of events leading to the appearance of a 'Neolithic' economy is well attested at the Haua Fteah cave. By about five thousand BC the faunal remains from the occupation layers show that 80% of the meat eaten came from domestic sheep or goats, a high proportion of which were juveniles. This clearly 'Neolithic' economy is in marked contrast to the situation in the underlying hunting/gathering occupation layers (Libyco-Capsian) where it was bovids and the wild Barbary sheep (*Ammotragus*)—identified on the larger mean size of the bones—that provided most of the meat. A study of the bovid remains from both horizons shows no indications that domestic cattle were present.[15]

In Cyrenaica there is, thus, no evidence of the gradational stages of domestication seen in southwest Asia and the stock and cultural equipment appear suddenly. The 'Neolithic' tool-kit of this time in Cyrenaica shows no fundamental break with what had gone before and combines conventional microlithic elements, burins and end-scrapers, with certain new forms and techniques—pressure flaking, pottery, tanged and leaf-shaped arrowheads, flat knives, the ground stone axe, numerous grindstones and a bone industry. This is taken to indicate that there was no significant change in the ethnic composition of the population and that the appearance of Neolithic technology and stock-raising was the result of diffusion, presumably westwards from the Nile valley. There is, however, no evidence for cultivation unless it be the so-called 'hoe blades' of limestone, and flint blades with a gloss on the cutting edge, like the sickle blades on the Egyptian sites, are conspicuous by their extreme rarity.[16]

The material culture, in particular the pottery, shows appreciably more in common with the Maghreb, however, than it does with the Nile valley (Merimde) or the Fayum, although the finds at Siwa Oasis in the desert midway between attest that some contact took place between east and west at that time.[17] The Maghrebian form of the 'Neolithic' is founded upon the Capsian tradition of stone-working and dates mostly from the late fourth millennium where it is associated with the rock-art tradition of the southern slopes of the Atlas range and the northern Sahara.[18] Two phases have been distinguished—one associated with the rock art on the plateau and Atlas slopes but with little pottery and another with a more northern distribution extending to the coast where the arrowheads are absent but pottery is fairly abundant. Remains of sheep and goat have been identified from a cave on the Algerian plateau (Rhar oum el-Fernan) with a 'Neolithic' assemblage.

There is evidence for geometric line engraving on ostrich egg-shell water containers and on slabs of chalky limestone, as well as some carving in the round, associated with the Capsian and dating from the seventh and eighth millennia[19] but as yet there is no indication that the naturalistic art on rocks in the open or on cave and shelter walls is as old as this. It could well be so, however, for isolated large animal engravings have now been found in Upper Egypt[20] and Cyrenaica.[21] In Nubia three main engraving groups have been distinguished.[22] The oldest group shows only hunting scenes with large game, including the ele-phant and giraffe which had certainly disappeared from the Nile valley by early Dynastic times (about 2900–2600 BC). Most of this north African rock art, however, probably dates between the sixth and the third millennium. It reaches its zenith in the art styles—both engravings and paintings—in the Sahara, particularly in the Tassili range and it is spread from one end of the desert to the other wherever suitable canvasses were to be found—rock shelters and caves for paintings and flat or vertical rocks in the open for engravings.[23]

Plate 47

Besides depicting the wild Sudanic fauna, the art includes many scenes showing herds of domestic cattle as well as sheep and this is of considerable interest with regard to the origins of the African domestic cattle. Contrary to what is often said, both large (*Bos primigenius*) and small (*Bos ibericus*) species of wild cattle existed in north Africa since early in the Pleistocene so that it is not beyond the bounds of possibility that they may have been domesticated there.[24] There is, however, no certain identifi-cation of domestic *Bos* in Egypt before the Predynastic period when ritual burials attest the emergence of a cattle cult.[25] One

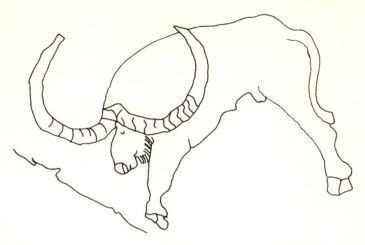

Fig. 62 Engraving of the extinct giant buffalo (Homoioceras *sp.*) *from site in southern Oran. (After C. B. M. McBurney, 1960)*

Saharan rock-shelter site (Uan Muhuggiag) at the eastern end of the Tassili range has, however, produced the skull of what has been described as the domestic *Bos brachyceros* dated to early in the fifth millennium or late in the sixth millennium BC (about 4000± 120 BC)[26], and domestic cattle may also be present in the lowest layers dating to about 5500 BC.

Although certainly a significant find, this needs to be confirmed by additional remains if the theory of an independent domestication centre in north Africa is to be seriously considered. The spread of cattle from Asia into Egypt and the Sahara is the most likely explanation at present but it has also been suggested that the rapid spread of 'Neolithic' culture in the Aegean and along the northern shores of the Mediterranean, which led to the occupation of southern Italy and Malta by the middle of the fifth millennium, if not before, might have similarly brought cattle by sea to northeastern Tunisia, thus initiating from the

Fig. 63 Painting in one of the earlier 'Round Head' styles showing a negro-like mask and costume from Aouanrhet. (After H. Lhote, 1963)

Maghreb an eastward and southward spread of pastoral groups with cattle.[27] It is from this time also that the obsidian from the Aeolian Islands[28] makes its appearance in north Africa, but only further finds, particularly, of course, a good pair of horn cores, can resolve the dilemma.

Whatever the origin of their stock, the first 'Neolithic' pastoralists appear in the Sahara in the fifth millennium BC, perhaps earlier. They drove herds of long- and short-horned cattle and goats and flocks of sheep and continued there until the increasing desiccation after two thousand five hundred BC forced some of them to move out. Though much remains to be learned, we now know not a little from the art about the way of life of the 'Neolithic' pastoralists of the desert, some of whom were of Afro-Mediterranean, others of negroid stock, as we have already seen. They were semi-nomadic and lived in light, movable shelters, camping in the open or in rock shelters and penning their stock in fenced enclosures. Sometimes they fought and always they hunted extensively—the elephant, rhinoceros, hippo, giraffe and the now extinct giant buffalo and many larger antelopes. They also fished the lakes. They sometimes dressed and ornamented themselves elaborately and their art depicts many domestic

Fig. 62

scenes and others of religious ritual. These communities occupied   *Fig. 63*
the Sahara for more than two thousand years during the optimum
climatic conditions that pertained before two thousand BC.

THE DEVELOPMENT OF AGRICULTURE

The distinctive Saharan 'Neolithic' culture tradition using
chert and chalcedony is subdivisible into several facies; it stretched
no further south than the northern edge of the present-day
savanna belt at $15°$ North. There it is replaced by various   *Fig. 64*
microlithic industries using quartz and these, clearly, are the
cultural expressions of two very different ecological zones. It is
in the latter region that Professor Murdock[29] has postulated that
agriculture developed independently between four thousand and
five thousand BC, at the same time, that is, as it was seemingly
being introduced into Egypt from southwest Asia. Factual
evidence to support this claim is, as yet, lacking but in recent
years a considerable amount of new information has become
available that does help to throw light on the origins of domestication south of the desert.   *Fig. 65*

Excavations in Sierra Leone, Ghana and Nigeria show that
about three thousand BC, mostly a little after that, the 'Later
Stone Age' microlithic tradition became enriched by the addition
of 'Neolithic' traits such as ground and polished stone axes and
pottery.[30] It seems reasonable to interpret this as indicating that
some of the savanna and forest peoples were now engaging in
cultivation and probably had some domestic stock. This is,
of course, later than the first appearance of domesticated plants
and animals in north Africa, so a knowledge of domestication
and some of the products thereof were presumably diffused south
some time after five thousand BC.

The main north/south lines of communication were, no doubt,
the same as those later followed by the chariot routes (see page 207)
and the nature of their habitat meant that the 'Neolithic' communities of the desert must have been highly mobile. Movement

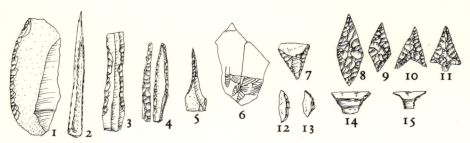

Fig. 64 Neolithic of Capsian tradition from Redeyet, southern Tunisia (1–15) (after R. Vaufrey, 1955) : 1 side scraper; 2 bone awl; 3 double concave scraper; 4 drill; 5 awl; 6 engraved ostrich eggshell; 7, 14, 15 triangular and tranchet arrowheads; 8–11 hollow-based and tanged arrowheads; 12, 13 lunates. Flint. Neolithic of Borku, southern Tibesti, Tchad (16–24) (after J. Courtin, 1966): 16–19, 23 lunate, deep crescent, triangles and tranchet; 20 backed flake; 21, 22 drills; 24 potsherd with 'dotted wavy line' decoration. Quartzite and chert. Neolithic of Ténéré, Central Sahara, Niger (25–34) (after G. Joubert and R. Vaufrey, 1946 and J. Tixier, 1962): 25 backed bladelet; 26 drill; 27 triangle and lunate; 28 end scraper; 29, 30 hollow based arrowheads; 31 tanged arrowhead; 32 polished adze; 33 disc knife; 34 gouge, polished on the ventral face, similar to those with the Khartoum Neolithic. Jasper.

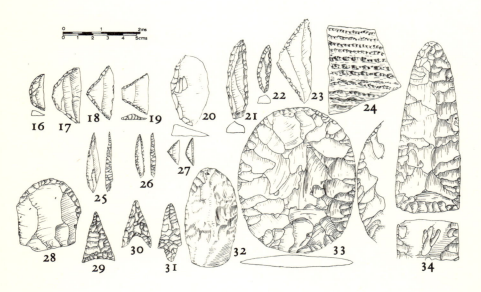

from the Nile westwards to the northern oases is attested at Kharga and Siwa while the Wadi Howar would at one time have provided a natural route westwards at the latitude of Meroe from the Nile to the savanna belt. Indeed, the wide spread of the Khartoum Wavy Line Pottery tradition, as far as the Hoggar highlands and Wanyanga in Tibesti, as well as the extensive trade in amazonstone from Tibesti, right across the Sahara from

Fig. 65 West African Neolithic Industries: 1–12 from Bosumpra Cave, Abetifi, southern Ghana (after C. T. Shaw, 1944): 1, 2 convex scrapers; 3 micro-flake core; 4–7 tranchets and deep crescents; 8, 9 lunates; 10 biconically pierced quartz pebble. 11, 12, ground and polished celts; 11, 12 greenstone, others quartz. 13–20 from Ntereso, northern Ghana (after O. Davies, 1966): 13 bone fish-hook; 14 bone harpoon; 15 fragment of stone 'cigar' (grater); 16 fragment of slate bracelet; 17 polished celt; 18–20 arrowheads of Sahara type, shale. Rare iron implements were found at Ntereso, except with the earliest occupation, but there is no evidence of metal working

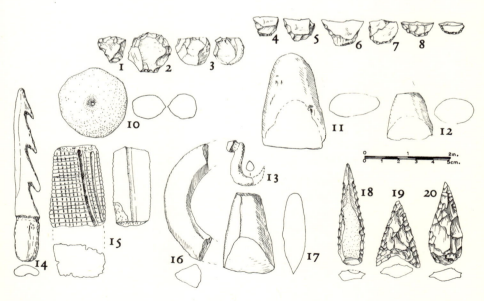

the west coast to the Nile, show that knowledge of plant cultivation as well as domestication of animals could equally have been
diffused to the limits of the savanna at this time.[31] Why, therefore, we may ask, did it take a further two thousand years before
a Neolithic technology, normally associated with food production, makes its appearance in west Africa?

There were probably several reasons. The habitat already
provided an inexhaustible supply of meat and plant food—
more than was necessary for the needs of the communities living
there. There was, therefore, no particular incentive at first to
change to raising crops and animals, especially since Neolithic
equipment cannot have been particularly advantageous in an
environment of high rainfall, hardwood forests and rapid regeneration. The chief reason, however, is likely to have been
because the crops grown in Egypt and north Africa were winter-
rainfall crops—wheat and barley—which are unsatisfactory under
tropical summer-rainfall conditions.

Moreover, there is, as yet, not a single piece of convincing
evidence that the Sahara pastoralists themselves cultivated crops
until quite late times. All the carbonized seeds and grains that
have been found there associated with the 'Neolithic' are from
wild forms and the grinding equipment that occurs on these sites
must, therefore, be presumed to have been used for preparing
these in the same way as the Tuareg still collect and use the wild
kreb grasses today.[32]. Only in southern Mauretania about eleven
hundred BC at the late 'Neolithic' settlements at Tichit Walata is
there evidence, recovered in 1968, for the cultivation of bullrush

Plate 41   millet (*Pennisetum*).[33] This is especially interesting since the wild
form is believed to be native to the savanna so that the *Pennisetum* must have been cultivated there first and then carried
northwards into the desert.

It is also possible that the wild-grass ancestors of bullrush
millet, sorghum and other cereals may have occurred in the Nile
valley as weed plants associated with the cultivation of the Asian

cereal crops. In such circumstances they may have undergone selective changes that rendered them suitable as domesticates in their own right. If this was so, the evidence still remains to be produced and it is more generally assumed that the wild species from which the African millets and sorghum are derived are indigenous to the sub-Saharan Sudan belt.

It is apparent, therefore, that much experimentation must have been necessary with potential savanna domesticates before suitable cultigens were produced. How long a time this would have taken is unknown—one thousand years? two thousand? There can, however, be little doubt that in the second and third, as well probably as in the fourth millennium BC, the cultivated forms of the indigenous food plants of west Africa, the Sudan and Ethiopia were first developed: Guinea rice and *fonio* in west Africa; bullrush millet and sorghum in the Sudan; finger millet, *teff* and *ensete* in Ethiopia, in addition to wheat and barley which were also early introduced onto the high plateau where the climate is suitable for their cultivation without the need for irrigation. All these are still grown today, many of them under slash-and-burn methods of cultivation, and compete with the introduced Asian and American food plants. However, with the exception of sorghum and some of the millets which were carried south, the use of most of these African cultigens would now seem to be restricted to those regions where they were first domesticated. Whether plant geneticists will ever be able to trace the initial stages in the domestication of some of these plants remains to be seen. Doubtless it was the necessity first to produce efficient local cultivated species that delayed the appearance of fully food-producing cultures in Africa south of the Sahara. At the same time the fact that so many plants *were* successfully domesticated serves to emphasize the ingenuity of the Negro and Cushitic populations.

The great advantage of livestock is, of course, the reserve supply of meat it provides and it is estimated that up to fifty per cent or more of the animals would be surplus to herd maintenance and so could be slaughtered every year.[34] We may then ask why there was no success in domesticating some of the large mammals of the Ethiopian fauna—there are probably more potential domesticates here than in any other continent. Certainly there are representations dating to Predynastic and Old Kingdom times in Egypt of what looks like experimental domestication of a number of different animals—gazelle, oryx, ibex, hyaena and, perhaps, even the giraffe—and this kind of symbiotic existence with animals must have extended much further back in time. However, the introduction of domestic sheep and goats and, especially, cattle—not forgetting the dog—appears effectively to have eclipsed any further attempts at domestication of African species excepting the ass, the cat and the guinea fowl. African experiments in the domestication of food animals came too late, therefore, to compete with the Asian ones but the success of modern experimental domestication of the eland suggests that, if this species had existed in the Nile valley in Neolithic times, it might also have been domesticated and might today have been competing successfully with cattle.

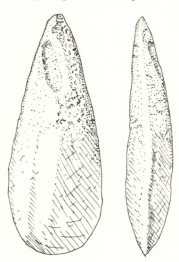

Fig. 66   Ground and polished celt of haematite from Hikita, Uele basin, northeastern Congo. (After F. van Noten, 1968)

THE 'NEOLITHIC' IN WEST AFRICA

In the west African rain-forest lived peoples with a 'Neolithic' technology, from the third millennium onwards. Some of their sites are now covered by secondary, or even by what is considered to be primary forest. Unless we consider the forest not to have been there at that time, which seems unlikely, the effective clearing of rain-forest for cultivation purposes presupposes the availability of quite a large labour force. Since sorghums and the other west African domesticated grains do not do well in humid rain-forest, what then was the staple food that supported these large populations? There is good reason to infer that it was yam cultivation and oil from the oil palm.

Until recently it was supposed that cultivated yams were of Asian origin and introduced into Africa some time after five hundred BC. However, it is now accepted by most botanists that the commonest yam grown in west Africa (*Dioscorea cayenensis*) is not of Asian origin but is derived from a local wild species.[35] The early domestication of this yam may therefore well account for the 'Neolithic' settlements in the forests. The distribution and nutritional value of the oil-palm nut needs no amplification.

These 'Neolithic' cultivators not only spread throughout the length of the west African forest region, as the distribution map shows, but it seems possible that they also spread southwards into the northwestern and northeastern parts of the Congo basin. Stone axes and pottery are found there, which, although they are very inadequately known and dated and have, up to now been considered to be late, could equally well represent an early southward movement of 'Neolithic' cultivators in the first millennium BC. (The map shows the clear differences between the desert and forest/savanna cultures and the areas in the Congo basin which were also probably occupied at this time.)

Fig. 42
Fig. 66

Indirect evidence is now available also to suggest that it was the first millennium BC when the extensive forest clearance first began in the Lake Victoria basin and in the west and south of that of the Congo. About three thousand years ago, as cores from Lake Victoria indicate, pollens of forest species show a sharp decline with a corresponding rise in grass pollens while another pollen species (*Acalypa*), which is an early-stage pioneer in the regeneration of forest after gardens have been abandoned, also increases in abundance.[36] In northeast Angola, the clogging of the stream courses with sand washed in from the sides of the valleys is not associated with any known climatic fluctuation and is believed to reflect the result of soil erosion following clearing of the woodland and forest for cultivation that began in the first millennium BC.[37] It certainly now begins to look as if the first millennium BC was the time when cultivators began to attack the Equatorial forests.

The presence of tsetse fly in most of west Africa and Equatoria effectively precludes the keeping of all except small stock and dwarf, tsetse-immune cattle in parts of west Africa, so that the later prehistoric peoples that occupied these regions must be considered to have been sedentary village cultivators who obtained most of their meat by hunting.

THE EAST AFRICAN HIGH GRASSLANDS

Plate 4

It is a different picture on the east side of the continent where pastoral peoples have been long established in the Horn and east Africa. Settlements of village farmers, basically 'Neolithic' but who also used some copper and presumably cultivated crops, are known from the plateau in northeastern Ethiopia where the material culture shows affinities with that of the C-group peoples who moved into Nubia from the western desert about two thousand five hundred BC.[38] If they were the same peoples as are depicted in the rock paintings in the eastern parts of Ethiopia and Somalia, they were 'Libyans'—the word is deliberately used in quotes—from the west and they owned herds of long-horned, humpless cattle that are shown in art styles reminiscent of those of the eastern Sahara.[39]

Fig. 67

Fig. 67   Long-horned, humpless cattle and herdsmen. Painting at Genda-Biftou (Sourré) Dire Dawa, Ethiopia. (After H. Breuil, 1934)

An influx of north Africans into the Sahara in the first millennium BC may also have helped to turn some of the 'Neolithic' communities there to moving southwards. The chariot routes that traverse the desert to the Niger bend are marked by engravings and paintings of light, two-wheeled chariots drawn by horses. They are associated with the Garamantes and Pharusii, knowledge of whom, after the fifth century BC, comes from classical authors. These chariots used to run down the troglodytes of the desert, and other scenes in the later rock art document the ousting of the 'Neolithic' pastoralists by militant, metal-using immigrants—ancestral Berber peoples, perhaps?[40] Incidentally, these chariots are the first indirect evidence for trans-Saharan trade—the possibilities they suggest are for the routes and not, of course, for what they, themselves, could carry.

Fig. 68

These population movements, that brought some of the desert pastoralists into the Nile valley and Ethiopia and probably turned others of them southwards from the Chad basin into the Central African Republic and down the drier lands of the

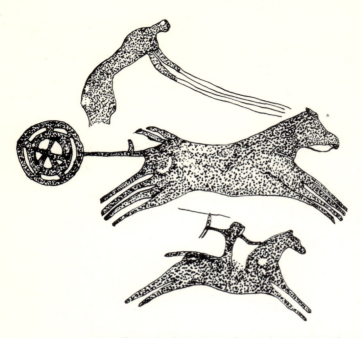

*Fig. 68   Light chariot drawn by two horses. Tin-Abou Teka, Tassili, Sahara.
(After H. Lhote, 1963)*

southern Sudan and northern Uganda into the high grasslands
of the Rift Valley in Kenya and northern Tanzania, are likely
also to be in some measure due to the more rapid desiccation of
the Sahara after two thousand five hundred BC and the probable
southward retreat of the tsetse-fly belt at this time.

By the end of the first millennium BC, if not earlier, Afro-
Mediterranean peoples, perhaps ancestral Nilotic groups, owning
sheep and cattle were in occupation of the East African Rift
Valley. There is no evidence yet that they did any cultivation,
though some planting of millet is not unlikely, and the thick
stone platters and bowls after which their cultures are named,
were probably used for cooking meat rather than grain.[41] Their

stone bowls and other traits, including burial customs, suggest links with the southern Sudan and the eastern Sahara but the associated obsidian industry of long blades and microliths, while it emphasizes the importance of hunting, shows a continuation with existing tradition. This suggests a basic, ethnic continuity, with which one would expect the long-headed element of the population to be associated, while the meso- to brachycephalic element that is now also present may be that associated with the newcomers.

Plates 43–45

Fig. 69

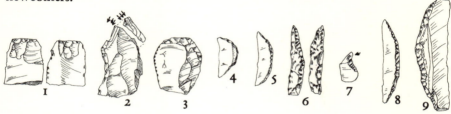

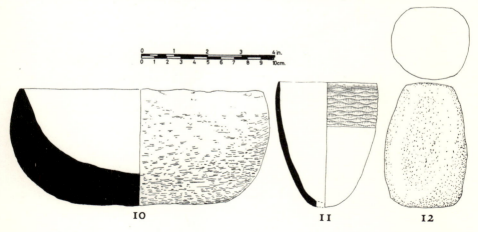

Fig. 69   Tools of the Stone Bowl Industry (Hyrax Hill Variant) from the Neolithic occupation site and cemetery, Hyrax Hill, Nakuru, Kenya (after M. D. Leakey, 1945): 1   scaled piece (outil écaillé); 2   dihedral burin; 3   shot end scraper; 4, 5   lunates; 6   borer; 7   micro- burin; 8, 9   backed blades (all obsidian); 10   stone bowl of lava; and on a larger scale: 11 ovoid beaker with decoration of festooned bands and impressions; 12   pestle-rubber

These peoples continued in occupation of the Kenya high-lands until the middle of the sixteenth century AD when they were replaced by Iron Age Negro peoples.[42] This early southward movement of pastoral, long-headed nomads drove a wedge into what at that time were the exclusively hunting and gathering populations of eastern Africa and can, it is believed, be associated with a southward movement of peoples speaking a Cushitic language.[43] This was not the 'Master Race' bringing civilization to Black Africa that the 'Hamitic myth' would have us believe, even if some later Cushitic immigrants into eastern Africa were able to establish themselves, though losing their language, as the ruling group over some Bantu-speaking peoples—a rule, inci-dentally, that is fast coming to an end. Although there are still groups of Cushitic-speakers as far south as central Tanganyika, the Cushitic element here was later fragmented and mostly replaced by Bantu-speaking Negroes. An even more southerly penetration at this time down the drier corridor separating western and eastern Africa, into the southwestern dry-lands of the Kalahari may have been responsible for introducing cattle and sheep, pottery and even stone bowls and other traits to groups of large Khoisan people living in South West Africa whose descendants we know today as the historic Hottentots.[44]

As we have seen, Khoisan-speakers were at one time much more widely spread over the southern and eastern parts of the continent than they are now. The Hadza and the Sandawe in northern and central Tanzania still speak 'click' languages but over most of the rest of east, central and southern Africa, except for the Kalahari and drier parts of South West Africa, they have been replaced by Bantu-speakers.

THE SPREAD OF BANTU

Fig. 71   The origins and spread of the Bantu is one of the most intriguing and challenging problems in African studies today and it is only through a correlation of many lines of evidence that the main

Fig. 70   Tall and steatopygous human figures with domestic sheep, in red and white pigment. Ruchera Cave, Mtoko, Rhodesia. (After Elizabeth Goodall, 1959)

theme of this will be made known. The dividing line between history and prehistory was never a very closely drawn one in Black Africa where the interests of scholars in both the human and natural sciences constantly overlap, and it is their combined researches that together will show the achievements and variety of Africa's past.

Linguistic data provide a measure for ethnic movement in prehistoric times as well as demonstrating the antiquity of the African languages and, when correlated with the contributions of other disciplines, the chronological, ethnic and cultural affiliations also become clearer. Recent linguistic work indicates that Bantu and Negro languages shared a common homeland in the eastern part of west Africa in the region of Chad and Cameroon[45] and, further, that there was a nuclear centre where 'Proto-Bantu' was spoken, in the southern part of the Congo basin.[46] From here the language spread in most directions at different times.[47] A western and an eastern dialect area, separated by the Rift Valley, are also well attested. It is now the responsibility of the ethnographer and the prehistorian to place these events in their correct perspective and to establish their significance for the culture history of the Bantu peoples. In rural central Africa today is preserved a living record of Iron Age society and technology

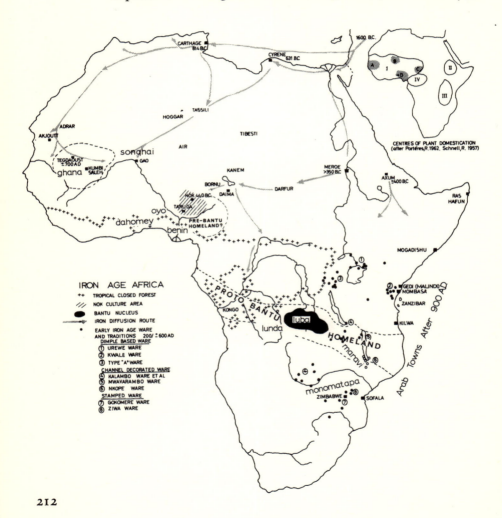

CENTRES OF PLANT DOMESTICATION
(after Portéres,R.1962, Schnell,R.1957)

IRON AGE AFRICA
++ TROPICAL CLOSED FOREST
/// NOK CULTURE AREA
BANTU NUCLEUS
IRON DIFFUSION ROUTE
• EARLY IRON AGE WARE
AND TRADITIONS 200/ ± 600 AD
DIMPLE BASED WARE
① UREWE WARE
② KWALE WARE
③ TYPE "A" WARE
CHANNEL DECORATED WARE
④ KALAMBO WARE ET AL
⑤ MWAVARAMBO WARE
⑥ NKOPE WARE
STAMPED WARE
⑦ GOKOMERE WARE
⑧ ZIWA WARE

Fig. 71 Iron Age Africa. Inset map: centres of plant domestication in sub-Saharan Africa (after R. Portères, 1962 and R. Schnell, 1957)

1. **West African centre**

A. *Senegambia region*
            Sorghum :   Sorghum gambicum
            Millet :   Pennisetum *(4 species)*
                          Digitaria exilis *(fonio)*
            Rice :   Oryza glaberrima *(secondary centre)*

B. *Central Niger region*
            Sorghum :   Sorghum *(5 species)*
            Millet :   Pennisetum cinereum
            Rice :   Oryza glaberrima

C. *Chad/Nile region*
            Millet :   Pennisetum *(3 species)*

D. *Sub-equatorial region*
    (Nigerian forest zone)   *Yams :*   Dioscorea cayenensis *and* D. dumetorum
            Oil Palm : Elaesis guineensis

2. **Nile/Ethiopian centre**

A. *Nile region*
            Sorghum :   Sorghum durra *and 3 other species*
            Millet :   Pennisetum *(4 species)*
            Oil plants : Sesamum *(3 species)*

B. *Abyssinian region*
            Teff :   Eragostris abyssinica
            Barley :   Hordeum distichum *(secondary centre)*
            African
            Banana :   Ensete edulis

3. **East African centre**
            Sorghum :   Sorghum *(5 species) (secondary centre)*
            Millet :   Pennisetum *(5 species)*
                          Eleusine corcorana *(secondary centre)*

4. **Central African centre**
            Ground bean : Voandzeia subterrannea
            Livingstone potato : Coleus *(2 species)*
            Oil palm : Elaeis guineensis

almost unique in its completeness. This is the basis from which reconstruction and interpretation of cultural relationships must begin.

Recent work to determine the degree of biological similarity between ethnic groups, so as to evaluate a general distance between them for a set of biological variables, has produced results in broad agreement with the linguistic data which indicates that a large part of the ancestral Bantu stock comes from the savanna lands north of the rain-forest. From here groups crossed the forest, rather than moving round its eastern borders, to a similar habitat in the southern Congo, from where there later began the widespread expansion into east and southern Africa.[48]

The rapidity of the movement from this nuclear centre finds ample support in the archaeological evidence though this is still very incomplete. At present, though it may seem a paradox, we chiefly lack evidence from the Congo basin itself. It may not be too far from the truth to suggest, however, that the ancestors of the 'Proto-Bantu' speakers, who were primarily cultivators of root crops, sorghums and millets, made their way into the western and northeastern parts of the Congo basin, perhaps in the second, but more likely in the first millennium BC when there is some evidence, as we have seen, for forest clearance. The stone equipment indicates a strong element derived from the later hunting/ gathering traditions of the Congo. Then, around the beginning of the present era, the introduction of metallurgy and, in particular, an iron technology, triggered-off rapid and widespread movements from the heartland south of the forests.

METALLURGY

The date at which a knowledge of iron-working reached sub-Saharan Africa has long been a matter for conjecture, equally with the source of this skill. Very recently the date has been moved down to the middle of the first millennium BC when iron was being smelted in northern Nigeria in the country between the Niger and the Benue by the Negro peoples whose culture is named from the site of Nok.[49] The Nok culture was fully iron-using and its main part seems to lie between five hundred BC and two hundred AD. There can, however, be no doubt that it began earlier and continued later, since the superb terracotta heads and figurines for which it is famous can now be shown to be ancestral to the Yoruba art that produced the famous Ife bronze heads.[50] North of Nok and approximately contemporary with this later stage is another culture area and, at Yelwa by the Niger dam, another large settlement site has been excavated dating from AD one hundred to four hundred and sixty and has produced figurines of a style different from those of Nok.[51]

It is apparent that the settlements were now large and they bear witness to lengthy occupation in the savannas and forests of west Africa. It can be expected that they will be found to group into a number of independent, though related, culture areas, each with its own artistic tradition. Possibly, by this time, we may speak of tribal entities but whether there were any tribal societies with centralized political government, we have no means of knowing. Perhaps, however, on the evidence of one date from the site at Ife where the heads of the kings of Benin were sent for burial, the Yoruba dynasty may have been established there by AD five hundred and sixty. Confirmation for the traditional foundation of the Benin dynasty about AD one thousand also comes from this site.[52]

Whether the knowledge of metallurgy spread to west Africa from the Nubian kingdom of Meroe or was transmitted across the Sahara by Berbers in touch with the classical Mediterranean world, it certainly proceded to revolutionize the way of life of the savanna and forest Negroes. In the now desert country of Borku, north of Lake Chad, iron makes its appearance in the first few centuries AD. The earliest iron artifacts from the occupation mound at Daima in the steppe country south of the lake are dated about the fifth and sixth centuries AD. However, in view of the evidence from Nok, it is not impossible that iron was already in use here several centuries earlier.[53] Iron-working makes its appearance in east and southern Africa at about the same time.

The earliest iron-smelting communities responsible for what is known as the Dimple Based, Channelled and Stamp-decorated pottery wares made their appearance at much the same time, between about AD one hundred and three hundred in Rwanda/ Burundi, Kenya, Tanzania, Zambia, Malawi and Rhodesia.[54] Although they have not yet been dated, those in the Katanga probably began about the same time.[55] They are thus spread around the periphery of the Congo basin as well as inside it and reach to the coast in the region of Mombasa. One fairly large village of this time is known from the Kalambo Falls and others in Rhodesia indicate smaller communities of several huts.[56] These people were fully in the Iron Age. The wide distribution of their characteristic pottery wares and the increasing number of dates now being obtained show that the spread must have been a particularly rapid one. It is most likely to have radiated out from the Bantu nuclear centre, though, until this region is better known archaeologically, there can be no certainty, and an unrelated movement associated especially with the spread of the sorghums, millets and cattle, down the line of the great lakes, also remains a possibility.

Iron technology introduced appreciably more efficient hunting and fighting equipment and tools for forest clearance. Added to this, the possession of plant and probably cereal crops, perhaps the introduction or adoption of the Asian food plants (yams, taro and bananas), and an ability for social and political organization appear to have been the reasons for the rapidity of the spread of Bantu.[57]

It has, of course, been argued that the language and culture were spread by large numbers of Negroid people moving into areas occupied by Khoisan- and Cushitic-speakers. The compounded evidence does not support this view. The large-scale

Fig. 72

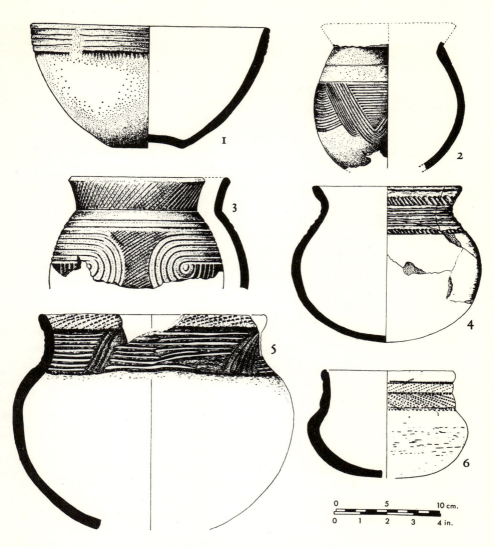

Fig. 72 Early Iron Age pottery from sub-Saharan Africa (after M. Posnansky, 1968; J. D. Clark and B. M. Fagan, 1965; K. R. Robinson, 1963): 1–3 dimple based ware from Lolui Island, Uganda; 4 pot with channel decoration, Machili, Zambia; 5, 6 stamped ware from Gokomere, Rhodesia

movements of the earlier part of the last century in southern Africa, or those of the sixteenth century in east Africa and the Congo were founded upon a specialized military organization for which there is as yet no evidence in the first millennium south of the Sahara. Rather do the cultural and skeletal remains and oral tradition suggest a gradual infiltration of small groups who settled in the areas most favourable for cultivation and who were welcomed for their superior abilities and techniques by the indigenous hunting or pastoral inhabitants.[58]

It was just such a situation as the coming of small groups or individual families that welded the Nyasa/Tanganyika corridor people into tribal units with chiefs after the sixteenth century.[59] Since the second World War the gradual infiltration of Mwiko (that is Lovale and Lochaze) peoples from northwestern Barotse-land to the southern plateau of Zambia, or of Hutu into western Uganda from the Congo, probably demonstrates very well the initial way in which the Bantu language and culture spread. Occupation of an empty or sparsely populated habitat, together with socially selective practices affecting the whole breeding population, can be expected to have resulted in a rapid increase in the numbers of the immigrant group. Also intermarriage and hybridization would lead to the breeding-out of the less desirable characteristics of the indigenous group and the breeding-in of the preferred ones which were those of the newcomers, as also the adoption of their Bantu language. The mixed Negro and Khoisan physical characteristics shown by the skeletal remains from sites in Zambia, Rhodesia and the northern Transvaal, show just such an hybridization. Indeed, this is the most likely explanation of why it is not possible to speak of a Bantu physical type. Bantu-speakers from east Africa exhibit as many differences among themselves, for example, as do those from central and southeastern Africa from one another. This must be due largely to their mixed genetic composition as well as to environmental adaptation.

The many kinds of ecological circumstances in which the Bantu language and Iron Age technology developed and the variable composition of the gene pool resulted in the proliferation of a large number of tribal units after AD one thousand. Not until the eleventh century in the subcontinent do we begin to see the onset of competition for land and this rivalry was probably one of the reasons for the growth of a number of centralized autocracies which maintained their individuality by conquest, trade and religious ties. Each had a cultural entity of its own but was capable of being grouped within larger units exhibiting a common broad pattern of culture.

Although the conception of culture areas is now rather out of fashion, nevertheless it is still very valid and, as has been said, it is essential for the understanding of the African way of life, that the analysis should focus on culture where language and physical type are such unpredictable variables.[60] In this way, the similarities and differences in culture can be seen in continental perspective, each of the main areas being capable of subdivision.

The powerful Luba and Lunda empires of the Katanga and Kasai, the Kingdom of Kongo[61] and the Empire of Mono-matapa[62] were major influences on the history of events in central Africa into historic times, partly because of their ability to canalize trade into their own hands, partly because of the organiza-tional ability of the ruling group. It is not possible to make more than a very brief mention of the important effects of the overland trade northwards in gold, ivory and other merchandise and southwards in salt, between north Africa and the kingdoms of west Africa, the first of which was that of ancient Ghana, established in the savanna and steppe country between the Niger and Senegal rivers before AD seven hundred.[63]

Was it the establishment by Berbers and Arabs of trading cities south of the desert and the opportunities for culture contact with literate peoples that gave rise to the city states and despotic principalities and empires of the savanna and forest zones, some time after AD five hundred⁵ Or do these owe little to north African culture? The effects of the Arab invasions of north Africa after the seventh and eighth centuries, as also the impact of Axumite civilization after the first century on Ethiopia are readily apparent; but how much, for example, did the west and central African communities owe to the diffusion, first of the Asian and later of the American food crops? Or how much did expansion of the Kanem-Bornu empire in the thirteenth century owe to contacts with the Nile and Tripoli? Or the early Luba copper- and iron-working centres of the eighth and ninth centuries in the Katanga owe to the copper trade with the Indian Ocean ports? To what extent also did the medieval Arab settlements on the Indian Ocean coast influence, through the gold and ivory trade, the character of the 'Monomatapa-Zim-babwe' confederacy on the Rhodesian plateau after the tenth century? Only further research will give us the answers but, at the present time, it would seem that, while these influences may have provided the impetus—perhaps the initial incentive—the characteristic form each of these cultures took is peculiarly its own and wholly African.

The 'Monomatapa-Zimbabwe' culture is a typical, if one of the more spectacular examples. High on a precipitous kopje in Mashonaland, first settled in AD three hundred by peoples making Stamp-decorated pottery, were built after eleven hundred the massive dry-stone walls that housed the ruler and many of the sacred objects and regalia of the confederacy of peoples governed by the Monomatapa. He was an autocratic monarch who, through his provincial governors, controlled a large part of Mashonaland from the Zambezi to the Limpopo as well as the gold mines of Butua to the west. The 'Lord of the Mines' traded his gold and the ivory that was not used locally with the Arabs, Indians and (later) the Portuguese at the city ports of Sofala and Kilwa and, in exchange, received not only trade goods—cloth

Plate 48

and glass beads, for example—but knowledge of the ways of the Oriental and Arab worlds.[64]

Perhaps it was acquaintance with the stone-built mosques and palaces of the medieval Arab cities that suggested the monumental architecture of Zimbabwe—the elliptical building with its huge, free-standing wall or the parallel passage and conical tower. This may well have been so, as there is no history of stone building in this part of Africa, but in interpretation and construction and the uses to which they were put, these buildings are essentially African. The elliptical building, for example, is a royal palace, closely resembling in ground plan that of the Paramount Chief of Barotseland today.[65] The walls and terraces of Zimbabwe and of some three hundred other stone ruins of this kind bear silent witness to the administrative and creative ability of the Mashona peoples whose *Mambo* continued to rule the watershed country between the rivers until the Roswi confederacy was destroyed in 1822 by the regiments of Zwengendaba and his Shangaans erupted from Natal.

The history of this state typifies the general pattern of that of other Bantu-speaking kingdoms in central Africa. Initially, it was a strong and vigorous central authority, no doubt established and held together by the personalities of its rulers who maintained control of rich economic resources distributed by networks of local and long-distance trade routes. The ultimate destruction and disappearance of the state followed weakening of the central power through a series of ineffectual rulers and the facility with which the provincial tribal authorities were then able to make themselves autonomous in a tropical environment where no proper communications system existed. Sometimes a satellite state, the outcome of this 'hiving-off process', was the cause of the eclipse of the parent authority. Sometimes, as with the Roswi state, it was foreign military superiority. In the nineteenth century it was a new element—the slave trade and the scramble for ivory—that disrupted the pattern of traditional authority in the interior and so prepared the way for colonial rule.

THE SIGNIFICANCE OF PREHISTORY IN AFRICA

Since the focus of African history has now shifted from that of the colonizing power to the African peoples themselves, it is also time for a more objective approach to the *pre*history of the continent, unencumbered by preconceptions inherited from an early emphasis on the cultural sequence of western Europe. Because the success with which cultural changes were made only becomes apparent when the material remains are studied in relation to the ecological and biological factors peculiar to the region from which they derive, a critical re-examination of this archaeological material in its natural and chronological setting can be expected to provide an appreciably better understanding of the causes and effects of the many differences that this material exhibits. Although still very far from comprehensive, the picture that is emerging is very different from the previously painted one of isolation and stagnation interspersed with spasmodic stimulation from foreign migrants. While the peoples of Africa have not been slow to take advantage of the opportunities for cultural exchange with non-African peoples, this exchange operated not merely in one direction but in both and the world in general, as well as Africa, is thereby the richer.

Ideas, inventions, techniques and material things diffused and were adapted to local needs, so becoming part of the traditional pattern, thereby often losing much of their original significance but acquiring a new one. In the other direction, the original home of man now looks to have been somewhere in Africa's tropical savanna lands and the contribution of this continent to the world of art, to take but one other example, needs no elaboration.

Even though there are, from time to time, some who think they can get along without it, a feeling for history lies deep in us all. This is hardly surprising since every society has its behaviour determined by the traditions that have grown out of the circumstances of its past. There is no part of the world where this is appreciated more than in Africa. It is precisely here that prehistory is making one of its most significant contributions, since it alone can provide the time-depth and knowledge of all except the more recent past from which present-day culture derives. New patterns are developing, new goals are being set and new leaders are rising up to effect the changes, but every year the increasing awareness of the importance of the past becomes more apparent in the greater emphasis that is being placed upon the traditional inheritance and the traditional way of life. Continuity through the African past is the clue to the changes taking place in the new Africa today.

Notes on the Text

CHAPTER I

1   Wheeler, Sir Mortimer. 1955. *Archaeology from the earth.* Oxford. pp. 2–3.

2   Martin, P. D. 1872. Stone implements and shell caves. *Cape Monthly Magazine* (N.S.) V. 25. July, 1872. pp. 53–5.

3   Sampson, H. F. 1948. Phoenician shipwreck on the Cape Flats. *South African Archaeological Bulletin,* III, 10. June, 1948. pp. 34–40.

4   Clark, J. D. 1959. *The prehistory of southern Africa.* Harmondsworth, London, p. 290.

5   Summers, R. 1963. *Zimbabwe: A Rhodesian mystery.* Cape Town, p. 19.

6   Cooke, H. B. S. 1967. The Pleistocene sequence in South Africa and problems of correlation. *In :* Bishop, W. W. and J. D. Clark, *eds. Background to Evolution in Africa.* Chicago. pp. 175–84.

7   Leakey, M. D. 1967. Preliminary survey of the cultural material from Beds I and II, Olduvai Gorge, Tanzania. *In :* Bishop, W. W. and J. D. Clark, *eds. Background to Evolution in Africa.* Chicago. pp. 417–46, see especially pp. 439 and 442–6.

8   Oakley, K. P. and B. G. Campbell, *eds.* 1967. *Catalogue of fossil hominids, Part I, Africa.* London. pp. 25, 66, 122.

9   Brown, F. H. In the press. Observations on the stratigraphy and radiometric age of the Omo Beds, southern Ethiopia. *Congrès Pan-Africain de Préhistoire et de l'Etude du Quaternaire, VIe Session, Dakar, 1967.*

10   Evernden, J. F. and G. H. Curtis. 1965. Potassium-argon dating of Late Cenozoic rocks in East Africa and Italy. *Current Anthropology,* 6, pp. 343–85.

11   Funnell, B. M. 1964. The Tertiary period. *Quarterly Journal of the Geological Society of London,* 120 S, pp. 179–91.

12   Bakker, E. M. van Zinderen. 1967. Upper Pleistocene and Holocene stratigraphy and ecology on the basis of vegetation changes in sub-Saharan Africa. *In :* Bishop, W. W. and J. D. Clark, *eds. Background to Evolution in Africa,* Chicago. pp. 125–47.

13   Leakey, L. S. B. 1965. *Olduvai Gorge, 1951–61.* Cambridge. pp. 73–85.

14   Leakey, L. S. B. 1959. Appendix *in* Clark, J. D. Further Excavations at Broken Hill, Northern Rhodesia. *Journal of the Royal Anthropological Institute,* 89(2), pp. 225–30.

15   Hay, R. L. 1967. Revised stratigraphy of Olduvai Gorge. *In:* Bishop, W. W. and J. D. Clark, *eds. Background to Evolution in Africa.* Chicago. pp. 221–5.

16   Brain, C. K. 1958. The Transvaal ape-man-bearing cave deposits. *Transvaal Museum Memoir No. 11.* pp. 1–131.

17   Brain, C. K. 1967. Procedures and some results in the study of Quaternary cave fillings. *In:* Bishop, W. W. and J. D. Clark, *eds. Background to Evolution in Africa.* Chicago. pp. 285–301.

18   Bond, G. 1957. The geology of the Khami Stone Age sites, Southern Rhodesia. *Occasional Papers of the National Museums of Southern Rhodesia,* No. 3. pp. 44–55.

19   Bishop, W. W. and J. D. Clark. 1967. *Background to Evolution in Africa.* Chicago. Discussions on terminology, pp. 861–901.

20   McBurney, C. B. M. 1967. *The Haua Fteah (Cyrenaica).* Cambridge.

21   Brain, C. K. 1967. a. Bone weathering and the problem of bone pseudo-tools. *South African Journal of Science,* 63, 3. pp. 97–9. b. Hottentot food remains and their bearing on the interpretation of fossil bone assemblages. *Scientific Papers of the Namib Desert Research Station, Pretoria, South Africa,* No. 32, VI, pp. 1–7.

CHAPTER II

1   Simons, E. L. 1965. New fossil apes from Egypt and the initial differentiation of the Hominoidea. *Nature,* 205, 135–9.

2   Simons, E. L. 1963. Some fallacies in the study of Hominid Phylogeny. *Science,* 141 (3584) 879–89.

3   Washburn, S. L. 1968. *The study of human evolution.* Condon Lectures, Eugene, Oregon. p. 48

4   a. Chesters, K. I. M. 1957. The Miocene flora of Rusinga Island, Lake Victoria, Kenya. *Paläontographica, Stuttgart,* 101 B, 30–71. b. Bishop, W. W. 1968. The evolution of fossil environments in East

Africa. *Trans. Leicester Literary and Philosophical Society,* Vol. LXII, pp. 22–44.

5   a. Simons, E. L. 1961. The phyletic position of *Ramapithecus. Postilla,* New Haven, Connecticut, 57, 1–9.   b. Simons, E. L. 1969. Late Miocene hominid from Fort Ternan, Kenya. *Nature,* 221. 448–51. c. Tattersall, I. 1969. Ecology of north Indian *Ramapithecus. Nature,* 221, pp. 451–2.

6   *Op. cit.* (3). pp. 14–15.

7   Leakey, L. S. B. 1967. An early Miocene member of the Hominidae. *Nature,* 213 (5072) 155–63.

8   Washburn, S. L. 1967. Behaviour and the origin of man. Huxley Memorial Lecture, 1967. *Proc. of the Royal Anthropological Institute,* 21–7.

9   a. Klinger, H. P., J. L. Hamerton, D. Mutton and E. M. Lang. 1963. The chromosomes of the Hominoidea. *In :* Washburn, S. L. *ed. Classification and human evolution.* Wenner-Gren Foundation, Viking Fund Publications in Anthropology, No. 37, pp. 235–42.   b. Goodman, M. 1963. Man's place in the phylogeny of the primates as reflected in serum proteins. *In :* Washburn, S. L. *op. cit.* (9a) pp. 204–34.

10   a. Sarich, V. M. 1968. The origin of the Hominids: an immunological approach. *In :* Washburn, S. L. and P. C. Jay, *eds. Perspectives on human evolution, I.* New York, pp. 94–121.   b. Wilson, A. C. and V. M. Sarich, 1969. A molecular time scale for human evolution. *Proceedings of the National Academy of Sciences* (USA) Vol. 63, No. 4, pp. 1088–93.

The recently carried out quantitative comparisons of serum albumins, transferrins, haemoglobins and DNA show that man is genetically much closer to the African apes than are the apes to Old World monkeys. The close agreement between the haemoglobin and albumin results and the indications that molecular evolution rates are the same in all mammalian lineages that have been compared, make it possible that those of man and the African apes separated as recently as four to five million years ago.

11   *Op. cit.* (8) p. 23.

12   Leakey, L. S. B. 1961. A new Lower Pliocene fossil primate from Kenya. *American Magazine of Natural History,* Ser. 13. iv: 689–96.

13   Leakey, L. S. B. 1968. Bone smashing by Late Miocene Hominidae. *Nature,* 218, no. 5141, pp. 528–30.

14   *Op. cit.* (10).

15   L. S. B. Leakey—personal communication.

16   Tobias, P. V. and G. H. R. von Koenigswald, 1964. A comparison between the Olduvai hominines and those of Java and some implications for hominid phylogeny. *Nature,* 204, pp. 515–8.

17   Clark, Sir W. E. LeGros, 1967. *Man-apes or ape-men ?* New York. The literature on the Australopithecines and Lower Pleistocene Hominids is voluminous but this book provides the best overall summary of the evidence and the status of these fossils.

18   Brain, C. K. 1958. The Transvaal ape-man-bearing cave deposits. *Transvaal Museum Memoir No. 11,* pp. 1–131.

19   Ewer, R. F. 1967. The fossil Hyaenids of Africa: A reappraisal. *In :* Bishop, W. W. and J. D. Clark, *eds. Background to Evolution in Africa.* Chicago. pp. 109–22.

20   Cooke, H. B. S. 1963. Pleistocene mammal faunas of Africa, with particular reference to southern Africa. *In :* Howell, F. C. and F. Bourlière, *eds. African ecology and human evolution.* Wenner-Gren Foundation, Viking Fund Publications in Anthropology No. 36. pp. 65–116.

21   *Op. cit.* (18).

22   Tobias, P. V. 1967. *The cranium and maxillary dentition of Australopithecus (Zinjanthropus) boisei.* Cambridge.

23   Isaac, G. Ll. 1967. The stratigraphy of the Peninj Group—early Middle Pleistocene formations west of Lake Natron, Tanzania. *In :* Bishop, W. W. and J. D. Clark, *eds. Background to Evolution in Africa.* Chicago. pp. 229–57.

24   Leakey, L. S. B. 1960. Recent discoveries at Olduvai Gorge. *Nature,* 188, 1050–52.

25   Day, M. H. and J. R. Napier. 1964. Hominid fossils from Bed I, Olduvai Gorge, Tanzania: fossil foot bones. *Nature,* 201, 969.

26   Napier, J. R. 1962. Fossil hand bones from Olduvai Gorge. *Nature,* 196, 409–11.

27   Leakey, L. S. B., P. V. Tobias and J. R. Napier. 1964. A new species of the genus *Homo* from Olduvai Gorge. *Nature,* 202, 7–9.

28   Davis, P. R. *et al.* 1964. Hominid fossils from Bed I, Olduvai Gorge, Tanganyika: A tibia and fibula. *Nature,* 201, p. 967.

29   *Op. cit.* (17). pp. 103–6.

30   *Op. cit.* (27). pp. 8–9.

31 Coppens, Y. 1967. L'hominien du Tchad. *Actas del V congreso panafricano de prehistoria y de estudio del Cuaternario.* Tenerife (1963). pp. 329–30.

32 Robinson, J. T. 1953. Telanthropus and its phylogenetic significance. *American Journal of Physical Anthropology,* 11, pp. 445–501.

33 Howell, F. C. 1969. Remains of Hominidae from Pliocene/Pleistocene formations in the lower Omo basin, Ethiopia. *Nature,* 223, 1234–9.

34 H. B. S. Cooke—personal communication.

35 *Op. cit.* (10a) p. 119.

36 *Op. cit.* (18) pp. 119–22.

37 a. Hay, R. L. 1967. Revised stratigraphy of Olduvai Gorge. *In: Op. cit.* at note (15) of Chapter I, p. 221. b. Coppens, Y. and J.-C. Koeniguer. 1967. Sur les flores ligneuses disparues Plio-Quaternaires du Tchad et du Niger. *C.R. Acad. Sc. Paris,* vol. 265, pp. 1282–5.

38 a. van Lawick-Goodall, J. 1968. A preliminary report on expressive movements and communication in the Gombe Stream chimpanzees. *In:* Jay, P. C., *ed. Primates.* New York, pp. 313–74. b. Goodall, J. 1964. Tool-using and aimed throwing in a community of free-living chimpanzees. *Nature,* 201. pp. 1264–6.

39 Kortlandt, A. 1968. Handgebrauch bei freilebenden Schimpansen. *In:* Rensch, B. *Handgebrauch und Verständigung bei Affen und Frühmenschen.* Stuttgart. pp. 59–102.

40 Reynolds, V. and F. 1965. Chimpanzees of the Budongo Forest. *In:* DeVore, I. *ed. Primate Behaviour.* New York. pp. 368–424.

41 Dart, R. A. 1957. The Makapansgat Australopithecine Osteodontokeratic Culture. *In:* Clark, J. D. and S. Cole, *eds. Proceedings of the 3rd Pan-African Congress on Prehistory, 1955, Livingstone.* London. pp. 161–71.

42 See Brain, C. K. 1967. *Op. cit.* (21a and b) Chapter I.

43 Ardrey, R. 1961. *African Genesis.* London and New York. pp. 293–306.

44 *Op. cit.* at note (7) of Chapter I, Leakey, M. D. 1967.

45 a. Woodburn, J. 1968. An introduction to Hadza ecology. *In:* Lee, R. B. and I. DeVore, *eds. Man the hunter.* Chicago. p. 51. b. Lee, R. B. 1968. What hunters do for a living or How to make out on scarce resources. *Op cit.* (a) above, p. 40.

46 a. Leakey, L. S. B. 1963. Very early East African Hominidae and their ecological setting. *In :* Howell, F. C. and F. Bourlière, *eds. African ecology and human evolution.* Wenner-Gren Foundation, Viking Fund Publications in Anthropology, No. 36. pp. 451–2. b. Leakey, M. D. 1967, p. 428 of *Op. cit.* at note (7) of Chapter I.

47 Mann, A. E. *The palaeodemography of* Australopithecus. Doctoral dissertation, Department of Anthropology, University of California, Berkeley. p. 64.

48 Leakey, M. D. 1967, p. 426 of *Op. cit.* at note (7) of Chapter I.

49 *Op. cit.* at note (47) above, p. 69.

50 *Op. cit.* (8).

CHAPTER III

1 McCall, G. J. H., B. H. Baker and J. Walsh. 1967. Late Tertiary and Quaternary sediments of the Kenya Rift Valley. *In :* Bishop, W. W. and J. D. Clark, *eds. Background to Evolution in Africa.* Chicago. pp. 191–220.

2 a. Hay, R. L. 1967. Hominid-bearing deposits of Olduvai Gorge. National Academy of Sciences, Washington, Publication no. 1469, *Time and stratigraphy in the evolution of man,* pp. 30–42. b. Leakey, M. D. 1967. *Op. cit.* at note (7) of Chapter I, pp. 417, 418 and 432.

3 Tobias, P. V. and G. H. R. von Koenigswald. 1964. *Op. cit.* at note (16) of Chapter II.

4 Leakey, L. S. B. 1961. New finds at Olduvai Gorge. *Nature,* 189, 649–50.

5 Isaac, G. Ll. 1967. *Op. cit.* at note (23) of Chapter II, pp. 245–50.

6 *Op. cit.* at (5) above, p. 244.

7 Clark, J. D. 1969. *Kalambo Falls prehistoric site,* Vol. I. Cambridge, Appendix J, p. 236.

8 a. Biberson, P. 1961. *Le cadre paléogéographique de la préhistoire du Maroc atlantique.* Pub. Serv. Ant. Maroc, Mem. 16. b. Biberson, P. 1961. *Le Paléolithique inférieur du Maroc atlantique.* Pub. Serv. Ant. Maroc, Mem. 17.

9 a. Campbell, B. G. 1966. *Human evolution : An introduction to man's adaptations.* Chicago. pp. 343–8. b. Clark, W. E. LeGros. 1964. *The fossil evidence for human evolution.* Chicago. pp. 95–114.

10 Leakey, M. D. 1967. *Op. cit.* at note (7) of Chapter I. pp. 431–40.

11 Isaac, G. Ll. 1969. Studies of early culture in East Africa. *World Archaeology*, I, 1, pp. 1–28.

12 Leakey, M. D. 1967. *Op. cit.* at note (7) of Chapter I. pp. 441–2.

13 Biberson, P. 1961. *Op. cit.* at note (8b) above, pp. 156–85.

14 Balout, L., P. Biberson and J. Tixier, 1967. L'Acheuléen de Ternifine (Algérie), gisement de l'Atlanthrope. *L'Anthropologie, Paris.* 71, 3–4, pp. 217–38.

15 Isaac, G. Ll. 1967. *Op. cit.* at note (23) of Chapter II, pp. 250–1.

16 Hay, R. L. 1967. *Op. cit.* at (2a) above, p. 37.

17 Isaac, G. Ll. 1969. *Op. cit.* at (11) above.

18 Robinson, J. T. and R. J. Mason, 1962. Australopithecines and artifacts at Sterkfontein. *South African Archaeological Bulletin,* 17. pp. 87–125.

During the course of a recent excavation programme over two thousand artifacts (nearly a hundred of which have breccia adhering) were recovered from the dumps in the immediate vicinity of the Extension and Type Sites. This indicates that many more may be expected to be found when excavation recommences in the 'middle breccia'. In the Type Site excavation, the believed identification of the place where the skull Sterkfontein V ('Mrs Ples') was found suggests that this may also belong in the 'middle breccia'. (Tobias, P. V. and A. R. Hughes, 1969 (February), 'The new Witwatersrand University excavation at Sterkfontein. Progress report, some problems and first results'. Paper presented at the Conference on the Quaternary in Southern Africa).

19 Tobias, P. V. 1965. *Australopithecus, Homo habilis,* tool-using and tool-making. *South African Archaeological Bulletin,* XX, 80, iv. pp. 167–92, especially p. 187.

20 a. Brain, C. K. 1958. *Op. cit.* at note (16) of Chapter I. p. 88. b. Robinson, J. T. 1961. The Australopithecines and their bearing on the origins of man and of stone tool-making. *South African Journal of Science,* 57, 1. pp. 3–13. c. Brain, C. K. 1967. The Transvaal Museum's fossil project at Swartkrans. *South African Journal of Science,* 63, 9. pp. 378–84.

21 Mason, R. J. 1962. *Prehistory of the Transvaal.* Johannesburg. pp. 119–43.

22 Leakey, M. D. 1967. *Op. cit.* at note (7) of Chapter I. p. 440.

23 Leakey, L. S. B. 1958. Recent discoveries at Olduvai Gorge,

Tanganyika. *Nature,* 181. 1099–1103, Fig. 4.

24 Robinson, J. T. 1959. A bone implement from Sterkfontein. *Nature,* 184. pp. 583–5.

25 Leakey, L. S. B. 1958. *Op. cit.* at (23) above. p. 1099.

26 Isaac, G. Ll. 1969. *Op. cit.* at (11) above.

27 a. Isaac, G. Ll. 1968. Traces of Pleistocene hunters: An east African example. *In:* Lee, R. B. and I. DeVore, *eds. Man the hunter.* Chicago. pp. 253–61, especially pp. 255–8. b. Isaac, G. Ll. 1967. *Towards the interpretation of occupation debris—some experiments and observations.* Kroeber Anthropological Society Papers, 37. Berkeley. pp. 31–9.

28 Howell, F. C. and J. D. Clark. 1963. Acheulian hunter-gatherers of sub-Saharan Africa. pp. 458–546 *In:* Howell, F. C. and F. Bourlière, *eds. Op. cit.* at note (46)(a) of Chapter II. See especially p. 520.

29 Clark, J. D. 1967. The Middle Acheulian occupation site at Latamne, northern Syria. *Quaternaria,* 9. Rome. pp. 1–68.

30 Lumley, H. de. 1969. A Palaeolithic camp at Nice. *Scientific American,* 220, 5. pp. 42–50.

31 Howell, F. C., G. H. Cole and M. R. Kleindienst. 1962. Isimila, an Acheulian occupation site in the Iringa Highlands, Southern Highlands Province, Tanganyika. *In:* G. Mortelmans and J. Nenquin, *eds. Actes du IVe congrès panafricain de préhistoire et de l'étude du Quaternaire,* Section III, pp. 43–105. Musée royal de l'Afrique centrale, Tervuren, Série in-8 , Sciences humaines, no. 40. See especially p. 67.

32 Isaac, G. Ll. 1968. *Op. cit.* at (27a) above, p. 259.

33 Howell, F. C. 1966. Observations on the earlier phases of the European Lower Palaeolithic. *In:* Special Number of the *American Anthropologist,* edited by Clark, J. D. and F. C. Howell, 68, 2. pp. 88–201. See especially pp. 121–31.

34 Chavaillon, J. 1967. La préhistoire Ethiopienne à Melka Kontouré. *Archeologia,* 19. pp. 57–63.

35 Kleindienst, M. R. In the press. Report on excavations at Site JK2, Olduvai Gorge, Tanzania, 1961–2. *In: Compte rendu du VIe congrès panafricain de préhistoire et de l'étude du Quaternaire, Dakar, 1967.*

36 Clark, J. D. 1959. Further Excavations at Broken Hill, Northern Rhodesia. *Journal of the Royal Anthropological Institute,* 89 (2). pp. 201–24.

37 Clark, J. D. 1968. Further Palaeo-anthropological studies in northern Lunda. *Lisbon, Museu do Dundo, Publicações culturais,* no. 78.

pp. 19–51.

38 Söhnge, P. G., D. J. L. Visser and C. van Riet Lowe. 1937. The geology and archaeology of the Vaal river basin. p. 70. *Geological Survey Mem. no. 35,* Pretoria.

39 Mason, R. J. 1962. *Op. cit.* at (21) above. pp. 169–81.

40 Brain C. K. and R. J. Mason. 1955. A later African Chelles-Acheul site near Nakop, southern Kalahari. *South African Archaeological Bulletin,* 10 (37) 22–5.

41 Biberson, P. 1965. Recherches sur le Paléolithique inférieur de l'Adrar de Mauretanie. *In :* Cuscoy, L. D. *ed. Actas del V congreso panafricano de prehistoria y de estudio del Cuaternario. Tenerife, Museo arqueológico.* Vol. I. pp. 173–89. See especially p. 184.

42 Isaac, G. Ll. 1968. *Op. cit.* at (27a) above, p. 259.

43 Woodburn, J., 1968. *Op. cit.* at note (45a) of Chapter II. p. 51; and personal communication.

44 *Op. cit.* at (38) above, pp. 34, 69. The site at Pniel Estates, opposite Barkley West, was subsequently named after A. J. Power, the large collections being housed in the McGregor Museum, Kimberley, of which he was Director.

45 *Op. cit.* at note (7) above, pp. 104–9 and 172–4.

46 Clark, J. D. and C. V. Haynes. 1970. An elephant butchery site at Mwanganda's village, Karonga, Malawi, and its relevance for Palaeolithic archaeology. *World Archaeology,* I, 3, pp. 390–411.

47 Bond, G. 1948. Rhodesian Stone Age man and his raw materials. *South African Archaeological Bulletin,* III, 11, pp. 55–60, see especially p. 56.

48 Oakley, K. P. 1955. Fire as Palaeolithic tool and weapon. *Proceedings of the Prehistoric Society,* Vol. XXI, pp. 36–48.

49 Baker, Sir Samuel W. 1890. *Wild beasts and their ways : Reminiscences of Europe, Asia, Africa and America.* London. Vol. I. pp. 100–1.

50 Leakey, L. S. B. 1958. *Op. cit.* at (23) above. pp. 1099–1100.

51 Campbell, B. G. 1966. *Op. cit.* at (9a) above, p. 311.

CHAPTER IV

1 Bakker, E. M. van Zinderen. 1967. *Op. cit.* at note (12) of Chapter I.

2 a. Coetzee, J. A. 1967. Pollen analytical studies in east and southern

Africa. *In:* Bakker, E. M. van Zinderen, *ed. Palaeoecology of Africa, Volume III.* Balkema, Cape Town. b. Lawton, R. M. 1963. Plaeoecological and ecological studies in the Northern Province of Northern Rhodesia. *Kirkia,* Rhodesia, 3. pp. 46–77.

3 Bakker, E. M. van Zinderen. 1963. Analysis of pollen samples from northeast Angola. *In:* Clark, J. D. *Prehistoric cultures of northeast Angola and their significance in tropical Africa.* Lisbon, Museu do Dundo, Publicações culturais, no. 62. Appendix pp. 213–7.

4 Clark, J. D. 1967. Compiler. *The Atlas of African prehistory.* Chicago. Map 5 and Overlays 12 and 13.

5 Goodwin, A. J. H. and C. van Riet Lowe. 1929. The Stone Age cultures of South Africa. *Annals of the South African Museum,* 27. pp. 71–94. As yet, no precise definition exists of a Fauresmith aggregate from a sealed site in the type area.

6 Mason, R. J. 1962. *Op. cit.* at note (21) of Chapter III. pp. 159–69 and 181–4.

7 Keller, C. M. In the press. Montagu Cave. *In: Op. cit.* at note (9) of Chapter I.

8 Clark, J. D. 1964. The Sangoan culture of Equatoria: The implications of its stone equipment. *In:* Ripoll Perelló, E., *ed. Miscelanea en Homenaje al Abate Henri Breuil.* Barcelona. Vol. I. pp. 309–23.

9 a. Guichard, J. and G. 1968. Contributions to the study of the early and middle Paleolithic of Nubia. *In:* Wendorf, F., *ed. The Prehistory of Nubia.* Volume I. Fort Burgwin Research Center and Southern Methodist University Press. pp. 148–93, but especially pp. 183–93. b. Marks, A. E. 1968. The Mousterian industries of Nubia. *In: Op cit.* at (a) above, pp. 194–314.

10 McBurney, C. B. M. 1967. *Op. cit.* at note (20) of Chapter I. pp. 105–34.

11 a. Gobert, E. G. 1962. La Préhistoire dans la zone littorale de la Tunisie. *Quaternaria,* 6. Rome. pp. 271–307. b. Balout, L. 1965. Le Moustérien du Maghreb. *Quaternaria,* 7. Rome, pp. 43–58.

12 Gruet, M. 1954. Le gisement moustérien d'El Guettar. *Karthago,* V. pp. 1–79.

13 a. Ennouchi, E. 1963. Un gisement de Néanderthaliens Nord-Africains. *Actes du 88e congrès national des sociétés savantes.* Clermont-Ferand. pp. 49–62. b. Balout, L. 1965. Données nouvelles sur le

problème du moustérien en Afrique du nord. *In : Op. cit.* at note (41) of Chapter III. pp. 137–46.

14　Pycraft, W. P. *et al.* 1928. *Rhodesian man and associated remains.* British Museum (Nat. Hist.) London.

15　Vallois, H. V. 1951. La mandibule humaine fossile de la grotte du Porc-épic, près Diré-Daoua (Abyssinie). *Anthropologie,* Paris, 55. pp. 231–38.

16　Weinert, H. 1939. *Africanthropus njarasensis :* Beschreibung und phyletische Einordung des ersten Affenmenschen aus Ostafrika. *Z. Morph. Anthrop.* 38, pp. 252–307.

17　Leakey, L. S. B. and M. D. 1964. Recent discoveries of fossil hominids in Tanganyika: at Olduvai and near Lake Natron. *Nature,* 202, 4927, pp. 3–9, see p. 5.

18　Singer, R. 1954. The Saldanha skull from Hopefield, South Africa. *American Journal of Physical Anthropology,* 12, pp. 345–62. Elandsfontein is the name of the farm on which the site and fossils occur. Hopefield is the name of the nearest town and Saldanha that of the coastal bay some fifteen miles to the northwest.

19　Clark, J. D. *et al.* 1947. New studies on Rhodesian man. *Journal of the Royal Anthropological Institute,* 77, pp. 7–32. The industry was known previously as 'Proto-Stillbay'.

20　Clark, J. D. *et al.* 1968. Rhodesian man: Notes on a new femur fragment. *Man* (new series) 3 (1) pp. 105–11.

21　a. Cooke, H. B. S. 1963. *Op. cit.* at note (20) Chapter II, pp. 98–101.　b. Singer, R. and J. R. Crawford. 1958. The significance of the archaeological discoveries at Hopefield, South Africa. *Journal of the Royal Anthropological Institute,* 88 (1). pp. 11–19.　c. Singer, R. and J. Wymer. 1968. Archaeological investigations at the Saldanha skull site in South Africa. *South African Archaeological Bulletin,* 23 (III), pp. 63–74.

22　a. Leakey, L. S. B. 1935. *The Stone Age Races of Kenya,* London, pp. 27–9.　b. Tobias, P. V. 1962. Early members of the genus *Homo* in Africa. In Gotfried Kurth. *Evolution and Hominisation.* Stuttgart, pp. 191–204.

23　Leakey, R. E. F., K. W. Butzer and M. H. Day. 1969. Early *Homo sapiens* remains from the Omo river region of southwest Ethiopia. *Nature,* 222: 1137–1143.

24 Brothwell, D. R. 1963. Evidence of early population change in central and southern Africa: Doubts and problems. *Man,* LXIII, no. 132. pp. 101–4.

25 Arkell, A. J., D. M. A. Bate, L. H. Wells and A. D. Lacaille. 1951. The Pleistocene fauna of two Blue Nile sites. *In : Fossil mammals of Africa,* No. 2. British Museum (Nat. Hist.), London.

26 a. Keller, C. M. *Archaeological investigation of Montagu Cave, Republic of South Africa.* Doctoral dissertation, Department of Anthropology, University of California, Berkeley, 1967. b. Mason, R. J. 1962. *Op. cit.* at note (21) of Chapter III, pp. 232–89. c. Miller, S. F. *The Nachikufan industries of the Later Stone Age in Zambia.* Doctoral dissertation, Department of Anthropology, University of California, Berkeley, 1969.

27 a. Balout, L. 1955. *Préhistoire de l'Afrique du Nord.* Arts et Métiers graphiques, Paris. pp. 269–334. b. Caton Thompson, G. 1946. The Aterian industry: Its place and significance in the Palaeolithic world. *Journal of the Royal Anthropological Institute,* 76(ii), pp. 87–130. c. Tixier, J. 1967. Procédés d'analyse et questions de terminologie concernant l'étude des ensembles industriels du Paléolithique récent et de l'Epipaléolithique dans l'Afrique du nord-est. *In : Op. cit.* at note (6) to Chapter I, pp. 771–820. See especially pp. 786–97.

28 Caton Thompson, G. 1952. *Kharga Oasis in prehistory.* London. pp. 81–90 and 116–23.

29 Arkell, A. J. 1962. The Aterian of Great Wanyanga (Ounianga Kebir). *In : Op. cit.* at note (31) of Chapter III, pp. 233–42.

30 a. Marks, A. E. 1968. The Khormusan: An Upper Pleistocene industry in Sudanese Nubia. *In : Op. cit.* at note (9a) above, pp. 315–91. b. Marks, A. E. 1968. The Halfan industry. *In : Op. cit.* at (a) above, pp. 392–460.

31 McBurney, C. B. M. 1967. *Op. cit.* at note (20) of Chapter I. pp. 135–228.

32 Clark, J. D. 1954. *The prehistoric cultures of the Horn of Africa.* Cambridge. pp. 160–225.

33 Anthony, B. In the press. The Stillbay Culture. *In : Op. cit.* at note (9) of Chapter I.—with further reference to the aggregates from Prospect Farm, Kenya.

34 Cooke, C. K. 1963. Report on excavations at Pomongwe and Tshangula Caves, Matopo Hills, Southern Rhodesia. *South African*

Archaeological Bulletin, 18 (71). pp. 73–151.

35 a. *Op. cit.* at (26b) above. b. Mason, R. J. 1967. Analytical procedures in the earlier and middle stone age cultures in southern Africa. *In:* *Op. cit.* at note (6) of Chapter I. pp. 737–64. c. Sampson, C. G. 1968. *The Middle Stone Age Industries of the Orange River Scheme Area.* National Museum, Bloemfontein, Memoir No. 4. Bloemfontein.

36 a. Jolly, K. 1948. The development of the Cape Middle Stone Age in the Skildergat Cave, Fish Hoek. *South African Archaeological Bulletin,* 3, 12. pp. 106–7. b. B. Anthony, personal communication.

37 Keller, C. M. 1969. Mossel Bay: A redescription. *South African Archaeological Bulletin,* 23, IV, pp. 131–40.

38 a. Mortelmans, G. 1962. Vue d'ensemble sur la préhistoire du Congo occidental. *In:* *Op. cit.* at note (31) of Chapter III, pp. 129–64. b. Clark, J. D. 1963. *Op. cit.* at (3) above.

39 a. Cooke, H. B. S. 1963. *Op. cit.* at note (20) chapter II. pp. 98–101. b. H. B. S. Cooke, unpublished report.

40 *Op. cit.* at note (46) of Chapter III.

41 McBurney, C. B. M. and R. W. Hey. 1955. *Prehistory and Pleistocene geology in Cyrenaican Libya.* Cambridge. pp. 141–56.

42 Mason, R. J., R. A. Dart and J. W. Kitching. 1968. Bone tools at the Kalkbank Middle Stone Age site and the Makapansgat Australopithecine locality, central Transvaal. *South African Archaeological Bulletin,* 13 (51) pp. 85–116.

43 Merrick, H. and A. Pastron, *Contributions to a colloquium on History of diet and subsistence in Africa.* 1969 meeting of the Bay Area Africanists, University of California, Berkeley.

44 Clark, J. D. 1968. *Op. cit.* at note (37) of Chapter III, pp. 130–32 and 156–7.

45 Clark, J. D. 1955. A note on a wooden implement from the level of Peat I at Florisbad, Orange Free State. *Researches of the National Museum, Bloemfontein* 1, (6) pp. 135–40.

46 a. Howell, F. C. and Clark, J. D. 1963, *Op. cit.* at note (28) of Chapter III, pp. 520–21. b. Clark, J. D. 1955. The stone ball: Its associations and use by prehistoric man in Africa. *C. R. Congrès panafricain de préhistoire, Alger,* 1952. pp. 403–17.

47 Campbell, B. G. 1966. *Op. cit.* at note (9a) of Chapter III, p. 315.

48 See (47) above pp. 320–21.

49   Stewart, T. D. 1958. The restoration and study of the Shanidar 1 Neanderthal skeleton in Baghdad, Iraq. *Yearbook of the American Philosophical Society.*

50   Lancaster, J. B. 1968. Primate communication systems and the emergence of human language. *In :* Jay, P. C. *ed. Primates : Studies in adaptation and variability.* New York. pp. 439–57.

CHAPTER V

1   Bakker, E. M. van Zinderen. 1967. Upper Pleistocene and Holocene stratigraphy and ecology on the basis of vegetation changes in sub-Saharan Africa. *In : Op. cit.* at note (6) of Chapter I, pp. 125–47.

2   De Ploey, J. 1965. Position géomorphologique, genèse et chrono-logie de certains dépôts superficiels au Congo occidental. *Quaternaria, 7.* Rome. pp. 131–54.

3   a. Coetzee, J. A. 1967. *Op. cit.* at note (2a) of Chapter IV. b. Kendall, R. L. and D. A. Livingstone. In the press. Paleoecological studies on the east African plateau. *In : Op. cit.* at note (9) of Chapter I.

4   Richardson, J. L. 1966. Changes in level of Lake Naivasha, Kenya, during post-glacial times. *Nature, 209.* 290–1.

5   Butzer, K. W., n. d. Climatic changes in the arid zones of Africa during early to mid-Holocene times. *In : Royal Meteorological Society Proceedings of the International Symposium on World Climate (1966) from 8000 to 0 B.C.* pp. 72–82. See p. 75.

6   Monod, Th. 1963. The late Tertiary and Pleistocene in the Sahara. *In : Op. cit.* at note (20) of Chapter II, pp. 119–229. See especially pp. 119–66.

7   Mori, F. 1965. *Tadrart Acacus : Arte rupestre e culture del Sahara preistorico.* Turin. pp. 215–40.

8   Hugot, H. J. *Ed.* 1962. *Missions Berliet Ténéré, Tchad.* Paris. pp. 235–76 and 313–28.

9   a. Grove, A. T. and R. A. Pullan. 1963. Some aspects of the Pleistocene paleogeography of the Chad basin. *In : Op. cit.* at note (20) of Chapter II. pp. 230–245. b. Monod, Th. 1963. *Op. cit.* at (6) above, pp. 170–90.

10   The name given to this industry is a corruption of *Jebel abd el Qadir,* the name of the hill near where it was first recognised.

11 Fagan, B. M. and F. L. van Noten. 1966. Wooden implements from Late Stone Age sites at Gwisho hot-springs, Lochinvar, Zambia. *Proceedings of the Prehistoric Society,* new series XXXII, pp. 246–61. See page 255.

12 Fagan, B. M.—unpublished manuscript on the vegetal remains from Gwisho hot-springs, Lochinvar, Zambia and personal communication.

13 a. Vaufrey, R. 1955. Préhistoire de l'Afrique, Vol. I. *Publications de l'Institut des hautes études de Tunis,* IV. pp. 257–90. b. Tixier, J. 1967. *Op. cit.* at note (27)(c) of Chapter IV, pp. 797–808.

14 McBurney, C. B. M. 1967. *Op. cit.* at note (20) of Chapter I. pp. 185–228.

15 Wendorf, F. 1968. Site 117: A Nubian final Palaeolithic graveyard near Jebel Sahaba, Sudan. *In :* Op. cit. at (9a) of Chapter IV. Volume II, pp. 954–95.

16 *Op. cit.* at (13a) above, pp. 127–254.

17 a. Deevey, E. S. *et al. eds. Radiocarbon,* Volume 8, 1966. Yale University. p. 158. b. Washburn, C. K. 1967. Lake levels and Quaternary climates in the eastern Rift Valley. *Nature,* 216. pp. 672–3. c. Leakey, L. S. B. 1931. *The Stone Age cultures of Kenya Colony.* Cambridge. pp. 90–171.

18 *Op. cit.* at note (32) of Chapter IV, pp. 218–25.

19 a. Clark, J. D. 1959. *The prehistory of southern Africa.* Harmondsworth. pp. 166–84. b. Cole, G. H. 1967. A re-investigation of Magosi and the Magosian. *Quaternaria,* 9, Rome. pp. 153–67.

20 Clark, J. D. 1963. *Op. cit.* at note (3) of Chapter IV. Volume I, pp. 171–83 and Volume II, plates 79 and 80.

21 Tobias, P. V. 1962. Early members of the genus *Homo* in Africa. *In :* Kurth, G. *Evolution and hominisation.* Stuttgart. pp. 191–204. See p. 197.

22 a. *Op. cit.* at (21) above, p. 199. b. Wells, L. H. 1950. The fossil human skull from Singa. *In : British Museum (Nat. Hist.) Fossil Mammals of Africa,* No. 2. pp. 29–41.

23 Louw, J. T. 1960. *Prehistory of the Matjes river rock shelter.* National Museum, Bloemfontein, Mem. 1.

24 a. Keith, A. 1931. *New discoveries relating to the antiquity of man.* London. b. Toerien, M. J. and A. R. Hughes. 1955. The limb bones

of Springbok Flats man. *South African Journal of Science,* 52, (5) pp. 125–7.

25 a. Oakley, K. P. and B. G. Campbell, *eds.* 1967. *Op. cit.* at note (8) of Chapter I, p. 48. b. Shaw, T. In the press. Finds at the Iwo Eleru rock shelter, western Nigeria. *In :* *Op. cit.* at note (9) of Chapter I.

26 Twiesselmann, F. 1958. Les ossements humains du gîte Mésolithi⁄que d'Ishango. *Exploration du Parc national Albert, Mission J. de Heinzelin de Braucourt, 1950.* Volume 5, Institut des parcs nationaux du Congo belge, Brussels.

27 Chamla, M.⁄C. 1968. Les populations anciennes du Sahara et des régions limitrophes: Etude des restes osseux humains Néolithiques et protohistoriques. *Mémoires du centre de Recherches anthropologiques, pré⁄historiques et ethnographiques en Algérie.* Volume IX. Paris. pp. 15–99.

28 Deevy, D. E. 1949. Report on the human remains. *In :* Arkell, A. J. *Early Khartoum.* Oxford.

29 a. Briggs, L. C. 1955. *The Stone Age races of northwest Africa.* American School of Prehistoric Research, Harvard, Bulletin no. 18. b. Ferembach, D. 1962. *La nécropole épipaléolithique de Taforalt (Maroc oriental) : Etude des squelettes humains.* Casablanca.

30 a. Vallois, H. V. 1950. Le squelette d'Ain Méterchem. *Atti del Primo Congr. Intern. de Preistoria e Protostoria Mediterranea.* Florence, pp. 102–4. b. Balout, L. 1949. Découverte d'un squelette humain pré⁄historique dans la région de Tébessa. *Bull. Soc. Hist. Nat. de l'Afrique du nord,* 40, pp. 193–5.

31 a. Leakey, L. S. B. 1935. *The Stone Age races of Kenya.* Oxford. b. Wells, L. H. 1957. Late Stone Age human types in central Africa. *In :* *Op. cit.* at note (41) of Chapter II, pp. 183–5. c. Coon, C. S. 1962. *The origin of races,* New York. pp. 634–6.

32 a. Singer, R. and J. S. Weiner. 1963. Biological aspects of some indigenous African populations. *Southwest Journal of Anthropology,* 19, pp. 168–76. b. Tobias, P. V. 1966. The peoples of Africa south of the Sahara. *In :* Baker, P. T. and J. S. Weiner, *eds.* *The biology of human adaptability.* Oxford. pp. 112–200.

33 Hiernaux, J. 1966. Peoples of Africa from 22°N. to the equator. *In :* *Op. cit.* at (32b) above. pp. 92–110. See p. 100.

34 a. *Op. cit.* at (5) above, p. 74. b. Smith, P. E. L. 1966. The late Palaeolithic of north east Africa in the light of recent research. *Op. cit.* at

note (33) of Chapter III, pp. 326–55.

35 *Op. cit.* at note (9) of Chapter IV, with reference to the gathering and grinding of wild grasses see Volume II, pp. 940–6.

36 Wendorf, F. 1968. *Op. cit.* at (15) above, pp. 954–95.

37 a. Arkell, A. J. 1966. *Early Khartoum.* Oxford. b. Wendt, W. E. 1966. Two prehistoric archaeological sites in Egyptian Nubia. *Postilla,* no. 102, pp. 1–46. c. Monod, Th. 1963. *Op. cit.* at (6) above, pp. 170–90.

38 Robbins, L. H. 1967. A recent archaeological discovery in the Turkana district of northern Kenya. *Azania,* 2. pp. 69–73.

39 Oakley, K. P. 1961. Bone harpoon from Gamble's Cave, Kenya. *Antiquaries Journal,* 41, 86–7.

40 Heinzelin de Braucourt, J. de. 1957. Les Fouilles d'Ishango. *Exploration du Parc National Albert, 1950,* Volume 2. Brussels, Institut des parcs nationaux du Congo belge.

41 Louw, J. T. 1960. *Op. cit.* at (23) above.

42 a. Goodwin, A. J. H. *et al.* 1938. Archaeology of the Oakhurst Shelter, George. *Trans. Royal Society of South Africa,* XXV, III, pp. 17–324. b. Fagan, B. M. 1960. The Glentyre shelter and Oakhurst re-examined. *South African Archaeological Bulletin,* XV, 59, pp. 80–94. c. Schirre, C. 1962. Oakhurst: A re-examination and vindication. *South African Archaeological Bulletin,* XVII, 67 pp. 181–95.

43 a. Breuil, H. 1945. Sea animals amongst the prehistoric rock paintings of Ladybrand. *South African Journal of Science,* XLI, pp. 353–60. b. Goodwin, A. J. H. 1949. A fishing scene from east Griqualand. *The South African Archaeological Bulletin,* IV, 14, pp. 51–3.

44 Some radiocarbon dates for early examples of 'Later Stone Age' blade technology:—

Kisese Rockshelter, Tanzania, early 'Later Stone Age', av. 14,550 ± 213 years, BP.

Prospect Farm, Kenya, Kenya Capsian, 10,560 ± 1650 years BP.

Iwo Eleru, Nigeria, unnamed microlithic industry, 11,200 ± 2000 years BP.

Calonda I, Angola, Lower Tshitolian, 12,970 ± 250 years BP.

Mwela Rocks, Zambia, Nachikufan I, 10,820 ± 340 years BP and 11,700 ± 280 years BP.

Nachikufu Cave, Zambia, post-Nachikufan I, 9,720 ± 550 years BP.

Leopard's Hill Cave, Zambia, Nachikufan I, 16,715± 95 years BP and proto-'Later Stone Age', 21,550± 950 BP and 23,600± 360 years BP.
Pomongwe Cave, Rhodesia, Pomongwan, 9,400   100 years, BP.
Tshangula Cave, Rhodesia, Pomongwan, 12,200   250   ears BP.
Matjes River, Cape, South Africa, 'Smithfield A', 11,250± 400 years BP.
45   a. Willett, F. 1962. The microlithic industry from Old Oyo, western Nigeria. *In: Op. cit.* at note (31) of Chapter III, pp. 261–71.
b. Fagg, B. E. B. 1944. Preliminary report on a microlithic industry at Rop rockshelter, northern Nigeria. *Proceedings of the Prehistoric Society,* 10, pp. 68–9.
46   a. Bequaert, M. and G. Mortelmans. 1955. Le Tshitolien dans le bassin du Congo. *Mém. Acad. royale Sciences Colon. Mém. in 8°,* Nouv. Série. II(5).   b. Clark, J. D. 1963. *Op. cit.* at note (3) of Chapter IV, Vol. I, pp. 153–70 and Vol. II, Plates.
47   a. Clark, J. D. 1950. The newly discovered Nachikufu culture of Northern Rhodesia and the possible origin of certain elements of the South African Smithfield culture. *South African Archaeological Bulletin,* 5, 86–98.   b. Miller, S. F. 1969. *Op. cit.* at note (26c) of Chapter IV.
48   a. *Op. cit.* at (47b) above.   b. Nachikufan I layer Y 807 charcoal 10,820± 340 years BP. Mwela Rocks 4′ 6″–7′ alk 11,700± 280 years BP.
49   Inskeep. R. R. 1967. The Late Stone Age in southern Africa. *In: Op. cit.* at note (6) of Chapter I, pp. 557–82.
50   a. Sampson, C. G. 1967. *Excavations at Zaayfontein shelter, Norvalspont, northern Cape.* Researches of the National Museum, Bloemfontein, II, 2, no. 4.   b. Sampson, C. G. 1967. Excavations at Glen Elliot shelter, Colesberg district, northern Cape *and* Zeekoegat, 13: A Later Stone Age open-site near Venterstad, Cape. *Op. cit.* at (50a) above, nos. 5 and 6.   c. Sampson, C. G. and M. n.d. *Riversmead shelter: Excavations and analysis.* National Museum, Bloemfontein, Memoir 3.
51   a. Fosbrooke, H. A. *et al.* 1950. Tanganyika rock paintings: A guide and record. *Tanganyika Notes and Records,* Dar-es-Salaam.   b. Summers, R. *ed.* 1959. *Prehistoric Rock Art of the Federation of Rhodesia and Nyasaland.* National Publications Trust, Salisbury, Rhodesia.   c. Willcox, A. R. 1963. *The rock art of South Africa.* Johannesburg.
52   *Op. cit.* at (51)(c) above.
53   Sierts, W. 1968. How were rock engravings made? *South African*

Journal of Science, 64, 7. pp. 281–5.

54 Noten, F. van. 1965. Nouvelles fouilles à Lochinvar, (Zambia) 1964. *Africa-Tervuren*, XI (1). pp. 16–22. See p. 19.

55 Clark, J. D. In the press. *Kalambo Falls Prehistoric Site, Volume II*. Cambridge.

56 MacCalman, H. R. and B. J. Grobbelaar. 1965. *Preliminary report of two stone-working OvaTjimba groups in the Northern Kaokoveld of South West Africa*. Cimbebasia, State Museum, Windhoek, No. 13.

57 Laughlin, W. S. 1968. Hunting: An integrating biobehavior system and its evolutionary importance. *In: Op. cit.* at note (45)(a) to Chapter II. pp. 304–20.

CHAPTER VI

1 Renfrew, C., J. E. Dixon and J. R. Cann. 1966. Obsidian and early cultural contact in the Near East. *Proceedings of the Prehistoric Society*, XXXII, pp. 30–72.

2 a. Wendorf, F. and R. Said. 1967. Palaeolithic remains in Upper Egypt. *Nature*, 215, 5098, pp. 244–7. b. Butzer, K. W. and C. L. Hansen. 1968. *Desert and river in Nubia*. University of Wisconsin Press. pp. 171–4.

3 Herodotus, *The Histories*. Translated by Aubrey de Sélincourt. Harmondsworth. 1959 reprint, page 135.

4 Heinzelin, J. de. 1967. Discussion following Mauny, R. L'Afrique et les origines de la domestication. *In: Op. cit.* at note (6) of Chapter I, p. 598.

5 *Op. cit.* at (2b) above, pp. 163–8 and 176–7.

6 Arkell, A. J. 1953. *Shaheinab*. Oxford. pp. 15–16.

7 Caton Thompson, G. and E. W. Gardner. 1934. *The Desert Fayum*. London. 2 vols. Royal Anthropological Institute.

8 Vandier, J. 1952. *Manuel d'archéologie égyptienne, Vol. I Les époques de formation, la préhistoire*. Paris.

9 Kantor, H. J. 1965. The relative chronology of Egypt and its foreign correlations before the late Bronze Age. *In:* Ehrich, R. W. *ed. Chronologies in Old World archaeology*. Chicago. pp. 1–46.

10 Trigger, B. G. 1968. *Beyond history: The methods of prehistory*. New York. pp. 77–86.

11 *Op. cit.* at (10) above, pp. 76–77.

12 Greenberg, J. H. 1963. *Languages of Africa*. Indiana University Research Center in Anthropology, Folklore and Linguistics, Pub. 25. pp. 42–65.

13 *Op. cit.* at (10) above, pp. 85–6.

14 a. Arkell, A. J. 1961. *A history of the Sudan to 1821*. London. p. 166. b. Shinnie, P. L. 1967. *Meroe, a civilization of the Sudan*. London and New York. pp. 100–22. c. Davidson, B. 1964. *The African past: Chronicles from antiquity to modern times*. London. pp. 48–50.

15 McBurney, C. B. M. 1967. *Op. cit.* at note (20) of Chapter II, 313–19.

16 *Op. cit.* at (15) above, pp. 285 and 298.

17 McBurney, C. B. M. and R. W. Hey. 1955. *Op. cit.* at note (41) of Chapter IV. pp. 251–62.

18 a. Balout, L. 1955. *Op. cit.* at note (27a) of Chapter IV, pp. 449–91. b. Vaufrey, R. 1939. L'art rupestre nord-africain. *Arch. de l'Institut de Pal. hum.* Mem. 20. Paris.

19 Camps-Fabrer, H. 1966. Matière et art mobilier dans la préhistoire nord-africaine et saharienne. *Mémoires du C.R.A.P.E., Algiers,* V. pp. 241–47 and 354–69.

20 Smith, P. E. L. 1968. Problems and possibilities of the prehistoric rock art of northern Africa. *African Historical Studies,* I, 1, pp. 1–39.

21 Paradisi, U. 1965. Prehistoric art in the Gebel el-Akhdar (Cyrenaica). *Antiquity,* 39. pp. 95–101.

22 Winckler, H. A. 1938–39. *Rock drawings of southern Upper Egypt.* 2 vols. London.

23 *Op. cit.* at (20) above for recent general review of the north African rock art.

24 Higgs, E. S. 1967. Early domesticated animals in Libya. *In:* *Op. cit.* at note (6) of Chapter I, pp. 165–71.

25 a. Brunton, G. and G. Caton Thompson. 1928. *The Badarian civilisation.* London. p. 91. b. Mauny, R. 1967. L'Afrique et les origines de la domestication. *In: Op. cit.* at note (6) of Chapter I, pp. 583–99. See p. 587.

26 Mori, F. 1965. *Op. cit.* at note (7) of Chapter V, pp. 225–6 and 234.

27 McBurney, C. B. M. 1967. *Op. cit.* at note (20) of Chapter I, p. 313.

28 Camps, G. 1960. Les traces d'un âge du bronze en Afrique du

nord. *Revue africaine, Algiers,* 104, p. 47.

29 Murdock, G. P. 1959. *Africa : Its peoples and their culture history.* New York. pp. 64–8.

30 a. Coon, C. S. 1968. *Yengema cave report.* Philadelphia Museum Monographs, and J. Atherton, personal communication. b. Flight, C. In the press. The prehistoric sequence in the Kintampo area of Ghana. *In : Op. cit.* at note (9) of Chapter I. c. Shaw, T. 1968. *Radiocarbon dating in Nigeria.* Ibadan University Press, Nigeria. p. 8. Four radiocarbon dates suggest that the earlier Buobini industry was superseded by the Kintampo industry about 1450 BC. No date is available for the beginning of the Buobini industry but dates from the White Volta site of Nteresa corroborate the existence of Kintampo industry elements in Ghana about 1500 BC.

31 Arkell, A. J. and P. J. Ucko. 1965. Review of Predynastic development in the Nile Valley. *Current Anthropology,* vol. 6, 2. pp. 145–165. See pp. 147–8.

32 a. Gast, M. 1968. Alimentation des populations de l'Ahaggar. *Mémoires du CRAPE, Algiers,* VIII. pp. 208–18. b. Monod, Th. 1963. *Op. cit.* at note (6) of Chapter V, pp. 194–7.

33 Munson, P. J. 1968. Recent archaeological research in the Dhar Tichitt region of south-central Mauretania. *West African Archaeological Newsletter,* No. 10. Ibadan, Nigeria. pp. 6–13 and personal communication.

34 McBurney, C. B. M. 1967. *Op. cit.* at note (20) of Chapter I, p. 314.

35 Coursey, D. G. 1965. *Yams in west Africa.* Institute of African Studies, University of Ghana, Legon.

36 Kendall, R. L. and D. A. Livingstone. In the press. *Op. cit.* at note (3b) of Chapter V.

37 Clark, J. D. 1968. *Op. cit.* at note (37) of Chapter III, pp. 142–8.

38 Arkell, A. J. 1954. Four occupation sites at Agordat. *Kush,* II, pp. 33–62.

39 a. Clark, J. D. 1954. *Op. cit.* at note (32) of Chapter IV, pp. 295–315 and Plates 47–52. b. Graziosi, P. 1964. New Discoveries of rock paintings in Ethiopia. Parts I and II. *Antiquity,* XXXVIII, pp. 91–8 and 187–90.

40 Law, R. C. C. 1967. The Garamantes and Trans-Saharan enterprise in classical times. *Journal of African History,* 8, 2. pp. 181–200.

41   a. Cole, S. 1963. *The prehistory of east Africa.* New York. (2nd edition). pp. 282–98.   b. Leakey, L. S. B. and M. D. 1950. *Excavations at the Njoro River cave, stone age cremated burials in Kenya colony.* Oxford. pp. 15–16.

42   Posnansky, M. 1967. Excavations at Lanet, Kenya, 1957. *Azania,* II, pp. 89–114. See pp. 108–9.

43   a. Greenberg, J. H. 1963. *Op. cit.* at note (12) above, pp. 48–51. b. Oliver, R. and G. Mathew. 1963. *History of East Africa.* Oxford. Vol. I. pp. 198–203.

44   Clark, J. D. 1964. Stone vessels from Northern Rhodesia. *Man,* 88, pp. 69–73.

45   Greenberg, J. H. 1963. *Op. cit.* at note (12) above, pp. 30–41.

46   Guthrie, M. 1962. Some developments in the prehistory of the Bantu languages. *Journal of African History,* III, 2, 273–82.

47   Oliver, R. 1966. The problem of the Bantu expansion. *Journal of African History,* VII, 3, pp. 361–376.

48   Hiernaux, J. 1968. Bantu expansion: The evidence from physical anthropology confronted with linguistic and archaeological evidence. *Journal of African History,* IX, 4. pp. 505–15.

49   Fagg, B. E. B. 1969. Recent work in west Africa: new light on the Nok Culture. *World Archaeology,* I, 1, pp. 41–50.

50   Willett, F. 1967. *Ife in the history of west African sculpture.* London. pp. 119–28.

51   Shaw, T. 1968. *Op. cit.* at note (30c) above, p. 12.

52   *Op. cit.* at (51) above, p. 14.

53   a. Huard, P. 1966. Introduction et diffusion du fer au Tchad. *Journal of African History,* VII, pp. 377–404.   b. Schneider, J. L. 1967. Evolution du dernier lacustre et peuplements préhistoriques aux pays-bas du Tchad. *ASEQUA,* 14–15. pp. 18–23.   c. Connah, G. 1968. Radiocarbon dates for Benin city and further dates for Daima, N.E. Nigeria. *Journal of the Historical Society of Nigeria,* 4, 2. pp. 313–20. See pp. 316–20.

54   a. Fagan, B. M. 1966. Early Iron Age pottery in eastern and southern Africa. *Azania,* I., pp. 101–10.   b. Robinson, K. R. and B. Sandelowsky. 1968. The Iron Age of northern Malawi: Recent work. *Azania,* III, pp. 107–46.   c. Soper, R. C. 1967. Kwale: An early Iron Age site in south-eastern Kenya. *Azania,* II, pp. 1–18.   d. Soper, R. C. 1967. Iron

Age sites in north-eastern Tanzania. *Azania,* II. pp. 19–36.

55   Nenquin, J. 1961. Dimple-based pots from Kasai, Belgian Congo. *Man,* 59, 242.

56   a. *Op. cit.* at note (55) of Chapter V.   b. Robinson, K. R. 1961. An early Iron Age site from the Chibi district, Southern Rhodesia. *South African Archaeological Bulletin,* 16, 62, pp. 75–102.   c. Robinson, K. R. 1963. Further excavations in the Iron Age deposits at the Tunnel site, Gokomere Hill, Southern Rhodesia. *South African Archaeological Bulletin,* 18, 72, pp. 155–72.

57   Oliver, R. 1966. *Op. cit.* at note (47) above.

58   Clark, J. D. 1970. African prehistory: Opportunities for collaboration between archaeologists, ethnographers and linguists in Dalby, David, ed. *Language and History of Africa.* London.

59   Wilson, M. 1958. The peoples of the Nyasa-Tanganyika corridor. *Communications from the School of African Studies,* University of Cape Town, no. 29, new series.

60   Herskovits, M. J. 1962. *The human factor in changing Africa.* New York. pp. 51–9.

61   Vansina, J. 1966. *Kingdoms of the savanna.* Wisconsin. pp. 37–97.

62   a. Robinson, K. R. 1966. The archaeology of the Rozwi. *In:* Stokes, E. and R. Brown, *eds. The Zambesian Past.* Manchester. pp. 3–27. b. Abraham, D. P. 1966. The roles of 'Chaminuka' and the Mhondoro-cults in Shona political history. *In:* *Op. cit.* at (62a) above, pp. 28–46.

63   Mauny, R. 1961. Tableau géographique de l'ouest africain du moyen âge d'après les sources écrites, la tradition et l'archéologie. *Mémoires de l'IFAN, Dakar,* no. 61. pp. 71–4, 469–73, 480–2.

64   Fagan, B. M. 1969. Early trade and raw materials in south central Africa. *Journal of African History,* Vol. X, 1. pp. 1–14.

65   Clark, J. D. 1959. *Op. cit.* at note (19a) of Chapter V. p. 291.

Appendix

COMPOSITION OF SOME AFRICAN PREHISTORIC INDUSTRIES:
PERCENTAGES OF SHAPED TOOL CATEGORIES

East Africa

OLDOWAN. Date: From? 2.0–2.5 million to? ± 1 million years BP. *Industry from DK I, Lower Bed I, Olduvai.* Percentages: Choppers 11.9; Polyhedrons 10.3; Discoids 11.3; Spheroids 0.6; Scrapers 1.8; Miscellaneous tools 2.1; 'Anvils' 5.5; Hammerstones 14.6; Utilized heavy duty 31.1; Utilized light duty 10.3.

DEVELOPED OLDOWAN. Date: From? ± 1 million to? ± 600,000 years BP.
Industry from BK II, Upper Bed II, Olduvai. Percentages: Choppers 9.5; Proto-handaxes 1.9; Polyhedrons 1.9; Discoids 5.4; Spheroids 24.8; Scrapers 8.9; Points 5.2; Miscellaneous tools 4.4; Modified Battered Pieces 8.1; Anvils 2.2; Hammerstones 4.4; Utilized heavy duty 3.5; Utilized flakes, etc. 19.0.

LOWER ACHEULIAN. Date: From? ± 1 million to? ± 0.5 million years BP.
Industry from EF-HR, Middle Bed II, Olduvai. Percentages: Choppers 10.5; Handaxes 38.9; Discoids 1.0; Spheroids 11.5; Scrapers 1.0; Miscellaneous tools 8.4; Hammerstones 7.3; Utilized heavy-duty 22.1.

UPPER ACHEULIAN. Date: From? ± 500,000 to 60,000 years BP. *Industry from Isimila Occupation Area K14.* Percentages: Handaxes 13.6; Cleavers 40.0; Knives 0.8; Discs 1.6; Core Scrapers 0.8; Picks 1.6; Choppers 9.6; Spheroids 7.2; Small scrapers 13.6; Other small tools 8.0.

Northwest Africa

ATERIAN. Date: From > 30,000 to < 19,000 years BP.

Industry from Ain Fritissa, eastern Morocco. Percentages: Levallois flakes 13.70; Levallois blades 3.20; Levallois points 1.05; Pseudo-Levallois points 0.58; Mousterian points 4.65; Limaces 0.05; Side scrapers 48.55; Bifacially retouched side scrapers 1.20; Core scrapers 1.65; End scrapers 2.85; Burins 0.38; Borers 0.66; Naturally backed knives 1.05; Backed knives 0.85; *Raclettes* 0.05; Truncated flakes 0.85; Notched pieces 2.20; Denticulate pieces 6.75; Choppers 0.58; Tanged flakes and points 0.90; Flakes with partial bifacial retouch 1.09; Splintered pieces 0.09; Bifacially retouched tools 2.20; Polyhedrals 0.35; Miscellaneous 4.52.

ORANIAN (Ibero-Maurusian). Date: From > 12,000 to 10,000 years BP.

Industry from Layer VIII, Taforalt Cave, Morocco. Percentages: Burins 0.8; Denticulates 8.0; End scrapers 1.8; Truncated pieces 0.5; Utilised flakes 4.7; Microburins 18.6; Backed bladelets 60.2; Miscellaneous 5.4.

CAPSIAN. Date: *Capsien typique,* From ?($\pm$ 10,000) to 8500 years BP. Upper Capsian, From *c.* 8500 to *c.* 6500 years BP.

Typical Capsian Industry from Ain Metterchem, Tebessa, Tunisia. Percentages: Backed blades 33.25; Burins 6.65; End scrapers 5.75; Obliquely truncated blades 0.25; Notched and denticulate pieces 9.60; Convex backed bladelets 23.55; Lunates 2.42; Triangles 1.27; Trapezes 0.64; Truncated bladelets 2.67; shouldered bladelets 1.14; Drills 0.64; Microburins 11.05; Upper and lower grindstones 0.50; Bone points 0.12; Miscellaneous including pigment 0.50.

Northeast Africa

LEVALLOIS-MOUSTERIAN. Date: From > 60,000 to $\pm$ 55,000 years BP.

Industry from Layer XXXIII, Haua Fteah Cave, Cyrenaica. Percentages: Points 8; Side scrapers 19; End scrapers 10; Miscellaneous scrapers 13; Burins 2; Notched pieces 44; Chisels and *lames écaillées* 2; Awls 2.

NUBIAN MOUSTERIAN, TYPE A. Date: From > 47,000 to < 35,000 years BP.

Industry from Site 1010–8, east of Wadi Halfa, Sudan. Percentages: Levallois flakes 16.2; Levallois points 0.6; Pseudo-Levallois points 1.1; Side scrapers 12.7; End scrapers 7.5; *Raclettes* 0.6; Burins 1.7; Borers 5.8; Truncated pieces 7.5; Notched pieces 9.2; Denticulate pieces 13.9; Bec burins 4.6; Inversely retouched 6.9; Tayac points 1.1; End-notched 5.8; Miscellaneous 4.6.

DABBAN. Date: From ± 40,000 to 15,000 years BP.
Early Dabban Industry from Layers XX/XXI interface, Haua Fteah Cave, Cyrenaica. Percentages: Backed blades 47.1; Burins 17.82; Chamfered blades 7.10; End scrapers 16.30; Miscellaneous scrapers 8.20; Awls 2.72; *Lames écaillées* 0.38; Flaked adzes 0.38.

KHORMUSAN. Date: From > 22,000 to < 18,700 years BP.
Industry from Site 34A, Dibeira East, Nubia. Percentages: Levallois flakes 57.8; Levallois blades 2.9; Levallois and pseudo-Levallois points 4.4; Burins 3.3; End scrapers 1.2; Side scrapers 8.9; Notched pieces 5.0; Denticulates 7.1; Retouched flakes 4.1; Truncated pieces 0.9; Cortex backed knives 0.3; Strangulated pieces 2.9; Miscellaneous 1.2.

HALFAN. Date: From *c.* 20,000 to 17,000 years BP.
Stage II Industry from Site 1020, Wadi Halfa, Sudan. Percentages: Halfa flakes 52.5; Levallois flakes 2.0; End scrapers 2.5; Core scrapers 3.0; Side scrapers 1.5; Borers 0.5; Burins 6.5; Denticulates 6.0; Notched pieces 6.5; Truncated flakes 2.5; Cortex- and parti-backed knives 6.0; Backed bladelets 2.0; Retouched bladelets 2.0; Retouched flakes 4.5; Miscellaneous 0.5.

SEBILIAN. Date: From *c.* 15,000 to 11,000 years BP.
Early Sebilian Industry from Site 1042, near Mirgissa, Wadi Halfa, Sudan. Percentages: Levallois flakes and blades 21.6; Levallois points 3.1; Side scrapers 0.7; Notched pieces 4.1; Denticulates 1.0; Burins 0.3; Cortex backed knives 1.0; Basal truncations 27.1; Basal and oblique truncations 15.4; Oblique truncations 11.1; Backed flakes and blades 6.5; Backing and basal truncations 7.2; Other Sebilian types 0.3; Microburins 0.3.

QADAN. Date: From *c.* 14,500 to *c.* 6400 years BP.
Industry from Site ANE–1, Halfa Dequim, south of Wadi Halfa, Sudan.
Percentages: Levallois flakes 0.1; Nosed scrapers 0.6; End/end and side
scrapers 4.9; Side scrapers 7.5; Multiple edged scrapers 1.8; Other
scrapers 0.1; Core scrapers 0.9; Denticulates 3.8; Notched pieces 4.3;
Burins 3.9; Truncated pieces 8.9; Backed flakes 11.0; Borers 0.1;
Backed blades and knives 3.8; Cortex backed knives 0.3; Lunates 23.0;
Geometric microliths 8.1; *outils écaillés* 3.3; Points 5.4; Retouched flakes
and blades 5.7; Miscellaneous 1.6; Groovers 0.5; Grindstones (five
fragments).

Central and West Africa

SANGOAN. Date: From ± 46,000 to ± 37,000 years BP.
Industry from Floor B2/59/4, Kalambo Falls, Zambia. Percentages: Handaxes 2.45; Cleavers 1.10; Knives 2.45; Picks 0.74; Core-axes 6.5;
Choppers 2.20; Large scrapers 3.70; Small scrapers 63.10; Core
scrapers 8.50; Other large tools 0.38; Other small tools 8.5; Spheroids
0.38.

LUPEMBAN. Date: From *c.* 36,000 to *c.* 14,000 years BP.
Upper Lupemban Industry from Matafari, Dundo, northeast Angola. Percent-
ages: Handaxes 3.25; Other bifaces 11.1; Choppers 2.6; Picks 9.1;
Flake scrapers 25.3; Core-axes 36.3; Points 4.55; Tranchets 0.65;
Polyhedrals 3.25; Hammerstones, grindstones and anvils 3.9.

TSHITOLIAN. Date: From *c.* 13,000 to 4500 years BP.
Industry from 10m. terrace, Cauma Mine, northeast Angola. Percentages:
Handaxes 2.3; Choppers 0.8; Core-axes 16.1; Small bifaces 0.8;
Utilized flakes 3.3; Core scrapers 0.3; Flake scrapers 15.1; Backed
blades and flakes 1.3; Microliths 0.8; Simple truncated pieces 23.4;
Petit tranchet truncations 31.6; Grindstones, hammer and pestle stones,
anvils 4.1; Miscellaneous 0.5.

WEST AFRICAN MICROLITHIC. Date: [5] ± 4000 years BP.
Industry from Old Oyo Rockshelter, southeastern Nigeria. Percentages:
Lunates and trapezes 62.35; Backed bladelets 5.20; Scrapers 7.30;
Borers 3.13; Points 12.36; Burins 2.14; Rods 1.10; *Outils écaillés* 2.14;
Microburins 2.14; Miscellaneous 2.14.

CHARAMAN (= 'Rhodesian Proto-Stillbay'). Date: From ± 42,000 to 36,000 years BP.
Industry from Charama Plateau, Gokwe, Rhodesia. Percentages: Picks 15.3; Handaxes 1.0; 'Points' 17.1; Scrapers 47.2; Utilized blades 8.3; Choppers, anvils, hammerstones, etc. 11.1.

BAMBATAN (= 'Rhodesian Stillbay'). Date: From 22,000 to ± 15,000 years BP.
Industry from Layer 7, Khami Waterworks Site, Rhodesia. Percentages: Unifaced points 10.45; Bifacial points 3.44; Scrapers 39.00; Backed blades 13.90; Large lunates 3.85; Burins 3.85; Saws 4.50; Flakes with inverse retouch (Kasouga) 1.02; Borers 0.34; Backed knives 1.36; Choppers 0.69; Spheroids 0.34; Hammerstones 9.70; Anvils 2.40; Fabricators 1.72; Pigment 3.44.

UMGUZAN (= 'Rhodesian Magosian').
Industry from Layer 6, Khami Waterworks Site, Rhodesia. Percentages: Points 15.89; Scrapers 19.00; *outils écaillés* 6.20; Saws 1.25; Burins 3.05; Backed and eared tools 7.15; Backed blades and lunates 36.05; Borers 2.70; Tranchets 1.25; Hammerstones 0.62; Bipolar anvils 1.56; Fabricators 2.17; Grooved stones 0.62; Choppers 0.62; Grindstones 1.25; Pigment 0.31; Miscellaneous 0.31.

POMONGWAN. Date: From *c.* 9400 to *c.* 7500 years BP.
Industry from Layers 7–10, Pomongwe Cave, Rhodesia. Percentages: Circular scrapers 89.15; Duckbill scrapers 1.90; Notched scrapers 0.39; Side scrapers 0.19; Burins 0.19; Choppers 0.19; Detaching hammers 2.85; Anvils 3.24; Fabricators 1.14; Bone points 0.57; Eyed needles 0.19.

MATOPAN (= 'Rhodesian Wilton'). Date: From *c.* 7500 to *c.* 1200 years BP.
Industry from Amadzimba Cave, Matopo Hills, Rhodesia. Percentages: Thumbnail scrapers 37.55; Other scrapers 9.22; Backed bladelets 12.23; Lunates 6.26; Trapeziums 0.18; Backed points 0.72; Burins 2.26; Pointed flakes 1.08; Borers 0.18; Hammerstones and mullers 3.75;

Anvils 1.26; Rubbing stones 2.26; Grooved stones 1.44; Ground slate fragment 0.18; Fabricators 0.90; Bone implements 14.73; Slate, bone, ivory ornaments excluding ostrich eggshell beads 4.36; Miscellaneous 1.44.

South Africa

FAURESMITH. Date: From ? ± 60,000 to ? ± 40,000 years BP.
Industry from Rooidam, northern Cape Province (all levels). Percentages: Handaxes 13.4; Cleavers 3.5; Choppers 4.6; Other bifaces 2.4; Backed knives 8.6; Concave scrapers 30.8; Denticulated scrapers 2.1; Discoids 32.5; Spheroids 1.1; Anvils 0.25; Points 0.75.

PIETERSBURG. Date: From > 40,000 to ± 15,000 years BP.
Lower Pietersburg Industry from Bed 4, Cave of Hearths, Transvaal. Percentages: Irregular end-struck flakes (*c.* 1/9th utilized) 49.5; Irregular side-struck flakes (some utilized) 4.8; Quadrilateral flakes (*c.* 1/6th utilized) 28.0; Triangular flakes (some utilized and retouched) 2.8; Single side scrapers 2.9; Side and end scrapers 0.2; Double side scrapers 0.8; End scrapers 0.2; Cuboids (?core scrapers) 2.7; Spheroids 1.8; *Outils écaillés* 0.3; Choppers 0.1; Anvils 0.2; Miscellaneous 3.5.
Middle Pietersburg Industry from Bed 5, Cave of Hearths. Percentages: Irregular end-struck flakes (*c.* 1/6 utilized) 51; Irregular side struck flakes (*c.* 1/3 utilized) 4.4; Quadrilateral flakes (*c.* 1/3 utilized) 31; Triangular flakes (*c.* 2/5 retouched, 2/5 utilized and 1/5 plain) 3.8; Single side scrapers 3.5; Side and end scrapers 1.0; Double side scrapers 0.9; End scrapers 0.4; Cuboids 1.5; Spheroids 0.4; Miscellaneous 3.2.
Upper Pietersburg Industry from Beds 6–9, Cave of Hearths. Percentages: Irregular end-struck flakes (some utilized) 36.5; Irregular side-struck flakes (some utilized) 10.5; Quadrilateral flakes (*c.* 1/6 utilized) 23.0; Triangular flakes (*c.* 2/3 retouched, 1/6 utilized and 1/6 plain) 5.1; Single side scrapers 5.8; Side and end scrapers 1.1; Double side scrapers 2.6; End scrapers 0.6; Cuboids 2.8; Spheroids 2.3; Grindstones 0.8; *Outils écaillés* 4.0; Backed flakes 0.2; Miscellaneous 4.8.

MOSSEL BAY. Date: From ? ± 35,000 to ± 15,000 years BP.
Industry from Layer C, Cape St Blaize Cave, Mossel Bay. Percentages: Points 8.2; Trimmed flakes 43.2; Trimmed chips and chunks 26.7;

Scrapers 12.3; Hollow scrapers 4.1; Obliquely truncated blades 3.1; Burins 1.1; Burin/Scraper 1.1.

SMITHFIELD A. Date: From ± 11,000 to ? > 3000 years BP.
Industry from the Lower Level, Zeekoegat 13, Orange Free State. Percentages: Convex scrapers 8.4; Trimmed flakes 52.1; Circular scrapers 1.4; Trimmed flake fragments (straight and convex) 15.5; Concave scrapers 2.8; Steep scrapers 2.8; End scrapers 4.2; Battered fragments 2.8.

SMITHFIELD C. Date: ± 3000 years BP.
Industry from Layer VIII, Glen Elliott Rockshelter, Orange Free State. Percentages: End scrapers 8.4; Side and end scrapers 5.1; Small end scrapers 1.7; Pebble adzes 3.4; Trimmed blades and flakes 16.9; *Outils écaillés* 6.8; Small convex scrapers 28.8; Straight backed points 8.5; Backed bladelets 15.2; Circular scrapers 3.4; Ground stones 1.7; Convex trimmed fragments 3.4; Steep scrapers 1.7; Battered fragments 1.7.

SMITHFIELD B. Date: From ? ± 1500 to ± 200 years BP.
Industry from Layer III, Glen Elliott Rockshelter, Orange Free State. Percentages: End scrapers 15.3; Side and end scrapers 14.1; Small end scrapers 12.3; Core hammers 3.0; Convex scrapers 3.0; Borers 4.9; Backed and pebble adzes 2.5; Trimmed flakes and blades 17.1; Small convex scrapers 1.2; Straight backed points 0.6; Backed bladelets 3.6; Concave backed fragments 0.6; Circular scrapers 0.6; Ground stones 0.6; Bone points and fragments 17.8; Reamers and fragments 1.2; Gouges 0.6.

WILTON. Date: From ? ± 7000 to 200 years BP.
Sample from Type Industry, Wilton Rock shelter, Eastern Cape Province. Percentages: End scrapers 17.4; Side and end scrapers 0.9; Small end scrapers 4.1; Core hammers 0.4; Convex scrapers 1.8; Backed adzes 3.3; Trimmed bladelets and flakes 31.0; *outils écaillés* 1.6; Small convex scrapers 22.3; Straight backed points 0.5; Backed bladelets 1.3; Lunates 1.6; Concave backed fragments 0.1; Bored and ground stones 0.7; Double crescents 1.3; Small double end and side scrapers 6.6; Small circular scrapers 1.5; Small side scrapers 3.7.

Bibliography

Below are listed some of the more general and specific journals and books recommended for further reading. Most of the specific references given in the Annotations are not repeated here and should, therefore, be read in conjunction with this general bibliography.

I GENERAL SOURCES

1 Journals and occasional publications devoted entirely to African archaeology and Quaternary studies.

North Africa
Kush, Antiquities Department, Khartoum, Sudan.
Libyca, Centre de Recherches anthropologiques, préhistoriques et ethnographiques (CRAPE), Algiers. Annually.

West Africa
ASEQUA, Journal of the Association sénégalaise pour l'étude du Quaternaire de l'ouest africain, Institut fondamental d'Afrique noire (IFAN), Dakar. Quarterly.
West African Archaeological Newsletter, Institute of African Studies, University of Ibadan, Nigeria. Periodically.

East Africa
Azania, Journal of the British Institute of History and Archaeology in East Africa, Nairobi. Annually.

Southern Africa
South African Archaeological Bulletin, South African Archaeological Society, Claremont, Cape Town.
Archaeologica Zambiana, Occasional newsletter from the Commission for the Preservation of Natural and Historical Monuments and Relics, Livingstone, Zambia.

2 Journals and occasional publications with regular contributions on African archaeology and Quaternary studies.

General
L'Anthropologie, Masson et Cie, Paris.
Journal of African History, School of Oriental and African Studies, University of London. Quarterly.
Quaternaria, Via G. Caccini, 1, Rome. Annually.
Man, Journal of the Royal Anthropological Institute, London, Quarterly.

Mostly North African
Bulletin de la Société Préhistorique française, Paris.
Etudes et travaux d'archéologie marocaine, Rabat.
Hesperis Tamuda, Archives Berbères et Bulletin de l'Institut des Hautes Etudes marocaines, Rabat.
Travaux de l'Institut de Recherches sahariennes, Algiers.
Mémoires du Centre de Recherches anthropologiques, Préhistoriques et Ethnographiques (CRAPE) Algiers.

West Africa
Notes Africaines, IFAN, University of Dakar, Senegal. Quarterly.
Bulletin d'IFAN, Dakar, Senegal.
Journal of the Historical Society of Nigeria, The Historical Society of Nigeria and the University of Ibadan Press.

East Africa
Annales d'Ethiopie, L'Institut éthiopien d'archéologie, Addis Ababa.
Journal of the Uganda Society, Kampala, Uganda.
Tanganyika Notes and Records, Dar-es-Salaam, Tanzania.
Journal of the East African Natural History Society, Nairobi, Kenya.

Equatoria
Africa Tervuren, Musée royal de l'Afrique centrale, Tervuren, Belgium. Quarterly.
Publicações Culturais do Museu do Dundo, Companhia de Diamantes de Angola, Lisbon, Portugal. Periodically.

Rhodesia and Zambia
Occasional Papers of the National Museums of Southern Rhodesia, Salisbury.

Arnoldia, Miscellaneous publications of the National Museums of Southern Rhodesia.

The Robins Series of works on central Africa published by Chatto and Windus, London, for the National Museums of Zambia.

Southern Africa

South African Journal of Science, South African Association for the Advancement of Science, Johannesburg.

Annals of the South African Museum, Cape Town.

Annals of the Cape Provincial Museums, published jointly by the Cape Provincial Museums at the Albany Museum, Grahamstown.

Mémoires of the Transvaal Museum, Pretoria.

Mémoires and *Researches* of the National Museum of the Orange Free State, Bloemfontein.

Journal of the South West African Scientific Society, Windhoek, South West Africa.

Cimbebasia, South West African Research, The State Museum, Windhoek.

Trabalhos do Instituto de investigação científica de Moçambique, Lourenço Marques, Moçambique.

II GEOGRAPHY AND ECOLOGY

DAVIS, D. H. S., *ed.* 1964. Ecological Studies in southern Africa. *Monographiae biologicae,* no. XIV, Junk, The Hague.

FITZGERALD, W. 1961. *Africa : A social, economic and political geography of its major regions.* New York (repr. of 9th ed., London 1934).

GROVE, A. T. 1967. *Africa south of the Sahara.* Oxford.

Oxford Regional Economic Atlas. 1965. *Africa.* Oxford.

TRAPNELL, C. G. 1953. *The soils, vegetation and agriculture of northeastern Rhodesia.* Lusaka.

TRAPNELL, C. G. and J. N. CLOTHIER. 1957. *The soils, vegetation and agricultural systems of northwestern Rhodesia.* Lusaka.

UNESCO. 1963. *A review of the natural resources of the African continent.* Paris.

III PALAEOECOLOGY AND POLLEN ANALYSIS

BAKKER, E. M. van Zinderen. Palaeoecology of Africa and the surrounding islands and Antarctica. *Balkema,* Cape Town. Published every two years giving summaries of recent researches.
Vol. I. (1950–63) 1966.
Vol. II. (1964 & 5) 1967.
Vol. III, 1967—Pollen analytical studies in east and southern Africa, by J. A. Coetzee.

IV GENERAL WORKS ON AFRICAN PALAEOANTHROPOLOGY
—containing many papers covering all aspects of Quaternary studies and archaeology in Africa

The Proceedings of the Pan-African Congress on Prehistory and the study of the Quaternary, held every four years.

1 LEAKEY, L. S. B. and S. COLE. 1952, eds. *Proceedings of the Pan-African Congress on Prehistory, Nairobi, 1947.* Oxford.

2 BALOUT, L., ed. 1955. *Actes du Congrès Pan-africain de Préhistoire, IIe session, Alger, 1952.* Paris.

3 CLARK, J. D. and S. COLE, eds. 1957. *Proceedings of the third Pan-African Congress on Prehistory, Livingstone, Northern Rhodesia, 1955.* London.

4 MORTELMANS, G. and J. NENQUIN, eds. 1962. *Actes du IVe Congrès panafricain de préhistoire et de l'étude du Quaternaire, Léopoldville, Congo, 1959.* Musée royal de l'Afrique centrale, Tervuren, Belgium, Annales, Série en–8° Sciences humaines, no. 40. 2 vols.

5 CUSCOY, L. D., ed. 1965. *Actas del V Congreso Panafricano de prehistoria y de estudio del Cuaternaria, Tenerife, 1963.* Museo arqueologico Santa Cruz de Tenerife. 2 vols.

6 HUGOT, H. J., ed. In the press. *Actes du sixième congrès panafricain de préhistoire et de l'étude du Quaternaire, Dakar, Sénégal, 1967.*

Howell, F. C. and F. Bourlière, eds. 1963. *African ecology and human evolution.* Chicago. Viking Fund Publications in Anthropology, no. 36.

Bishop, W. W. and J. D. Clark, *eds.* 1967. *Background to Evolution in Africa.* Chicago.

V PRIMATE STUDIES

DeVore, I., *ed.* 1965. *Primate behaviour—field studies of monkeys and apes.* New York.

Jay, P. C., *ed.* 1968. *Primates: Studies in adaptation and variability.* New York.

VI HUMAN EVOLUTION AND FOSSIL MAN

1 General

Campbell, B. G. 1966. *Human evolution, an introduction to man's adaptations.* Chicago.

Clark, W. E. LeGros. 1955. *The fossil evidence for human evolution: An introduction to the study of Palaeoanthropology.* Chicago.

Coon, C. S. 1962. *The origin of races.* New York.

Day, M. H. 1965. *Guide to fossil man: A handbook of human palaeontology.* London. Cleveland, Ohio, 1966.

Washburn, S. L., *ed.* 1961. *Social life of early man.* Chicago, Viking Fund Publications in Anthropology, no. 31.

Washburn, S. L., *ed.* 1963. *Classification and human evolution.* Chicago, Viking Fund Publications in Anthropology, no. 37.

Washburn, S. L. and P. C. Jay, *eds.* 1968. *Perspectives on human evolution, I.* New York.

2 Specifically African

Arambourg, C. and R. Hoffstetter. 1963. *Le gisement de Ternifine, 1.* Archives de l'Institut de Paléontologie humaine, Mem. 32. Paris.

Briggs, L. C. 1955. *The stone age races of northwest Africa.* American School of Prehistoric Research, Peabody Museum, Harvard, Bulletin, no. 18.

Broom, R. and G. W. H. Schepers. 1946. *The South African fossil ape-men, the Australopithecinae.* Transvaal Museum Mémoire no. 2. Pretoria.

BROOM, R., J. T. ROBINSON and G. W. H. SCHEPERS. 1950. *Sterkfontein ape-man*, Plesianthropus. Transvaal Museum Mémoire, no. 4. Pretoria.

BROOM, R. and J. T. ROBINSON. 1952. *Swartkrans ape-man*, Paranthropus crassidens. Transvaal Museum Mémoire, no. 6. Pretoria.

CHAMLA, M.-C. 1968. Les populations anciennes du Sahara et des régions limitrophes: Etude des restes osseux humains Néolithiques et protohistoriques. *Mémoires du CRAPE, Algiers*. vol. XI. Paris.

GALLOWAY, A. 1959. *The skeletal remains of Bambandyanalo*. Johannesburg.

CLARK, W. E. LeGROS. 1967. *Man-apes or ape-men? The story of discoveries in Africa*. New York.

OAKLEY, K. P. and B. G. CAMPBELL. 1967. *Catalogue of fossil hominids, Part I, Africa*. British Museum (Nat. Hist.) London.

ROBINSON, J. T. 1956. *The dentition of the Australopithecinae*. Transvaal Museum Mémoire no. 9. Pretoria.

TOBIAS, P. V. 1967. The cranium and maxillary dentition of *Australopithecus (Zinjanthropus) boisei*. Olduvai Gorge. vol. II. Cambridge.

VII HUMAN POPULATIONS OF AFRICA

BAKER, P. T. and J. S. WEINER, *eds*. 1966. *The biology of human adaptability*, Oxford. The section on African populations.

BRIGGS, L. C. 1958. *The living races of the Sahara desert*. Cambridge, Mass.

HIERNAUX, J. 1968. *La diversité humaine en Afrique subsaharienne*. Recherches biologiques, études ethnographiques, éditions de l'Institut de Sociologie, Université libre de Bruxelles, Belgium.

VILLIERS, H. DE. 1968. *The skull of the South African Negro—a biometrical and morphological study*. Johannesburg, San Francisco and New York.

VIII STRATIGRAPHY, FOSSIL FAUNAS, PALAEOCLI-
   MATOLOGY AND CHRONOLOGY

HOWELL, F. C. and F. BOURLIÉRE. 1963—see under IV, above, pp. 1–334.

BISHOP, W. W. and J. D. CLARK. 1967—see under IV, above, Parts 1 and 2 and summary review by F. C. Howell at end of volume.

1 General

BISHOP, W. W. 1968. The evolution of fossil environments in east Africa. *Transactions of the Leicester Literary and Philosophical Society,* vol. LXII, pp. 22–44.

COOKE, H. B. S. 1958. *Observations relating to Quaternary environments in east and southern Africa.* Du Toit Memorial Lecture, Geological Society of South Africa, vol. LX, annexure.

FLINT, R. F. 1959. Pleistocene climates in eastern and southern Africa. *Bulletin of the Geological Society of America,* 70, pp. 343–74.

HOWELL, F. C. 1967. Recent advances in human evolutionary studies. *Quarterly Review of Biology,* vol. 42, no. 4. pp. 471–513.

OAKLEY, K. P. 1964. *Frameworks for dating fossil man.* London and Chicago.

2 Fauna

CARTMILL, M. 1967. The early Pleistocene mammalian microfaunas of sub-Saharan Africa and their ecological significance. *Quaternaria,* vol. IX, pp. 169–98.

COOKE, H. B. S. 1968. Evolution of mammals on southern continents, II The fossil mammal fauna of Africa. *Quarterly Review of Biology,* vol. 43, 3. pp. 234–64.

LEAKEY, L. S. B. 1965. *Olduvai Gorge, 1951–60, Volume I : a preliminary report on the geology and fauna.* Cambridge.

3 Regional Stratigraphy and Quaternary Climates

BISHOP, W. W. and A. F. TRENDALL. 1967. Erosion-surfaces, tectonics and volcanic activity in Uganda. *Quarterly Journal of the Geological Society of London,* vol. 122, pp. 385–420.

BRAIN, C. K. 1958. *The Transvaal Ape-Man-bearing cave deposits.* Transvaal Museum Mémoire no. 11. Pretoria.

BUTZER, K. W. and C. L. HANSEN. 1968. *Desert and river in Nubia.* Madison.

CHAVAILLON, J. 1964. *Etude stratigraphique des formations quaternaires du Sahara nord-occidental.* Algiers.

CLARK, J. D. 1969. *Kalambo Falls Prehistoric Site.* vol. I. Cambridge.

4 Chronometric and Archaeological Dating

DEACON, J. 1966. An annotated list of radiocarbon dates for sub-Saharan Africa. *Annals of the Cape Provincial Museums,* vol. V, pp. 5–84.

———— 1968. Supplementary list and index to *op. cit.* above. Supplement to vol. V.

EVERNDEN, J. F. and G. H. CURTIS. 1965. The Potassium-argon dating of late Cenozoic rocks in east Africa and Italy. *Current Anthropology,* 6, pp. 343–85.

GARLAKE, P. S. 1968. The value of imported ceramics in the dating and interpretation of the Rhodesian Iron Age. *Journal of African History,* vol. IX, 1. pp. 13–34.

KANTOR, H. J. 1965. The relative chronology of Egypt and its foreign correlations before the late Bronze Age. *In :* Ehrich, R. W. *Chronologies in Old World archaeology.* Chicago. pp. 1–46.

MERWE, N. J. VAN DER and M. STUIVER. 1968. Dating iron by the carbon-14 method. *Current Anthropology,* 9, 1. pp. 48–58.

Radiocarbon published annually by the American Journal of Science at Yale University, New Haven, Connecticut.

Lists of radiocarbon dates for sub-Saharan Africa, compiled by B. M. Fagan, appear from time to time in the Journal of African History.

IX ARCHAEOLOGICAL TYPOLOGY AND TERMINOLOGY; INDUSTRIAL DISTRIBUTIONS

BISHOP, W. W. and CLARK, J. D. 1967. *Op. cit.* at IV above. The relevant papers.

BORDES, F. 1961. Typologie du paléolithique ancien et moyen. Bordeaux. 2 vols.

Bulletins of the Commission on Nomenclature of the Pan-African Congress on Prehistory and the Study of the Quaternary. Issued periodically from the bureaux at the Institut de Paléontologie humaine, Paris, and the Department of Anthropology, University of California, Berkeley.

CLARK, J. D. 1967. *Atlas of African Prehistory.* Chicago.

COOKE, H. B. S., R. SUMMERS and K. R. ROBINSON. 1966. Rhodesian prehistory re-examined, I The Stone Age; II The Iron Age. *Arnoldia,* vol. 2, nos. 12 and 17.

Fiches typologiques africaines, ed. L. Balout and G. Camps for the PanAfrican Congress, published by CRAPE, Algiers.

HEINZELIN DE BRAUCOURT, J. DE. 1962. *Manual de typologie des industries lithiques.* Brussels, Inst. roy. des sciences naturelles de Belgique.

Inventaria archaeologica africana, ed. by J. Nenquin, Tervuren, Belgium.

TIXIER, J. 1963. *Typologie de l'épipaléolithique du Maghreb.* Mémoires de CRAPE, Algiers, no. 2.

X ARCHAEOLOGY

1 General

ALIMEN, H. 1957. *The prehistory of Africa,* translated by A. H. Broderick. London and New York.

PERICOT, L. and M. TARRADELL. 1962. *Manual de prehistoria africana.* Madrid.

2 North Africa (General)

McBURNEY, C. B. M. 1960. *The Stone Age in northern Africa.* Harmondsworth.

North-west Africa

BALOUT, L. 1955. *Préhistoire de l'Afrique du nord: essai de chronologie.* Paris.

BIBERSON, P. 1961(a). *Le cadre paléogéographique de la préhistoire du Maroc atlantique.* Rabat, Service des Antiquités du Maroc.

——— 1961(b). *Le paléolithique inférieur du Maroc atlantique.* Rabat. Service des Antiquités du Maroc.

CAMPS-FABRER, H. 1966. *Matière et art mobilier dans la préhistoire nordafricaine et saharienne.* Mémoires du CRAPE, Algiers, vol. V.

HOWE, B. 1967. *The Palaeolithic of Tangier, Morocco, excavations at Cape Ashakar, 1939–47.* American School of Prehistoric Research, Peabody Museum, Harvard, Bull. no. 22.

ROCHE, J. 1963. *L'épipaléolithique marocain.* Foundation Calouste Gulbenkian, Paris.

VAUFREY, R. 1955. *Préhistoire de l'Afrique. I. Le Maghreb.* Publications de l'Institut des Hautes Etudes de Tunis, IV. Paris.

North-east Africa (Libya, Egypt and the Sudan)

ARKELL, A. J. 1949. *Early Khartoum*. Oxford.

────── 1953. *Shaheinab, an account of the excavation of a Neolithic occupation site carried out for the Sudan Antiquities Service in 1949–50*. Oxford.

────── 1961. *A history of the Sudan from the earliest times to 1821*. London.

CATON THOMPSON, G. and E. W. GARDNER. 1934. *The desert Fayum*. London.

CATON THOMPSON, G. 1952. *Kharga Oasis in Prehistory*. London.

McBURNEY, C. B. M. 1967. *The Haua Fteah (Cyrenaica) and the Stone Age of the south-east Mediterranean*. Cambridge.

McBURNEY, C. B. M. and R. W. HEY. 1955. *Prehistory and Pleistocene geology of Cyrenaican Libya*. Cambridge.

SHINNIE, P. L. 1967. *Meroe, a civilisation of the Sudan*. London and New York.

TRIGGER, B. G. 1968. *Beyond History, the methods of prehistory*. New York.

WENDORF, F., ed. 1968. *The Prehistory of Nubia*. 3 vols. Dallas.

The Sahara

HUGOT, H. J. 1963. *Recherches préhistoriques dans l'Ahaggar nord-occidental, 1950–57*. CRAPE, Algiers, Bulletin 1.

HUGOT, H. J., ed. 1962. *Missions Berliet Ténéré Tchad*. Paris.

3   West Africa

DAVIES, O. 1964. *The Quaternary in the coastlands of Guinea*. Glasgow.

────── 1967. *West Africa before the Europeans*. London.

MAUNY, R. 1961. *Tableau géographique de l'ouest africain du moyen âge d'après les sources écrites, la tradition et l'archéologie*. Mémoires de IFAN, Dakar, no. 61.

WILLETT, F. 1967. *Ife in the history of West African sculpture*. London and New York.

4   East Africa

CLARK, J. D. 1954. *The prehistoric cultures of the Horn of Africa*. Cambridge.

COLE, S. 1963. *The prehistory of east Africa*. New York.

LEAKEY, L. S. B. 1931. *Stone Age cultures of Kenya Colony*. Cambridge.

────── 1935. *Stone Age races of Kenya*. Oxford.

LOWE, C. VAN RIET. 1952. *The Pleistocene geology and prehistory of Uganda; Vol. II, Prehistory.* Mémoire no. 6. Geological Survey, Uganda.

POSNANSKY, M., ed. 1966. *Prelude to east African history.* Oxford.

5 Equatoria

CLARK, J. D. 1963. *Prehistoric cultures of northeast Angola and their significance in tropical Africa.* 2 vols. No. 62.

—— 1966. *The distribution of prehistoric culture in Angola.* No. 73.

—— 1968. *Further palaeo-anthropological studies in northern Lunda.* No. 78.

Publicações culturais do Museu do Dundo, Lisbon.

HEINZELIN DE BRAUCOURT, J. DE. 1957. *Les Fouilles d'Ishango.* Exploration du Parc National Albert, 1950, Volume 2. Brussels, Institut des parcs nationaux du Congo belge.

MOORSEL, H. VAN. 1968. *Atlas de préhistoire de la plaine de Kinshasa.* Université Lovanium. Kinshasa.

NENQUIN, J. 1963. *Excavations at Sanga (1957) the protohistoric necropolis.* Mus. roy. de l'Afr. cent., Tervuren, Belgium. Série in 8°. Sciences humaines, no. 45.

—— 1967. *Contributions to the study of the prehistoric cultures of Rwanda and Burundi.* Mus. roy. de l'Afr. cent. Tervuren. Belgium. Série en 8°, Sciences humaines, no. 59.

NOTEN, F. L. VAN. 1968. *The Uelian, a culture with a Neolithic aspect, Uele-Basin (northeast Congo Republic): an archaeological study.* Tervuren, Belgium, Série en 8°, Sciences humaines, no. 64.

6 Southern Africa

CATON THOMPSON, G. 1931. *The Zimbabwe Culture.* Oxford.

CLARK, J. D. 1950. *The Stone Age cultures of Northern Rhodesia.* South African Archaeological Society, Cape Town.

FAGAN, B. M. 1965. *South Africa during the Iron Age.* London.

—— 1966. *A short history of Zambia (from the earliest times until A.D. 1900).* Nairobi.

—— 1967. *Iron Age cultures in Zambia, Vol. I.* Robins Series, No. 5. London.

FAGAN, B. M., D. W. PHILLIPSON and S. G. H. DANIELS. 1969. *Iron Age cultures in Zambia, Vol. II.* Robins Series, London.

FOUCHÉ, L. 1937. *Mapungubwe, Vol. I.* Cambridge.

GABEL, W. C. 1965. *Stone Age hunters of the Kafue—the Gwisho A site.* Boston, Mass.

GARDENER, G. A. 1963. *Mapungubwe, Vol. II,* Van Schaik, Pretoria.

GOODWIN, A. J. H. and C. VAN RIET LOWE. 1929. *The Stone Age cultures of South Africa.* Cape Town. Annals of the South African Museum, no. 27.

MASON, R. J. 1962. *The Prehistory of the Transvaal.* Johannesburg.

ROBINSON, K. R. 1959. *Khami Ruins.* Cambridge.

ROBINSON, K. R., SUMMERS, R. and WHITTY, A. 1961. *Zimbabwe excavations, 1958.* Occasional Papers of the National Museums of Southern Rhodesia, no. 23 A. Cambridge.

SOHNGE, P. G., D. J. L. VISSER and C. VAN RIET LOWE. 1937. *The Geology and archaeology of the Vaal River Basin.* Pretoria.

SUMMERS, R. F. H. 1958. *Inyanga, ancient settlement in Southern Rhodesia.* London.

——— 1963. *Zimbabwe, a Rhodesian mystery.* Johannesburg.

WALTON, J. 1956. *The African village.* Pretoria.

WIESCHOFF, H. A. 1941. *The Zimbabwe-Monomatapa culture in southeast Africa.* Menashe, U.S.A.

XI ROCK ART

North Africa and Sahara

FROBENIUS, L. 1964. *Ekade Ektab, die Felsbilder Fezzans.* First published Leipzig, 1937, repr. Graz, 1964.

LAJOUX, J. D. 1962. *Merveilles du Tassili N'Ajjer.* Paris. Eng. trans. *Rock Paintings of Tassili.* London, 1963.

LHOTE, H. 1959. *The search for the Tassili frescoes.* Translated from the French. London and New York.

MORI, F. 1965. *Tadrart Acacus : Arte rupestre e culture del Sahara preistorico.* Turin.

RHOTERT, C. R. DE H. 1952. *Libysche Felsbilder.* Darmstadt.

TSCHUDI, J. 1955. Die Felsmalereien in Edjeri, Tamrit, Assakao, Meddak (Tassili-ni-Ajjer). *Proceedings of the Second Pan-African Congress on Prehistory, Algiers, 1952,* pp. 761–7.

VAUFREY, R. 1939. *L'art rupestre nord-africain.* Arch. de l'Institut de Paléontologie humaine, Paris, Mém. 20.

WINCKLER, H. A. 1938–9. *Rock drawings of southern Upper Egypt.* 2 vols. London.

East and Central Africa

BREUIL, H. 1952, Les figures incisées et ponctuées de la grotte de Kiantampo, Katanga. pp. 3–34. *Ann. du Mus. roy. du Congo Belge, Tervuren.* Sér. en 8° Sci. hum. Préhistoire, Vol. 1.

FOSBROOKE, H. A. *et al.* 1950. Tanganyika rock paintings: a guide and record. *Tanganyika Notes and Records,* Dar-es-Salaam.

KOHL-LARSEN, L. 1938. *Felsmalereien in Innerafrika.* Stuttgart.

MORTELMANS, G. 1952. Les dessins rupestres gravés, ponctués et peints du Katanga: essai de synthèse. pp. 35–52. *Op. cit.* at Breuil, H. above.

MORTELMANS, G. and R. MONTEYNE, 1962. La grotte peinte de Mbafu, témoignage iconographique de la première évangélisation du Bas-Congo. *Actes du IVe Congrès Pan-africain de Préhistoire,* vol. II. pp. 457–86.

SUMMERS, R., *ed.* 1959. *Prehistoric rock art of the Federation of Rhodesia and Nyasaland.* Salisbury, Rhodesia.

South and South-west Africa

BATTISS, W. W. 1939. *The amazing Bushman.* Pretoria.

BREUIL, H. 1955. *The white lady of the Brandberg.* London and New York, 1967.

———— 1957. *Philipp Cave* and subsequent volumes published by the 'Abbé Breuil Publications'. New York.

FROBENIUS, L. 1962. *Madsimu Dsangara, Südafrikanische Felsbilderchronik.* First published Berlin-Zurich, 1931, repr. Akademische Druck, Graz.

WILMAN, M. 1968. *The rock engravings of Griqualand west and Bechuana-land.* Balkema, Cape Town for the McGregor Museum, Kimberley. 2nd ed.

WILCOX, A. R. 1963. *The rock art of South Africa.* Johannesburg. New Jersey, 1964.

XII HISTORY AND ORAL TRADITION

DAVIDSON, B. 1964. *The African Past.* London and Boston, Mass.

FREEMAN-GRENVILLE, G. S. P. 1962. *The east African coast, select documents from the first to the earlier 19th century.* Oxford.

GABEL, W. C. and N. R. BENNETT, eds. 1967. *Reconstructing African culture history.* Boston University African Research Studies, no. 8. Boston, Massachusetts.

HONDIUS, J. 1952. *Klare besgryving van Cabo de bona esperança.* Facsimile of original 1652 edition with English translation published at Cape Town by the Book Exhibition Committee of the van Riebeeck Festival.

KIRKMAN, J. S. 1964. *Men and monuments on the east African coast.* London. New York, 1966.

HIRSCHBERG, W., ed. 1962. *Monumenta ethnographica, frühe völkerkundliche Bilddokumente, Vol. I, Black Africa.* Graz, Austria. Akademische Druck.

OLIVER, R. A. and G. MATHEWS, eds. 1963. *History of East Africa, Volume I.* Oxford.

VANSINA, J. 1965. *Oral tradition, a study in historical methodology.* Translated from the French by H. M. Wright. Chicago.

VANSINA, J. 1966. *Kingdoms of the savanna.* Wisconsin.

VANSINA, J., R. MAUNY and L. V. THOMAS, eds. 1964. *The historian in tropical Africa.* London.

XIII ETHNOGRAPHY AND CULTURAL ANTHROPOLOGY

BAUMANN, H. and D. WESTERMANN. 1957. *Les peuples et les civilisations de l'Afrique suivi de les langues et l'éducation.* French translation by L. Homburger. Paris.

BRIGGS, L. C. 1957. *Tribes of the Sahara.* Harvard.

CRÉAC'H, P. 1941. *Aliments et alimentation des indigènes du moyen Tchad (A.E.F.).* Marseille.

GABUS, J. 1951–2. *Contribution à l'étude des Nemadi.* Schweizerische Gesellschaft für Anthropologie.

GAST, M. 1968. *Alimentation des populations de l'Ahaggar, étude ethnographique.* Memoire no. VIII du CRAPE, Algiers. Paris, Arts et Métiers.

GIBBS, J. L., ed. 1965. *Peoples of Africa.* New York.

HERSKOVITS, M. J. 1962. *The human factor in changing Africa.* New York.

LEE, R. B. and I. DEVORE, *eds.* 1968. *Man the hunter.* Chicago.

MURDOCK, G. P. 1959. *Africa, its peoples and their culture history.* New York.

Royal Anthropological Institute, London, volumes in the *Ethnographic Survey of Africa.*

SCHAPERA, I. 1930. *The Khoisan peoples of South Africa—Bushmen and Hottentots.* London and New York.

————Ed. 1937. *The Bantu speaking tribes of South Africa.* London and New York.

SILBERBAUER, G. B. 1965. *Report to the Government of Bechuanaland on the Bushman Survey.* Bechuanaland Government, Gaberones.

THOMAS, E. M. 1959. *The harmless people : the Bushman of South West Africa.*

TURNBULL, C. M. 1962. *The forest people.* New York.

XIV LINGUISTICS

DALBY, D., *ed.* 1970. *Language and history in Africa.* London.

GREENBERG, J. H. 1963. *Languages of Africa.* Bloomington, Indiana.

GUTHRIE, M. 1968–9. *Comparative Bantu, Introduction to comparative linguistics and prehistory of the Bantu language.* 4 vols. London and Calif.

WESTPHAL, E. O. J. 1963. The linguistic prehistory of southern Africa: Bush, Kwadi, Hottentot and Bantu linguistic relationships. *Africa,* vol. XXXIII, 3.

Sources of Illustrations

The following persons, institutions and publishers kindly permitted use to be made of photographs taken or owned by them and their help is most gratefully acknowledged.
G. Ll. Isaac 4, 11, 28; M. R. Kleindienst 6; R. R. Inskeep 17; Dr C. B. M. McBurney, courtesy Cambridge University Press 18; P. A. Cole-King 19; Phyllis Dolhinow, courtesy Gombe Stream Research Centre 21; Maurice Wilson 22; Rona MacCalman 23, 24; J. Vicente Martius 25; C. K. Brain 26; Bruce Coleman Picture Researchers 27; A. R. Hughes, courtesy Dr M. Day, Dr L. S. B. Leakey and Cassell & Co. 29; C. Arambourg, courtesy Institut de Paléontologie humaine, Paris 30; Dr M. Day, Dr L. S. B. Leakey and Cassell & Co. 31, 32; courtesy the Trustees of the British Museum (Natural History) 33; Dr M. Day, Dr L. S. B. Leakey 34, 43–45; F. Wendorf 35; A. B. Elsaesser 38; R. J. Labuschagne, courtesy National Parks Board, Pretoria 39; J. de Heinzelin 40; P. Munson 41; A. Willcox 46; D. Mazonowicz 47; David Attenborough 48.

1

2

3

13

14

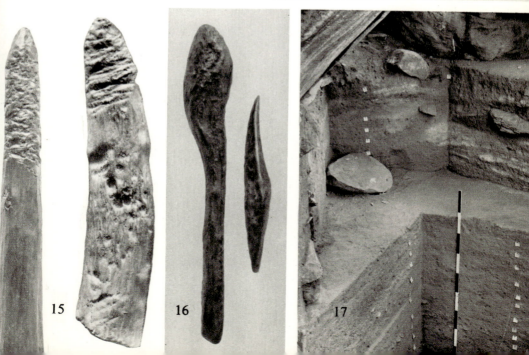

15   16   17

18

19

20

21

22

23

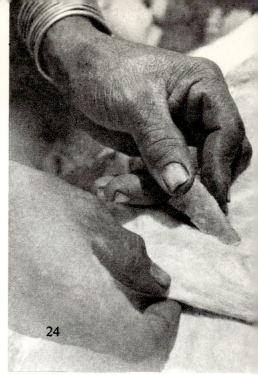

24

25

26

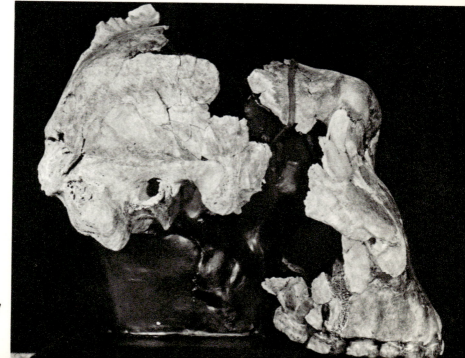

27

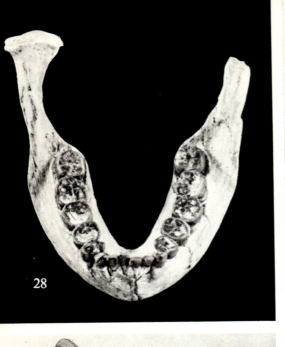

28

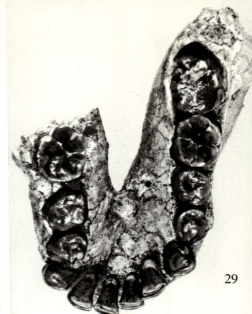

29

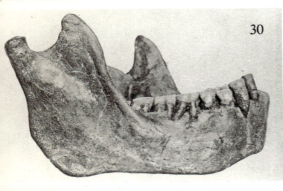

30

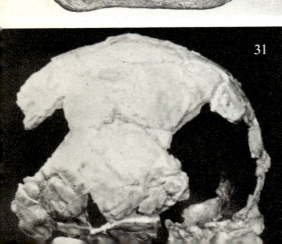

31

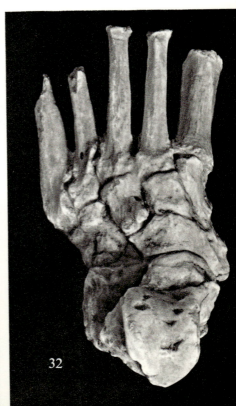

32

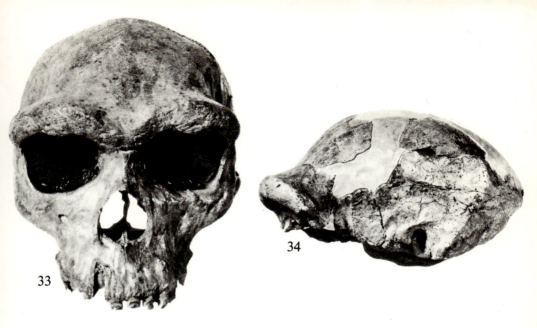

33

34

35

36

37

38

39

40

41

42

43

44

45

46

47

48

Notes on the Plates

1 Typical Karoo vegetation, Uniondale district, Cape Province, South Africa.

2 Pecked engraving of a warthog on dolerite outcrop at Stowlands on Vaal, Christiana, Transvaal, South Africa.

3 Three human figures in red paint from Kwa/Mateia rock shelter, Cheke area, Kisese, central Tanzania.

4 High grasslands at the south end of the Ngong Hills, Kenya. View over the Olorgesailie section of the Rift Valley; Olorgesailie Mountain in the background.

5 General view of the Olduvai Gorge, northern Tanzania, looking east towards the rim of the Ngorongoro caldera.

6 Circle of loosely piled lava blocks, apparently artificially constructed; associated with broken bones and many small artifacts of the Oldowan Industry. Living floor at Site DK I at the base of Bed I, Olduvai Gorge, February 1962.

7 General view of the concentrations of Upper Acheulian artifacts, manuports and bone debris at the DE/89 Site on Landsurface 7, by the edge of the Pleistocene freshwater lake at Olorgesailie, Gregory Rift Valley, Kenya.

8 Partially articulated skeleton of a Deinotherium associated with artifacts of the Oldowan Industry, from Site FLK II at the base of Bed II, Olduvai Gorge.

9 Close-up of part of the living floor at FLK I, Olduvai Gorge, on the

periphery of which has been found the skull of *Australopithecus (Zin-janthropus) boisei.* A lava chopper, quartz flakes and splinters can be seen associated with the horn cores of an extinct antelope and other broken and comminuted bone fragments.

10 General view from the Sterkfontein Extension Site, Transvaal, looking across the highveld grassland to Swartkrans. The large block of lime-stone in the foreground has fallen from the roof of the former cave, part of the wall of which is seen to the right.

11 Handaxes, spheroids and other tools with bones of the giant baboon Sinopithecus. At least fifty of these baboons were butchered by the makers of the Upper Acheulian industry at this site (Olorgesailie, Site DE/89).

12 Group of handaxes and other tools associated with tree trunks on Upper Acheulian living floor 5, Kalambo Falls, Zambia.

13 Fire charred logs from the Upper Acheulian living floor 6, Site B1, at Kalambo Falls, Zambia. Length of front piece approx. 40 cm.

14 Seeds of various edible fruits from the Upper Acheulian living floor 6, Site B1, at Kalambo Falls, Zambia. The trees from which these fruits came were growing in savanna and in montane forest. Approx. 3:2.

15 Right, butt end of a possible throwing stick from Peat I, Florisbad, showing cut marks, perhaps made to form a more secure grip for the hand; left, lower half of an Australian throwing stick for comparison.

16 A wooden club and a smoothed and pointed implement of wood from the Upper Acheulian living floor 5 at Site B2, Kalambo Falls, Zambia. Lengths 38 and 21 cm. respectively.

17 Kisese II rock shelter, Kondra district, Tanzania. The uniform deposits reached a depth of 20 feet and yielded a 'Later Stone Age' assemblage with microliths overlying older informal Archaeological Occurences with scrapers and *outils écaillés,* but only rare microliths. Radiocarbon

dates on burnt ostrich eggshell suggest the unbroken succession may have begun *c.* 30,000 years ago and that the transition to a fully micro‑lithic form took place *c.* 16,000 years ago. Wall paintings on scars left by exfoliated slabs found buried in the occupation midden all belong to the time represented by the uppermost two feet of deposit.

18 The Haua Fteah Cave, Cyrenaica, showing work in progress during the 1952 season.

19 *Brachystegia* woodland covers most of south central Africa and sup‑ported a considerable biomass of large game animals.

20 Commercial excavations to exploit the diamondiferous gravels at the base of the red redistributed Sands II of Kalahari‑type in north east Angola, have exposed Lupemban workshops and an industrial sequence covering most of Upper Pleistocene time. Mussolegi Mine, Luena Valley, Angola.

21 Chimpanzee termiting, Gombe Stream Reserve, Tanzania. Termites form a regular source of food and are extracted by selecting a twig or grass‑stem and inserting it into a tunnel in the nest. The termites adhering when the stick is withdrawn are licked off and eaten.

22 Reconstruction by Maurice Wilson of *Australopithecus robustus (Paran‑thropus)* holding a golden mole.

23 The power grip. An OvaTjimba man from the Baines Mountains, northern Kaokoveld, South West Africa, using a stone to break open a long bone and extract the marrow. This man belongs to one of the only two known groups in Africa still making and using stone tools.

24 The precision grip. An OvaTjimba man from the Baines Mountains, South West Africa, demonstrates the method of skinning a springbok with a quartz flake.

25 The method of making gun‑flints in the Lunda Province of north east Angola. Chalcedony and fine grained quartzite (grès polymorphe) are

used, the core being held by the heels and trimmed with a punch struck with a bar hammer. The flaking debris and the bifacial working of the gun-flints, comparable to that from Lupembo-Tshitolian and Tshitolian workshops, show that this technique is of considerable antiquity.

26 Skull of adult Australopithecine *(Australopithecus africanus)* from pink breccia at Sterkfontein Type Site, Transvaal.

27 Skull of juvenile robust Australopithecine *(Australopithecus (Zinjanthropus) boisei)* from the occupation site at FLK I, Bed I, Olduvai Gorge, Tanzania.

28 Mandible of robust Australopithecine *(Australopithecus (Zinjanthropus) sp.)* from the Humbu Formation (Middle Pleistocene), Peninj, Lake Natron basin, Tanzania. Overall length 13.5 cm.

29 Juvenile mandible of *Homo habilis* (Olduvai Hominid 7) from the site FLK NN I, Bed I, Olduvai Gorge, Tanzania. Overall length 8 cm.

30 Mandible No. III *(Homo (Atlanthropus) erectus)* from Ternifine, Algerian plateau.

31 Fragmentary skull (Olduvai Hominid 13) of juvenile *Homo habilis* from site MNK II, lower part of Bed II, Olduvai Gorge, Tanzania. Max. width 9.5 cm.

32 Foot bones of adult *Homo habilis* (Olduvai Hominid 8) from site FLK NN I, Bed I, Olduvai Gorge, Tanzania.

33 Skull of *Homo rhodesiensis* from cave at Broken Hill (now Kabwe), Zambia.

34 Calvaria of *Homo erectus* from site of LLK II in upper part of Bed II, Olduvai Gorge, Tanzania. Length approx. 21 cm.

35 Double burial of two adult males in a Final Palaeolithic cemetery at Site 117, Jebel Sahaba, Sudan. No. 20 had six and No. 21 had nineteen

microlithic stone artifacts in direct association with the body, including two embedded in the bones of No. 21, suggesting that these were the points and barbs of projectiles which had been the cause of death. 107 single and multiple burials were excavated; the artifacts belong to the Qadan Industry and the cemetery is dated to between 12,000 and 10,000 BC.

36 Dry-season fishing camp of BaTwa on Lochinvar Game Reserve, Kafue Flats, Zambia. The windbreak is constructed of *Phragmites* reeds and sacking. Note the centrally located fire-place, the long, bi- and tri-pronged fish spears, and the bent withy which forms part of the frame-work for 'dark entry' spearing of fish. Behind the men is a pile of peelings from water-lily bulbs which, with fish, form the staple food supply at the end of the dry season when the camps are established.

37 Rock shelter habitation of Rer Magno fishers at the mouth of the Nogal river, Mijertein, northern Somalia. Such sites will be occupied for up to ten years as long as the fishing remains good.

38 One of several collapsed windbreaks situated within the Big Elephant rock shelter in the Erongo Mountains, South West Africa, excavated to the original floor level. Much of the brush of the construction and cultural remains of wood and leather have been preserved by the dry climate. Charcoals gave a radiocarbon date suggesting an age between 500 BC and AD 500.

39 Bushman group with a recently killed and skinned springbok. Camp with grass-covered windbreaks in a trough between dunes, Gemsbok National Park, southern Kalahari, Botswana.

40 Baton or handle of bone 102 mm. long with a series of engraved lines and an unmodified quartz flake set in the end. The arrangement of the lines strongly suggests a simple notational system. From the main Ishango Industry horizon, Ishango, Lake Edward: extrapolated radio-carbon age *c.* 6,500–6000 BC.

41 The Neolithic village at the site of l'Ouadi is one of more than fifty such

villages with stone perimeter walls for defence. Built on the top of the Tichitt escarpment in south central Mauretania, they are estimated to have contained a population of 500–1,000 persons as well as cattle and goats. Evidence for cultivated *Pennisetum* also dates from this time: *c.* 1100 BC.

42 Galla man using a digging stick with a bored stone hafted on the upper end for breaking fresh ground for planting millet or coffee, Harar Plateau, Ethiopia.

43–45 Carbonised artifacts from cremation burials in the Njoro River Cave, Mau Escarpment, Kenya. Decorated wooden vessel from 'neolithic' cremation burial, associated with the Njoro Variant of the Stone Bowl Culture which dates to *c.* 970± 80 BC. (43) Fragment of a gourd (*Lagenaria* sp.). Note the decoration in white pigment. This is one of the earliest archaeological records of the gourd in the Old World. (44) Part of a large string bag. (45)

46 Polychrome painting of eland, the Eland Cave, Cathkin Area, Drak-ensberg, Natal.

47 Neolithic pastoral peoples of the Sahara herding cattle. Note the dog and the bow and arrow. In a rock shelter at Sefar, Tassili-n-Ajjer, central Sahara.

48 Zimbabwe 'Acropolis', Rhodesia, taken from the air.